The Basin of Mexico

D1328589

UNU Studies on Critical Environmental Regions
Edited by Jeanne X. Kasperson, Roger E. Kasperson, and B.L. Turner II

Note from the editors

This book is the fourth in a series from the United Nations University (UNU) research project, Critical Zones in Global Environmental Change, itself part of the UNU programme on the Human and Policy Dimensions of Global Change. Both endeavours explore the complex linkages between human activities and the environment.

The project views the human causes of and responses to major changes in bio-chemical systems – global environmental change broadly defined – as consequences of cumulative and synergistic actions (or inactions) of individuals, groups, and states, occurring in their local and regional settings. The study examines and compares nine regional cases in which large-scale, human-induced environmental changes portend to threaten the sustainability of an existing system. The aim is to define common lessons about regional trajectories and dynamics of change as well as the types of human actions that breed environmental criticality and endangerment, thereby contributing to global environmental change. The overall results of the comparative analysis are found in *Regions at Risk*, the initial volume in this series.

Titles currently available:

- Regions at Risk: Comparisons of Threatened Environments
- In Place of the Forest: Environmental and Socio-economic Transformation in Borneo and the Eastern Malay Peninsula
- Amazonia: Resiliency and Dynamism of the Land and its People
- The Basin of Mexico: Critical Environmental Issues and Sustainability
- The Ordos Plateau of China: An Endangered Environment

The Basin of Mexico: Critical environmental issues and sustainability

Exequiel Ezcurra, Marisa Mazari-Hiriart, Irene Pisanty, and Adrián Guillermo Aguilar

United Nations
University Press

TOKYO · NEW YORK · PARIS

United Nations University Press
The United Nations University, 53-70, Jingumae 5-chome, Shibuya-ku, Tokyo, 150-8925, Japan
Tel: +81-3-3499-2811   Fax: +81-3-3406-7345
E-mail: sales@hq.unu.edu
http://www.unu.edu

United Nations University Office in North America
2 United Nations Plaza, Room DC2-1462-70, New York, NY 10017, USA
Tel: +1-212-963-6387   Fax: +1-212-371-9454
E-mail: unuona@igc.apc.org

United Nations University Press is the publishing division of the United Nations University.

Cover design by Joyce C. Weston

Printed in the United States of America

UNUP-1021
ISBN 92-808-1021-9

Library of Congress Cataloging-in-Publication Data

The Basin of Mexico : critical environmental issues and sustainability / Exequiel Ezcurra
    p.   cm.
Includes bibliographical references (p.   ) and index. 1. Mexico City Metropolitan Area (Mexico) – Environmental conditions.
I. Ezcurra, Exequiel.
GE160.M6 B38 1999
363.7'00972'53 – dc21
99-6695
                                                                CIP

Contents

Acknowledgements

The authors thank Román Álvarez Béjar, Roberto Bonifaz, and Alma Luz Cabrera from the Instituto de Geografía, Universidad Nacional Autónoma de México (UNAM), for processing the imagery, and Lucero Rodríguez, Jorge Ortega, J. L. Pérez-Damian, and J. Gabriel for assistance in drawing and digitizing the figures. Marisa Mazari-Hiriart acknowledges financial support from the Dirección General de Asuntos del Personal Académico, UNAM. Adrián Guillermo Aguilar acknowledges the invaluable help of Irma Escamilla in the search for references and management of data bases. Exequiel Ezcurra thanks very especially Gonzalo Halffter and José Sarukhán, two outstanding Mexican ecologists who aroused his interest in the environmental future and sustainability of the Basin of Mexico.

Finally, the authors thank the research group at the Center for Technology, Environment, and Development (CENTED) at Clark University, especially Jeanne Kasperson, Roger Kasperson, and Billie Turner. It was their interest in critically endangered environmental regions that first brought the group together, and it was their enthusiasm that kept us going throughout the project. Thanks to their interest and support we learned to see with the eyes of a natural history researcher what previously had seemed to us only the city in which we lived. They brought a whole new perspective to our research, and we are grateful for it.

List of tables and figures

Tables

Figures

Preface

This landmark study is the outcome of a case study (Aguilar et al. 1995) prepared for the first book in the series UNU Studies on Critical Environmental Regions. Among the nine regions covered in that initial volume, *Regions at Risk: Comparisons of Threatened Environments* (Kasperson, Kasperson, and Turner 1995), only one (the Aral Sea basin) emerges more "at risk" than the Basin of Mexico, which, in short, exemplifies an endangered environment well on its way to criticality. At the helm of this dangerous course is Mexico City, that massive megalopolis in which dramatic concentrations of all kinds have coalesced to render an already precarious environment supremely capable of "biting back" and posing an immediate and long-term threat to human use, health, and well-being. The extraordinary pace of environmental changes is already depleting natural resources in the region and beyond and may be overwhelming local environmental sinks as well as institutional and societal capacities to cope. Indeed, an ever-increasing propensity to inhibit ongoing environmental degradation by enlisting imported resources and awaiting technological fixes may well have the effect of increasing overall risk. At the same time, however, the prospect of reversing the trajectory toward criticality is not altogether out of the question and may well be in progress in specific areas. Ezcurra and his colleagues rightly view the region as a laboratory engaged in testing many of the processes under way in the less developed regions of the world. The outcome of this experiment may signal the fate of other megacities across the globe.

As the world inches toward a new millennium, Mexico City stands out among "a number of urban agglomerations of a scale unprecedented in human history" (Fuchs 1994, 1). The present volume documents a lengthy history of environmental degradation exacerbated since the 1950s by the explosive growth of this decidedly primate city. Several major forces, typically at play in many developing countries, are driving the transformation. First, dating back to pre-Hispanic times, a long-standing state policy has promoted the capital as the financial, industrial, and cultural centre of Mexico and accordingly concentrated the nation's resources, as well as its economic-development efforts, in Mexico City. Second, owing in part to this colossal amassment of wealth, power, and services, staggering rural-to-urban migration has brought a relentless influx of rich and poor alike to the so-called "Mexico Megacity" (Pick and Butler 1997). They continue to arrive, some 1,500 daily, in search of jobs, education, medical care, sanitation, running water, and the general amenities attendant on urban life. They find all this and more, including a measure of prestige (life *is* easier in the city) albeit to starkly differential degrees. Here, as elsewhere, "the elite adopt affluent urban life styles amidst a growing underclass living in squalor, often with inadequate sanitary, health and educational services. Moreover, urban tensions foster the suburbanization process and the rise of the automobile culture with its toll on land, the environment and the social fabric" (Raskin et al. 1996, 10). Swelling a population already mounting owing to natural increase and declining mortality rates, these newcomers and their offspring aggravate the stress on a system already hard put to meet the everyday needs of some 15–20 million citizens.

The crushing scale of hyperurbanization translates into ever-higher levels of resource depletion, polluted air, contaminated water, and accumulated wastes and carries environmental implications for the entire Basin of Mexico as well as for people and ecosystems outside the region. It is not uncommon for wealthy cities to improve their own environmental situations by transferring certain environmental costs to other people, other regions, or other times (Haughton and Hunter 1994, 70; Satterthwaite 1997). Mexico City, albeit "wealthy" only in relative terms, has exercised its urban primacy (that "macro-cephalic domination of the country by its capital city" (Pezzoli 1998,

47)) to rob and pollute distant areas in a desperate attempt to coun-
teract its own formidable agglomeration of environmental ills. As the
city has grown, it has had to rely more and more on staggering subsidies from extraregional sources and from the nation at large in order
to sustain itself.

A reckless overexploitation of an otherwise renewable resource,
groundwater, has exceeded the rate of renewal attainable for the
aquifer underlying Mexico City. Similarly, the megacity's demand
for waste disposal has outpaced the assimilative capacity of the environment within the Basin of Mexico. Somehow policy makers have
managed to postpone the fashioning of appropriate governmental
policies to address these omens of criticality and simply exported the
problems. They draw down other river basins to offset the water
shortages attendant on population growth and urbanization. Mexican
taxpayers who reside far from the urban sprawl of the capital share
disproportionately the exorbitant (subsidized) costs of pumping
water uphill to a place that, at its lowest point, sits some 2,235 metres
above sea level. The discharge of largely untreated wastewater is fast
contaminating the involuntary recipient, the Tula Basin. And many
people who will rarely, if ever, make use of Mexico City's transport
system, or its medical facilities, nevertheless subsidize the provision
of such urban amenities, the likes of which lure people to the city in
the first place. Such extreme dependency can only worsen an already
high-risk situation and accelerate the race to criticality.

To be sure, the spectre of criticality that we ourselves saw hovering
over the Basin of Mexico in our overall assessment (Kasperson,
Kasperson, and Turner 1995; 1996) may be the inevitable outcome of
environmental degradation that "is likely to increase as Mexico City
expands (and implodes) without adequate facilities for sewage treatment, waste disposal, or policies to protect ecosystems" (Pezzoli
1998, 357). The urban ills that plague Mexico City may be so far
advanced as to preclude any viable rescue attempts. An ominous
prospect for a megalopolis that is paradigmatic of megacities
throughout the developing world (Ezcurra and Mazari-Hiriart 1996;
Konvitz 1996).

The authors of this volume sound a cautionary note that questions
the sustainability of such outlandish agglomerations. Yet this inter-
disciplinary team refuses to write off Mexico Megacity, prone as it is
to human-induced, natural, and technological disasters that conspire
with traditional driving forces of population, affluence, and technology to wreak environmental havoc in a closed hydrological system.

Rather, guarded optimism permits Ezcurra and his colleagues to spy glimmers of recovery attainable through recent environmental policies, the organized efforts of non-governmental organizations, technological innovations, and an ingeniously resilient citizenry.

Mexico as a nation has taken up the challenge of confronting its endangered environment and undertaken specific measures of redress. Although it is premature to suggest a complete turnaround, some signs of recovery are noteworthy. Reviewing the nation's "environmental performance," the Organisation for Economic Cooperation and Development (OECD) awarded Mexico high marks for its attempts to reverse serious environmental degradation through the launching of "new policies and programmes that are going in the *right direction* and in many ways are *exemplary*" (OECD 1998, 20). The same report lauds a stabilization in the rates of the legendary air pollution that is the most visible of Mexico City's environmental afflictions.

A four-day smog alert in May of 1998 prompted the mayor to implement a "good car/bad car policy, banning from the street during subsequent emergencies all pre-1991 automobiles not equipped with catalytic converters," which are now mandatory for some 125,000 taxis and minibuses in operation in Mexico City (Stevenson and Dabrowski 1998). Internet users have on-line access to data on the city's air quality (*www.calidad-del-aire.gob.mx* and *www.sima.com.mx*) and its air-pollution-control programmes (*www.ine.gob.mx*). These and an array of other attempts to cope with the unsavoury effects of air pollution are warranted and commendable, but they are prohibitively expensive and possibly misguided (Pezzoli 1998; Pick and Butler 1997; Stevenson and Dabrowski 1998), particularly in light of the severe water problems that lurk beneath the steadily subsiding metropolitan area.

As in much of the world, water supply and quality are in jeopardy in the Basin of Mexico. The primary source of water for Mexico City, the Mexico City Aquifer, is extremely vulnerable to contamination from various human activities above it, and it is difficult to predict its usable life with reliability (Joint Academies 1995, 79 [English]; 84 [Spanish]). The authors of this volume take pains to enumerate the sundry threats posed by inadequate treatment and disposal of hazardous wastes and wastewater, the numerous leaks in underground pipes, and the wholesale plunder of aquifers outside the basin. Overexploitation of the city aquifer has exacerbated a long-standing problem with land subsidence, thereby enhancing the risk of flooding as well as the vulnerability to contamination.

Recently, the premier research institutions of Mexico and the United States collaborated on a comprehensive study of the city's water supply and confirmed its precariousness (CNI 1995; Joint Academies 1995). The binational analysis commended Mexican authorities for taking steps to improve efficiency but went on to make a series of specific recommendations for managing water demand through the likes of pricing mechanisms, public-education campaigns, and conservation measures. The report also offers several general recommendations for improving understanding of regional hydrology, promoting reuse of wastewater, effecting institutional change, and addressing equity issues and human-health concerns (Joint Academies 1995, 78–87).

On the face of it, Mexico City is certainly receptive to heeding such advice. A recent flurry of environmental reforms speaks to a genuine attempt to streamline environmental decision-making, reduce inequities, and render both national and city authorities more responsive to public concerns (OECD 1998). The Federal Attorney for Environmental Protection (PROFEPA) takes pride in having handled more than 68 per cent of citizen complaints (e.g., 1,321 in 1992, 6,247 in 1996, and 3,893 in the first nine months of 1997) about "environmental irregularities" (OECD 1998, 137–138). In addition, many of the numerous environmental organizations in Mexico City are beginning to make headway in satisfying their demands for environmental justice (Pezzoli 1998). A prominent writer who wrote a novel depicting the city's water crisis (Arijdis 1993) is serving as president of the Group of 100, an environmental organization of local artists who are mobilizing social projects to combat environmental hazards and inequities (Living on Earth 1999). In 1998 public opposition succeeded in forcing the cancellation of plans to build another ring road around Mexico City (Stevenson and Dabrowski 1998, 10).

The foregoing examples suggest that it may still be possible to head off the march to criticality. Similar accounts of new initiatives, new attempts to enforce existing regulations, and new coalitions and networks of citizens' groups pepper this book. The Basin of Mexico is at least pointed in a direction that promises to "enhance its capacity to change in response to changing circumstances" (Rodger 1996, 18). Moreover, the resilient residents of Mexico City, much as they did in the aftermath of the 1985 earthquake, continue to develop that capacity for accommodating and adapting to the myriad environmental stresses that have transformed their surroundings. But are they adequately prepared to withstand the unexpected, the horrific surprise that may overpower their impressive store of resilience and adaptability?

It is too early to tell whether the ambitious reforms that are finally under way will have staying power and wind up embedded as routine practice. These measures have been unduly long in coming, despite an abundance of warning signs along the way (Ezcurra and Mazari-Hiriart 1996; United Nations 1991), and whether they are commensurate to the task at hand is an open question. But if Mexico City can avoid environmental criticality, "then the people and governments of the other megacities will have no excuse for doing less" (Konvitz 1996, 4). Thus the megacities of the world are watching from the wings to see how well Mexico City performs.

Jeanne X. Kasperson
Roger E. Kasperson
B. L. Turner, II

References

Aguilar, Adrián Guillermo, Exequiel Ezcurra, Teresa García, Marisa Mazari-Hiriart, and Irene Pisanty. 1995. The Basin of Mexico. In *Regions at risk: Comparisons of threatened environments*, ed. Jeanne X. Kasperson, Roger E. Kasperson, and B. L. Turner, II, 304–366. Tokyo: United Nations University Press.

Arijdis, Homero. 1993. *La leyenda de los soles*. Mexico City: Fondo de Cultura Economica.

CNI (Consejo Nacional de Investigación). 1995. *El agua y la Ciudad de México*. Mexico City: CNI.

Ezcurra, Exequiel, and Marisa Mazari-Hiriart. 1996. Are megacities viable? A cautionary tale from Mexico City. *Environment* 38, no. 1 (January/February): 6–15, 26–35.

Fuchs, Roland J. 1994. Introduction. In *Mega-city growth and the future*, ed. Roland J. Fuchs, Ellen Brennan, Joseph Chamie, Fu-Chen Lo, and Juha I. Uitto, 1–13. Tokyo: United Nations University Press.

Haughton, Graham, and Colin Hunter. 1994. *Sustainable cities*. Regional Policy and Development Series, 7. London: Jessica Kingsley Publishers.

Joint Academies Committee on the Mexico City Water Supply/Comitè de Academías para el Estudio de Suministro de Agua de la Ciudad de México. 1995. *Mexico City's water supply: Improving the outlook for sustainability/El suministro de agua de la ciudad de México: Mejorando la sustenabilidad*. Washington: National Academy Press.

Kasperson, Jeanne X., Roger E. Kasperson, and B. L. Turner, II, eds. 1995. *Regions at risk: Comparisons of threatened environments*. Tokyo: United Nations University Press.

Kasperson, Jeanne X., Roger E. Kasperson, and B. L. Turner, II. 1996. Regions at risk: Exploring environmental criticality. *Environment* 38, no. 10 (December): 4–15, 26–29.

Konvitz, Josef W. 1996. Mexico City: Metaphor for the world's urban future. *Environment* 38, no. 2 (March): 3–4.

Living on Earth [radio broadcast]. 1999. Top story: A thirsty city. Air date: week of February 19.

OECD (Organization for Economic Cooperation and Development). 1998. *Environmental performance reviews: Mexico*. Paris: OECD.

Pezzoli, Keith. 1998. *Human settlements and planning for ecological sustainability: The case of Mexico City*. Cambridge, MA: MIT Press.

Pick, James B., and Edgar W. Butler. 1997. *Mexico megacity*. Boulder, Colorado: Westview Press.

Raskin, Paul, Michael Chadwick, Tim Jackson, and Gerald Leach. 1996. *The sustainable transition: Beyond conventional development*. POLESTAR Series Report, no. 1. Stockholm: Stockholm Environment Institute.

Rodger, Allan. 1996. Urban directions for the 21st century: Visions and responsibilities, challenges and opportunities for ecologically and culturally sustainable urban development and redevelopment. In *Habitat II, dialogue 1: "How Cities Will Look in the 21st Century": Proceedings of ... 4 June 1996, Istanbul, Turkey*. UNCRD Proceedings no. 14. Nagoya, Japan: United Nations Centre for Regional Development.

Satterthwaite, David. 1997. Environmental transformations in cities as they get larger, wealthier and better managed. *Geographical Journal* 163, no. 2 (July): 216–224.

Stevenson, Mark, and Andrea Dabrowski. 1998. Mexico City's new mayor faces world-class environmental ills. *EcoAméricas* 1, no. 2 (December): 1, 10.

United Nations. 1991. *Population growth and policies in mega-cities: Mexico City*. Population Policy Paper, no. 32. New York: United Nations.

1

Introduction

Surrounded by the mountains of Mexico's Central Volcanic Axis, the Basin of Mexico remains, on all counts, the centre of the nation. It is also where one of the largest urban complexes in the world has developed and one of the most notorious examples of the phenomenon of urban concentration in third world countries. Old Tenochtitlan, the proud pre-Hispanic capital of the Aztec empire, the colonial "city of palaces" that astounded Alexander von Humboldt (1811), is today the paradigm of urban disaster, the archetype of the growing environmental and social problems of third world cities.

Indeed, one of the most notable global phenomena of the second half of the twentieth century has been the "rush to the cities" in developing countries, i.e. the concentration of the once-rural population in large urban areas. Although urbanization typically accompanies industrialization, the unbridled growth and development of large cities in the non-industrialized world presents a number of new characteristics that merit careful study. Perhaps the most noticeable attribute of this phenomenon is centralism, the "primate-city syndrome." Whereas the transition to an urban society in the developed world involved a large number of medium-sized cities, in the non-industrialized nations populations, wealth, and human activities

Table 1.1 **The 21 megacities whose population is expected to exceed 10 million by the year 2000, and their 1980–1990 growth rate**

Megacity (Country)	Estimated population 1990	Projected population 2000	Population growth rate 1980–1990	Per capita GNP 1991[a] (US$)
Tokyo (Japan)	25.0	28.0	1.4	26,824
São Paulo (Brazil)	18.1	22.6	4.1	2,920
Mexico City (Mexico)	16.8	20.1	2.0	2,971
New York (USA)	16.1	16.6	0.3	22,356
Shanghai (China)	13.4	17.4	1.4	364
Bombay (India)	12.2	18.1	4.2	330
Los Angeles (USA)	11.5	13.2	1.9	22,356
Buenos Aires (Argentina)	11.4	12.8	1.4	3,966
Seoul (Rep. of Korea)	11.0	12.9	2.9	6,277
Beijing (China)	10.9	14.4	1.9	364
Rio de Janeiro (Brazil)	10.9	12.2	2.2	2,920
Calcutta (India)	10.7	12.7	1.8	330
Osaka (Japan)	10.5	10.6	0.5	26,824
Jakarta (Indonesia)	9.2	13.4	4.4	592
Tianjin (China)	9.2	12.5	2.4	364
Manila (Philippines)	8.9	12.6	4.1	728
Cairo (Egypt)	8.6	10.8	2.3	611
New Delhi (India)	8.2	11.7	3.9	330
Karachi (Pakistan)	7.9	11.9	4.7	383
Lagos (Nigeria)	7.7	13.5	5.8	305
Dacca (Bangladesh)	6.6	11.5	7.2	205

Source: WRI (1994), except for Mexico City, which is based on this study.
a. The per capita gross national product is given for comparison purposes.

have concentrated in one or a few gigantic cities, frequently referred to as "megalopolises" or "megacities." The overwhelming immensity of these urban concentrations raises concerns about their long-term sustainability.

The world population in 1994/95 was estimated as 5.76 billion, and it is increasing by some 100 million annually (WRI 1994). Towards the year 2000 the majority of this population will be concentrated in urban areas. Of the 21 cities of the world that are expected to exceed 10 million inhabitants by the year 2000, only four are located in countries whose per capita gross national product (GNP) exceeds US$10,000 (table 1.1). Furthermore, a significant inverse relationship between GNP and population growth rate (fig. 1.1) indicates that the large cities of the poorer countries are growing at a much faster rate than similar megalopolises in the industrialized world (fig. 1.2) and

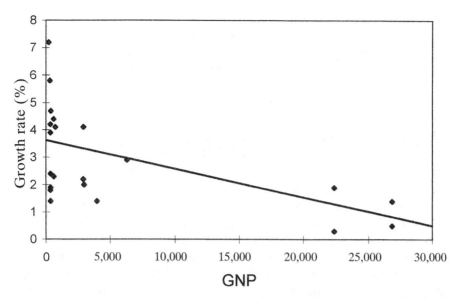

Fig. 1.1 **The inverse relationship between per capita gross national product and population growth rate for the 21 largest cities in the world ($r = -0.56$, $P = .008$. Source: WRI 1994)**

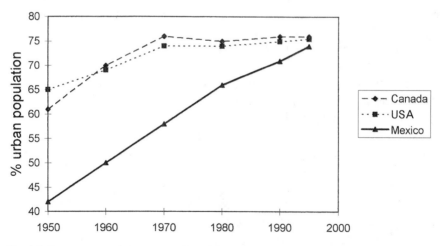

Fig. 1.2 **Percentage of the population living in urban areas in the three countries of North America (Note: the two industrialized nations – Canada and the USA – reached an asymptote of 75% around 1970, and since then have ceased to concentrate their population in urban areas; by contrast, Mexico is still rapidly concentrating its population in large cities. Source: CEC, in press)**

3

are creating an ever-increasing demand for urban services, which need to be supplied at a rate that often exceeds economic growth. Enter the mounting threats to air and water quality, the health problems attendant on environmental degradation, the enormous pressures on water, food, and energy supplies, and the increased risk of large-scale regional contamination by solid and liquid waste. Few of these issues have received adequate attention.

Following up and summarizing previous studies (Aguilar et al. 1995; Ezcurra and Mazari-Hiriart 1996), in this book we shall discuss the question of urban sustainability by concentrating on a paradigmatic case study: Mexico City, which is one of the world's largest megacities and is situated in problematic habitats. Its future carries a significance beyond Mexico, to numerous other megacities that are undergoing similar transformations. In short, Mexico City is an immense laboratory, an oversized mirror that reflects the environmental sustainability and the economic viability of the large cities of the developing world. The futures of the likes of São Paulo, Calcutta, Bombay, Jakarta, Buenos Aires, Rio de Janeiro, Manila, Caracas, Shanghai, or New Delhi are in many ways linked to the experiences generated by this huge empirical experiment. Like Mexico City, many of these cities lie rooted in old cultures and a long history of cycles of growth, grandeur, and collapse.

For many environmentalists, the urban and demographic growth of the Basin of Mexico is one of the main national worries, not only because of the attendant socio-economic consequences of such an immense concentration of population and the asymmetric relationship of the basin with the rest of the nation, but also because of the ominous ecological consequences that the clustering of some 18 million people may inflict on the use of natural resources. For many, this large human concentration is only the prelude to a great ecological catastrophe that will precipitate a forced decentralization of the basin. For others, the urban concentration of Mexico City is the logical result of the industrial development and the technological progress of the twentieth century, and does not represent a problem in itself. According to this view, technological development will provide the means to defeat the environmental and health problems spawned by unbridled urban growth.

We shall examine some of these questions in a historical perspective. Any discussion of an environmental crisis requires an analysis of the depletion and degradation of natural resources to levels that imperil the well-being and survival of large sectors of the population.

In a modern industrial city, an environmental crisis implies problems in safeguarding the supply and the quality of resources such as air, water, and soil. An ecological crisis in the Basin of Mexico will almost necessarily result from the exhaustion of the water supply, the degradation of air quality to unhealthy levels, the silting of the drainage system, and the flooding of the city as a result of deforestation, or some other similar problem.

Interestingly, the depletion of natural resources in the Basin of Mexico is not just a recent phenomenon. Deep in the historical past, it has triggered massive emigration and various socio-cultural collapses (Ezcurra 1990a, 1990b, 1992; Whitmore and Turner 1986; Whitmore et al. 1990). Yet the scale and pace of the changes currently under way are unprecedented and, given the basin's history, do not augur well for the future of Mexico City. Thus Mexico City and the Basin of Mexico at large pose a test of the sustainability of the environmental risks that threaten their populations.

Our methodology is based on the assumption that the history of the region has led to (and allows the understanding of) the current situation, both in terms of the social and economic structure of the basin and in terms of its natural resources. Within this historical framework, we essentially followed a "state–pressure–response" approach. This approach is reflected in the organization and order of the chapters.

We first analyse the environmental history of the Basin of Mexico (chap. 2) from the perspective of natural resource use and ecological sustainability. Our basic objective was to examine the pathway that led to the current environmental crisis, and to highlight past crises and their underlying causes. Then in chapter 3 we describe the current social and economic situation in the Basin of Mexico, and explain the process of metropolitanization and the consequences of political and economical centralism around Mexico City.

In chapter 4, we evaluate the magnitude of recent environmental changes in the Basin of Mexico in terms of population and natural resources. We include a detailed analysis of the problems, dealing with vegetation cover, water supply, waste, and air quality. We then describe the driving forces of environmental change, in terms of population change, governmental policies, and other interacting social and economic forces (chap. 5).

In chapter 6 we describe the environmental vulnerability of the basin. We assess the factors leading to environmental endangerment in terms of population and natural resources. Following the analysis of environmental changes presented in chapter 4, this chapter discusses the risks and hazards linked with disappearing vegetation cover, decreasing water supply, accumulating waste, and deteriorating air quality. Finally, we describe the responses to the environmental problem in Mexico City (chap. 7), analysing in detail the trends in both governmental institutions and non-governmental organizations.

In short, this book is an attempt to understand the environmental crisis in the Basin of Mexico. As already mentioned, opinion about the environmental situation in the Basin of Mexico is divided between those who believe the region to be critically unsustainable and those who believe that technological developments will solve the serious environmental problems of Mexico City. We have decided not to take sides in this debate. Rather, we have tried to present the information in an objective manner in the hopes that our readers will form their own opinion.

2

The environmental history of the basin

The ecological transformations of the Basin of Mexico

Immediately before the Spanish Conquest in 1519, the Basin of Mexico's population, upwards of 2 million according to some estimates (see Ezcurra 1992), occupied a series of towns and polities under the dominion of Tenochtitlan-Tlatelolco, sharing the cultural and technological components of their highly developed lacustrine civilization. Aztec agriculture was based on the cultivation of the *chinampas*, an intensive and highly productive agricultural system formed by a succession of raised fields within a network of canals dredged on the lake bed (frequently described as "floating gardens"). By harvesting aquatic products and by digging the muddy sediment from the canals and spreading it on the fields, the *chinampa* system was able to recycle in a very efficient manner the nutrients leached from the fertile soils of the agricultural fields. Thus, abundant harvests supplied many of the needs of the inhabitants of the basin.

The pre-Hispanic settlements, however, were already dependent on the import of products from outside the basin, which were collected forcibly in the form of tribute to the Aztec emperor. With the Spanish Conquest came the redesign of the urban areas of the basin according to the layout of Spanish towns and cities, and the lacustrine surface was considered incompatible with the new modalities of construction and land use. As early as the seventeenth century, drainage works of increasing size and complexity were built with the purpose of freeing the city of Mexico from the risk of floods and of drying the muddy subsoil of the old lake bed. These works, in turn, produced further changes in the environment of the basin. The progressive disappearance of the *chinampa* agriculture was one of the first consequences of these transformations.

These changes notwithstanding, the pace of environmental deterioration increased rapidly during the twentieth century. As in many other parts of Latin America, the industrialization of Mexico during this century accelerated migration towards the great city, where job opportunities were more plentiful. In its rapid growth, Mexico City started to engulf the satellite towns that surrounded the old Aztec capital, transforming itself into the immense megalopolis of today. The present urban conglomeration occupies most of the Federal District, as well as a large part of the neighbouring State of Mexico. The Basin of Mexico, with only 0.03 per cent of the nation's territory, is home to 20 per cent of the Mexican population and constitutes an environmental, social, and political problem of immense proportions. Even the mountain ranges south and west of the city, until the 1970s little affected by the process of urbanization, are now suffering the consequences of explosive urban growth.

All the residents of the basin are more or less aware of the serious problem of environmental pollution that has accompanied the growth of the megalopolis. Very few, however, realize that, environmentally, one of the most remarkable characteristics of the urbanization process is the basin's high degree of dependence on other ecosystems. Neither the city nor the Basin of Mexico is self-sufficient in any of its basic resource needs. On the contrary, their need for exogenous resources is growing steadily, and the import of these resources is generating environmental problems elsewhere in the country. It is known, for example, that the tropical forests of south-western Mexico have been logged intensively in the past decade. Few inhabitants of the basin, however, are aware that one of the main causes of this ecological disaster is the growing demand for beef by the urban middle class. Indeed, cattle breeding is the most notorious cause of deforestation in the Mexican tropical lowlands, where most of the forests logged are eventually transformed into tropical grasslands dedicated to raising cattle for large urban markets, particularly for the Basin of Mexico. In this book we shall discuss, from an ecological point of view, the growing dependency of the Basin of Mexico with respect to the rest of the country. We will attempt to analyse some aspects of the environmental history of the basin, as well as the present costs – both for its residents and for the nation at large – of maintaining this large megalopolis.

The environmental setting

The physical environment

The Basin of Mexico is a closed (but now artificially drained) hydro-logical watershed of approximately 7,000 km² (fig. 2.1). Its lowest part, a lacustrine plain, has an elevation of approximately 2,250 m above sea level. The basin is enclosed on three of its sides by a suc-cession of magnificent volcanic ranges of more than 3,500 m: the

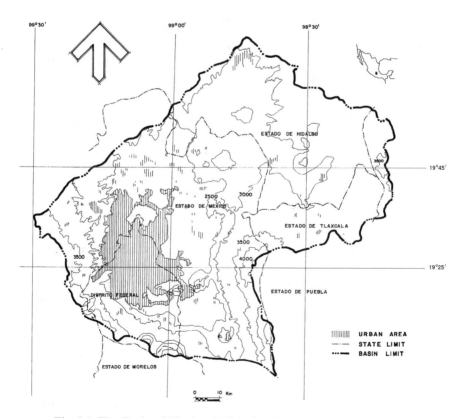

Fig. 2.1 **The Basin of Mexico: Political and geographical boundaries**

Ajusco towards the south, the Sierra Nevada to the east, and the Sierra de las Cruces to the west. To the north the basin is limited by a series of hills and low ranges (Los Pitos, Tepozotlán, Patlachique, and Santa Catarina, among others). The highest peaks – Popocatépetl and Iztaccíhuatl, with elevations of 5,465 and 5,230 m respectively – lie south-east of the basin, in the Sierra Nevada. A number of other peaks reach altitudes of more than 4,000 m. These circumscribing mountains represent an important physical boundary, limiting the expansion of the urbanized areas.

Geologically, the basin lies in the Transversal Volcanic Axis, a Late Tertiary formation, 20–70 km wide, that crosses the Mexican Republic from the Pacific to the Atlantic in a west–east direction (Mosser 1987). The proximity of the Basin of Mexico to the Pacific trench, the direct connection with the trench provided by the Volcanic Axis, and the numerous geological faults that occur along the axis have made earthquakes, volcanic eruptions, and tectonic instability in general a salient feature in the history of the region.

Before the rise of the Aztec state, around AD 1000, the lake system on the basin floor covered approximately 1,500 km^2 and was composed of five shallow lakes, linked from north to south: Tzompanco (Zumpango), Xaltocan, Texcoco, Xochimilco, and Chalco. The two southern lakes, Chalco and Xochimilco, and the two northern ones, Tzompanco and Xaltocan, were somewhat higher than Lake Texcoco, and their waters tended to flow into the latter, where they eventually evaporated into the atmosphere. Runoff water traversing rocks and hillsides towards the lower parts of the basin dissolves part of the minerals of the rocks and soil particles it finds in its way and transports these solutes in the form of mineral salts. In open basins, the final destination of these dissolved salts is the oceans, where brine has accumulated over millions of years. In closed watersheds such as the Basin of Mexico, however, the final destination of the salts dissolved in runoff water is the bottom of the basin, where the water eventually evaporates and the salts accumulate for thousands of years. Thus, the waters of Lake Texcoco were briny, and in terms of their geological origin they formed a true "interior sea," as Hernán Cortés so accurately described this large body of salt water (fig. 2.2).

Rainfall in the basin is concentrated in summer, mostly between June and September. There is a pronounced gradient of precipitation within the basin, from relatively rainy areas in the south-west (approximately 1,500 mm per year), to semi-arid areas in the north-east (around 600 mm). Mean annual temperature in the bottom of the

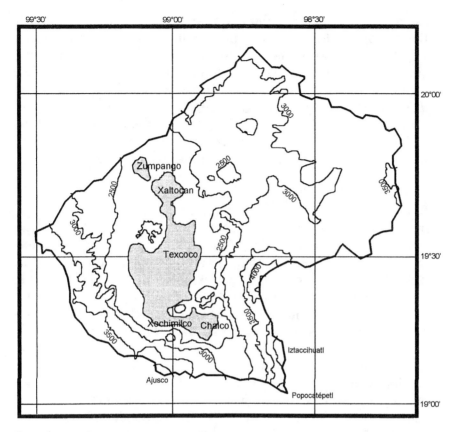

Fig. 2.2 **The lacustrine system of the Basin of Mexico in the sixteenth century, at the time of the arrival of the Spanish** *conquistadores*

basin is 15°C, with a variation of 8°C between summer and winter. Occasional night frosts occur throughout the basin, but their frequency increases with elevation and aridity (Jáuregui 1987).

In a detailed and outstanding study on the archaeology and the human use of the basin before the Spanish Conquest, Sanders, Parsons, and Santley (1979; see also Sanders, 1976a, 1976b, and Niederberger 1987a, 1987b) distinguished nine major environmental zones within the basin: (1) the lacustrine system, which represented a very important habitat for migratory waterfowl; (2) the salty lake shores, covered by halophilous plants; (3) the deep alluvial plains, dominated by sedges, willows (*Salix bomplandiana*), and *ahuehuetes* (*Taxodium mucronatum*); (4) the shallow alluvial plains, covered by grasslands and agaves; (5) the alluvial slopes, with oaks in the south

11

and south-western parts of the basin, and with acacias on the drier northern slopes; (6) the lower piedmont, with gentle slopes and vegetated by low oak (*Quercus* spp.) forests; (7) the mid piedmont, dominated by evergreen oaks with large leaves; (8) the upper piedmont, on slopes above 2,500 m, with dominance of oaks, alders (*Alnus* spp.), *tepozanes* (*Buddleia* spp.), and madrones (*Arbutus xalapensis*); and, finally, (9) the sierras, at elevations above 2,700 m, with pines (*Pinus* spp.), fir (*Abies religiosa*), junipers (*Juniperus deppeana*), and various species of tussock grasses or *zacatones*.

Vegetation

A rich flora evolved in the Basin of Mexico as a result of several ecological and historical factors. Among the most important factors are an inter-tropical location, the high-altitude temperate climate, the isolating effects of the surrounding mountain ranges and the altitudinal gradients they create, as well as the fact that the Central Volcanic Axis of Mexico is a boundary between the Nearctic and Neotropical biogeographic regions. The Basin of Mexico is not a continuous unit. Different geological origins, soil compositions, and climates determine a mosaic of environments, frequently characterized by different vegetation types.

Possibly the most exhaustive work on the vegetation of the basin is Rzedowski (1975; see also Sanders 1976b, and Sanders, Parsons, and Santley 1979), who recognizes 10 main vegetation types. Given the importance of vegetation for the environment of the basin as a regulator of the hydrological cycle, as habitat for wildlife, and as recreational wildlands and natural parks on the periphery of the large city, it is worth summarizing some of the most important aspects of Rzedowski's description of these vegetation types. The ecological zones, their main characteristics, and the vegetation associated with them are summarized in table 2.1.

Fir forest
Fir (*Abies religiosa*, known in Mexico as *oyamel*) is the dominant species at elevations of 2,700–3,500 m, where moisture conditions are more favourable. The firs form tall evergreen forests, 20–40 m in height, with a densely shaded understorey. Other important components of these communities are alders or *ailes* (*Alnus firmifolia*), white cedars (*Cupressus lindleyi*), oaks (*Quercus laurina*), spruces (*Pseudotsuga macrolepsis*), willows (*Salix oxylepis*), and *capulines* or

wild cherries (*Prunus serotina* spp. *capuli*), whose edible and tasty fruits are sold in traditional markets of Mexico. The understorey of this forest is scarce, and is formed by mosses and shade-tolerant plants.

Cloud forest

Broad-leaved cloud forests, also known as "mesophyllous" forests, are a rare community in the Basin of Mexico, occupying no more than 2 km² in the whole region. This forest develops in the ravines and on the protected slopes of the lower inclines of the Iztaccíhuatl volcano and the Sierra de las Cruces, at elevations of 2,500–3,000 m. Its most important characteristic is the abundance of epiphytes, especially mosses and ferns, and woody climbers that cover the branches and trunks of the dominant trees, which include genera such as *Quercus, Clethra, Fraxinus, Garrya, Ilex, Prunus*, and *Cupressus*, and several species of *Pinus*. The mesophyllous forest alternates, in a patchy distribution, with the drier and more frequent oak, pine, and fir forests. Affinities between the components of the mesophyllous forest and the forests of the nearby Balsas basin may be attributable to the connection between both basins about 1 million years ago. Some of the dominant trees are the *tlecuahuitl* (*Clethra mexicana*), an evergreen oak (*Quercus laurina*), and a holly (*Ilex tolucana*).

Pine forest

Different species of pine (*Pinus* spp.) form the most typical plant communities on the mountain slopes that surround the basin, especially in its southern part. These communities prosper at 2,350–4,000 m, with rainfall between 700 and 1,200 mm. The pines are the communities most frequently subject to forest fires, often induced by sheep herders between February and April to obtain a green and soft regrowth of the tussock grasses at the end of the dry season, when forage is most scarce. Among the most common species in these communities are *Pinus montezumae, P. hartweggii, P. teocote, P. pseudostrobus*, and *P. patula*. Their distribution is highly influenced by the altitudinal gradient.

The lowest pine forests are formed by *Pinus leiophylla*, frequently growing with oaks and forming open woodlands or woody grasslands. Displaced by the growth of Mexico City, these forests have now almost disappeared. The next altitudinal floor, at 2,500–3,100 m, is occupied by *ocote* (*Pinus montezumae*) in the southern part of the basin and by *Pinus radians* in the drier ranges of the north. Above

13

Table 2.1 **Vegetation zones in the Basin of Mexico**

Vegetation	Main species	Zone, altitude, precipitation	Additional information
Aquatic and subaquatic	*Typha latifolia* *Scirpus* spp. *Lemna* spp. *Eichhornia crassipes* *Juncus* spp. *Cyperus* spp. *Echinochloa* spp. *Hydrocotyle* spp. *Eleocharis* spp. *Bidens* spp. *Sagittaria* spp.	Lake system	Drastic reduction of the lakes has caused the disappearance of many species, allowing exotic species, particularly *Eichhornia crassipes*, to become dominant. The revegetation of the dry bed of Lake Texcoco allowed the establishment of halophilous grasses and herbs.
Halophytes	*Sporobolus* spp. *Distichlis* spp. *Typha* spp. *Atriplex* spp. *Eragrostis obtusiflora*	Saline and alkaline lake shores and dry beds of former lakes. c. 2,200 m	These species are frequently found as low grasslands growing in highly saline and badly drained soils. Soils along the former lake shores were used as salt sources in Aztec times.
Xerophytic scrub	*Opuntia streptacantha* *Mimosa biuncifera* *Hechtia podantha* *Jatropha dioica* *Eysenhardtia polystachya* Some former low tree communities were probably present, interspersed with grasses and shrubs.	Lowlands, on deep and thin soils. They can be found in different regions. In the southern part, they are characteristic of Pedregral de San Angel c. 2,250–2,700 m 400–700 mm	Develops in relatively dry flat zones surrounding the lake system. Soils are more or less deep except in the northern region, where they are very thin. Agriculture in this zone needs irrigation.

Grasslands	*Hilaria cenchroides* *Buchloe dactyloides* *Aristida adscensionis* *Bouteloua simplex* *Potentilla candicans* *Chalamagrostis tolucensis* *Festuca* spp.	Distributed through different environments with superficial or deep soils. 2,250–4,300 m 700–1,200 mm	In many cases, grasslands are secondary communities that can eventually be substituted by trees. In some cases they coexist with shrubs.
Scrub oak forests	*Quercus microphylla*	Found in the lower piedmont, on sandy loams. 2,300–3,100 m 700–900 mm	Probably a fire-induced community. Soils on these slopes are very vulnerable to erosion.
Juniper forests	*Juniperus deppeana*	Grows in the first part of the upper piedmont, characterized by shallow clay soils. 2,400–2,800 m 600–800 mm 11–14°C	Juniper forests are open, probably secondary communities. Owing to the low cover values, understorey species are abundant.
Oak forests	*Quercus* spp.	Found from the upper piedmont to the sierra regions. Inadequate forestry has reduced their original distribution area. Soils are shallow or deep, and frosts frequent. 2,350–3,100 m 700–1,200 mm	

Table 2.1 **(cont.)**

Vegetation	Main species	Zone, altitude, precipitation	Additional information
	Quercus laeta *Quercus deserticola* *Quercus crassipes* *Quercus obtusata*	Found at less than 2,500 m.	Low forests (5–10 m), with sparse canopies.
	Quercus rugosa *Quercus mexicana* *Quercus angustifolia*	Characteristic of the upper piedmont with deep or moderately shallow soils. 2,500–2,800 m 600–800 mm 11–14°C	Frequently the first species forms pure stands, but it can be found mingled with the other two.
Pine forests	*Pinus* spp.	Evergreen communities, growing in shallow, rocky, or deep soils in the sierra region. 2,350–4,000 m 700–1,200 mm	Agriculture, grazing, and timber logging have strongly disrupted these communities.
	Pinus leiophylla	This species coexists with several species of oaks, forming mixed communities. 2,350–2,600 m	Deeply disturbed communities, with severely eroded soils.
	Pinus montezumae *Pinus patula*	Relatively high and almost pure stands 2,500–3,100 m	

	Species	Conditions	Description
	Pinus hartweggii	This species can grow on steep slopes. 2,900–4,000 m	This forest marks the timberline in the higher part of the mountains.
Cloud forests	*Clethra mexicana* *Quercus laurina* *Prunus brachybotrya* *Alnus arguta* *Pinus* spp.	Upland alluvium. 2,500–3,000 m c. 1,000 mm	Found in restricted areas with deep soils and protected from strong winds and frosts. A high proportion of its original range has been transformed into agricultural areas.
Fir forests	*Abies religiosa*	Characteristic of the Sierra region. It grows on deep, well-drained, rich soils. 2,700–3,500 m 1,000–1,500 mm 7.5–13°C	Dense, high, and evergreen forests. Together with *Pinus hartweggii*, this forest reaches the timberline. It is used for pasturing herds and for wood extraction.

Sources: Sanders (1976a); Rzedowski (1975); Sanders, Parsons, and Santley (1979).

3,000 m are the open forests of *Pinus hartweggii*, the species that is most adapted to the extreme conditions of the upper altitudinal floors of the mountains that surround the basin. Supporting an understorey of large tussock grasses of the genera *Festuca* and *Muhlenbergia*, the forests of *Pinus hartweggii* are the habitat of the volcano rabbit or *zacatuche* (*Romerolagus diazii*), an endemic and highly endangered species of rabbit whose survival is currently threatened by the continuous burning of the grassy understorey.

Oak forest

As with the pine communities, a large number of oak species (*Quercus* spp.) occur in the Basin of Mexico and their distribution follows the altitudinal gradient. In previous centuries, the oak forests were widespread plant communities in the basin at elevations of 2,350–3,100 m, with annual rainfall in the range 700–1,200 mm. The environment in which oaks grow is similar to that of the drier pine species, and frequently both genera are found together, forming mixed forests. Oaks, however, generally form low forests, 5–12 m high, and usually constitute dense stands in the altitudinal floor immediately below the pine forests.

Below 2,500 m, the dominant species are *Quercus obtusata* and *Q. laeta*; at 2,500–2,800 m the most common oak is *Q. rugosa*, a species with wide rigid leaves, frequently associated with madrones (*Arbutus xalapensis*) and other less common oaks such as *Q. mexicana* and *Q. crassipes*. Above 2,800 m, the dominant oak species is *Q. laurina*, commonly associated with fir and pine forests. North of the basin, in the more arid ranges, low forests of *Q. microphylla* and *Q. gregii* are commonly found (Ezcurra 1990b). A spectacular mixed oak forest was found until recently in the lava badlands (*pedregal*) of San Angel, south of the basin. This forest has succumbed almost entirely to the advance of urban developments.

Juniper forest

Junipers (*Juniperus* spp.) are shrubs or low trees (less than 6 m high) forming open woodlands with an abundant herbaceous understorey. These forests are common in the northern and eastern parts of the basin, at elevations of 2,400–2,800 m. They develop on dry slopes and semi-arid plains, with annual rainfall of 600–800 mm. The dominant species is the *sabino* (*Juniperus deppeana*), a small tree some 4 m high, with green young stems and small scaly leaves. According to

Rzedowski, the juniper forests have in many cases been induced by the destruction of previously existing forests of pines and oaks.

Oak shrubland

This community is formed by dwarf oak (*Quercus microphylla*), a shrub that propagates vegetatively from root suckers and forms a dense thicket of low scrub 40–80 cm high. Two rosette plants frequently coexist with this oak: the *palmita* (*Nolina parviflora*) and the *sotol* (*Dasylirion acrotriche*). Like the juniper woodland, the dwarf oak scrub occurs in the north-east of the basin, in semi-arid areas with 700–900 mm of annual rainfall. Some evidence indicates that this community is also the result of the degradation of pine and oak forests. The disturbance factor that maintains this vegetation type is the occurrence of periodic fires.

Grassland

Grassland communities occur in various parts of the Basin of Mexico. The most important of these formations are the *Hilaria cenchroides* grasslands in the north-west of the basin, near Huehuetoca and Tepozotlán, and also in the foothills of the Sierra Nevada. This community grows on slopes and hills at altitudes of 2,300–2,700 m, with annual rainfall around 600–700 mm. In the plains of the centre and north of the basin, at 2,300–2,400 m, a grassland community is found in areas strongly disturbed by long human occupancy. The dominant species in these grasslands are annual grasses (*Aristida adscencionis* and *Bouteloua simplex*), frequently coexisting with the *pirú* (*Schinus molle*, a hardy drought-tolerant tree introduced from Peru during the early Spanish colonization) and prickly-pears (*Opuntia* spp.). These grassy plains are found mostly around Teotihuacan and northwards to Pachuca.

At much higher altitudes (2,900–3,500 m) in the oyamel forests, prairies of *sínfito* (*Potentilla candicans*) are found in valleys and high plains with clayey soil and poor drainage. During the dry season, these prairies are dominated by the creeping *Potentilla* plants with their lovely yellow flowers. During the rainy season, a dense carpet of grasses and sedges covers these valleys instead. At even higher elevations (4,000 m or more), above the timberline of the *Pinus hartweggii* forests, are alpine meadows of *Muhlenbergia* and *Festuca* (Beaman 1965). These hardy grasses with tussock growth form clusters of erect and tough leaves, 60–120 cm high. The dry tussocks burn very easily during the dry season and the community is a constant concern in terms of forest fires. Together with the open forests of *Pinus hartweggii*, these grasslands are the main habitat of the endangered volcano rabbit.

Xerophilous scrub

Xerophilous shrublands are quite common in the drier parts of the basin, including the northern region with its low rainfall and the *pedregales*, i.e. zones with porous basaltic substrates and hence with low capacities for retaining water. This vegetation type includes various shrub communities, dominated by dryland species. Its most distinctive characteristic is not the taxonomic identity of the component species, but rather its scrubby physiognomy and the adaptations of the plants to aridity. In general, these scrubs are found in the lower parts of the basin, at elevations of 2,250–2,700 m, in areas where annual precipitation is less than 700 mm.

The largest xerophilous community in the basin is formed by the *nopaleras* (prickly-pear scrub) of the north of the basin. In these areas the dominant species are the prickly-pear (*Opuntia streptacantha*), the cat-claw (*Mimosa biuncifera*), the desert palm (*Yucca filifera*), and the *cenicilla* (*Zaluzania augusta*). On some hillslopes of the north, an arid community of rosette plants is found, with dominance of the *guapilla* (*Hechtia podantha*) and the *lechuguilla* (*Agave lecheguilla*), which grow in association with sarcocaulescent (i.e. fleshy-stemmed) deciduous species such as *Jatropha dioica*.

In the Sierra de Guadalupe, in the central part of the basin, some remains of the *Eysenhardtia polystachya* community still occur, although this xerophilous association has almost disappeared under the pressure of urban expansion.

In the southern part of the basin, this xerophilous vegetation occurs mainly on land affected by the extensive lava flow that covered the Ajusco slopes after the eruption of the Xitle volcano some 2,000 years ago. This area is now known as El Pedregal de San Angel (the San Angel badlands). This unique ecosystem originally covered some 40 km^2, and its characteristically patchy distribution of species corresponded to an extremely varied environment (Rzedowski 1954).

In the lower part of El Pedregal, a very characteristic scrub was common until a few decades ago. Known locally as the *palo-loco* scrub, this community is characterized by the *palo-loco* (*Senecio praecox*), the *tepozán* (*Buddleia* spp.), *Wigandia urens*, various species of *copal* (*Bursera* spp.), *Eysenhardtia polystachya*, and a large number of herbaceous species, many of them endemic to these lava badlands.

In the higher parts, especially where the soil profile is not well developed, two smaller shrubs with similar growth habits (*Sedum oxypetallum* and *S. moranense*) dominate. The ability of these species to form clones from broken branches has contributed to their wide distribution in these habitats. Where the irregularities of the lava have allowed the accumulation and development of soil, oaks are often interspersed with a few individual trees of the rarer *Bursera fagaroides*. Above 2,800 m, pines (*Pinus hartweggii, P. rudis,* and *P. montezumae*) can be found in sedimentary soil pockets within the lava flow. The *tepozanes* (*Buddleia* spp.) that are common through-out the *pedregal* are indicators of environmental disturbance. Their long dormant periods, easy germination responses when conditions are favourable, and their formation of banks of small juveniles help to make these trees important secondary colonizers. Some species, including an orchid (*Tigridia pavonia*) and a cactus (*Mammillaria sanangelensis*), are endemic and are gravely endangered by the growth of the city.

El Pedregal now has been reduced to less than 3 km². The few existing remnants of the vegetation of these unique lava flows survive on the campus of the National Autonomous University of Mexico (UNAM), where an ecological reserve has been created to protect this fragile and endangered ecosystem.

Halophytic vegetation
Salt-loving vegetation currently dominates in the lower parts of the basin, mostly on the beds of the old lakes that now remain dry most of the year. Halophytes are particularly abundant in the area that was covered in former times by the briny waters of Lake Texcoco. Before the lakes dried up, these halophytes used to prosper only on the margins of the saltier bodies of water, but with artificial draining of the basin they have now extended their range into the former lake beds. The halophytic vegetation is threatened in part by the growth of the urban area, and even more by the discharges of waste water, some of which tend to accumulate in the lower parts of the basin.

The saline associations of the basin show the physiognomy of a low and dense grassland. These plant communities are dominated by grasses that multiply by stolons (*Distichlis spicata* and *Eragrostis obtusiflora*). There are also low shrubs such as *Atriplex* spp. and *Suaeda nigra*. The seedlings of this last species have been cultivated

for centuries by the *chinampa* farmers in Xochimilco, and are consumed as a tender vegetable. These seedlings, known locally as
romeritos, are one of the few known cases in which the seed for cultivation is extracted from wild adult plants, and not from the cultivated plants themselves.

Aquatic and sub-aquatic vegetation
Before the desiccation of the lakes, aquatic plants occupied large
areas of the basin. Swamp-cypress forests and willow stands were also
very important on the floodable lake margins of the alluvial plains.
Nowadays, however, they have been reduced to a minute fraction of
their original range.

The little aquatic vegetation that still remains is found in parts of
the former lakes of Texcoco, Zumpango, Xochimilco, and Chalco.
Until the middle of the twentieth century, emergent plant species (i.e.
rooted in the lake bottom but with aerial leaves) such as cattail or *tule*
(*Typha latifolia*) and rush (*Scirpus validus*) were commonly harvested as a source of fibres for roofing, mats, and chair seats. Small
sedge prairies are still found in some of the old lakes. Some native
free-floating species (*Lemna* spp. and *Azolla* spp.) are found in the
open water bodies that still exist. However, these floating species are
being quickly displaced by the weedy water hyacinth (*Eichhornia
crassipes*), a South American species that propagates vegetatively in
an extraordinary way and covers the water bodies completely, disrupting their light conditions and their oxygen content, and producing
serious disruptions in the life cycles of the native aquatic flora and
fauna.

Fauna

The fauna of the Basin of Mexico have suffered deep transformations
by human-induced environmental change, possibly deeper than those
experienced by the vegetation (Halffter and Reyes-Castillo 1975).
These transformations have been the product not only of modern
urban expansion, with the associated phenomena of pollution and
habitat degradation, but also of the long human occupancy of the
region, starting with the arrival of the first hunter-gatherers in the
New World. In a detailed study of the wild mammals of the basin,
Ceballos and Galindo (1984) described 87 species of mammals
recorded during the early 1980s, some of them present in very low
densities and identified through indirect evidence such as tracks or

Table 2.2 **Species richness of mammals in the Basin of Mexico in the early 1980s**

Order	No. of species
Marsupialia (opossums)	1
Insectivora (shrews)	5
Chiroptera (bats)	26
Edentata (armadillos)	1
Lagomorpha (rabbits and jackrabbits)	6
Rodentia (squirrels, mice, and gophers)	35
Carnivora (carnivores)	12
Artiodactyla (deer)	1

Source: Ceballos and Galindo (1984).

excrement, or indirect reports from third parties (table 2.2). The observed species are distributed among eight orders, of which the most abundant are rodents and bats.

The low number of large herbivores (Artiodactyla) in this list is striking. Based on historical and archaeological evidence, Niederberger (1987b) produced a similar list (table 2.3.), reconstructing the species richness of the basin in pre-Hispanic times. Whereas Niederberger's list is not exhaustive (it reports only those species for which there is archaeological evidence of their presence and emphasizes species used by human populations), Ceballos and Galindo's list tries to include all the mammal species found at present. Thus, those species cited in Niederberger but not listed in Ceballos and Galindo may have experienced local extinction. This certainly is the case for the ocelot, the pronghorn antelope, the mule deer, and the peccary. That is, the main differences between the two lists occur in the larger mammals, and principally in the large herbivores. Before the Conquest, these animals were highly valued as a source of protein, and since those times they have tended to vanish from the basin as a result of overhunting and land-use change. Similarly to the large herbivores, the wild turkey (*Meleagris gallopavo*) was also abundant in the forest ecosystems that surrounded the Basin of Mexico, and was an important game species until the seventeenth century (Niederberger 1987b). Its progressive disappearance in the region was mostly due to the intensive hunting pressure to which its wild populations were subjected. In the next chapter we shall discuss the problem of obtaining protein for the indigenous inhabitants of the basin. At this point, it is enough to note that, from the time of the first

Table 2.3 **Mammals present in the Basin of Mexico in pre-Hispanic times**

Order	Family	Species	Common names	Current presence[a]
Marsupialia	Didelphidae	*Didelphis marsupialis*	Opossum, *tlacuache*	*
Insectivora	Soricidae	*Sorex saussurei*	Shrew	*
Edentata	Dasypodidae	*Dasipus novemcinctus*	Armadillo	*
Lagomorpha	Leporidae	*Lepus callotis*	Jack-rabbit	*
		Sylvilagus floridanus	Cottontail, *tochtli*	*
		Sylvilagus cunicularius	Rabbit, *tochtli*	*
		Romerolagus diazi	Volcano rabbit, *Zacatuche*	*
Rodentia	Sciuridae	*Sciurus aureogaster*	Squirrel, *cuauhtechalote*	*
		Spermophilus mexicanus	Ground-squirrel, *motocle*	*
		Spermophilus variegatus	Rock squirrel, *techalote*	*
	Geomyidae	*Pappogeomys merriami*	Pocket gopher, *tuza*	*
		Pappogeomys tylorhinus	Pocket gopher, *tuza*	*
	Cricetidae	*Microtus mexicanus*	*Metorito, quimichin*	*
		Peromyscus melanotis	Black-eared mouse	*
		Peromyscus maniculatus	Deer mouse	*
		Peromyscus truei	Piñon mouse	*
		Neotomodon alstoni	Volcano rat	*
Carnivora	Felidae	*Felis concolor*	Puma	*
		Felis pardalis	Ocelot, *ocelotl*	
		Lynx rufus	Lynx	
	Canidae	*Canis latrans*	Coyote	*
		Urocyon cineroargenteus	Grey fox	*
	Procyonidae	*Bassariscus astutus*	Ringtail, *cacomixtle*	*
		Procyon lotor	Raccoon, *mapache*	*
	Mustelidae	*Mephitis macroura*	Hooded skunk	*
		Mustela frenata	Weasel	*
		Taxidea taxus	Badger, *tlalcoyote*	*

24

Artiodactyla	Antilocapridae	*Antilocapra americana*	Pronghorn, *berrendo*	*
	Cervidae	*Odocoileus virginianus*	White-tailed deer	
		Odocoileus hemionus	Mule deer, *bura*	
	Tayassuidae	*Pecari tajacu*	Peccary, *coyámetl*	

Source: Niederberger (1987b).

a. The asterisks indicate that the species has also been recorded recently. Species without an asterisk are now locally extinct (i.e. are not cited by Ceballos and Galindo, 1984, as currently present in the Basin of Mexico).

human settlements in the basin, the supply of animal protein became a logistical problem that induced, among other effects, a drastic local reduction in the wild populations of large game animals.

At the bottom of the basin, near or in the water bodies of the lakes, a rich fauna of waterfowl (including migrating species), reptiles, amphibians, fish, and aquatic invertebrates was found in pre-Hispanic and early colonial times. These groups of organisms were more difficult to eradicate through overhunting, and for centuries they represented the most abundant and dependable source of animal protein for the inhabitants of the basin. In the twentieth century, the drying of the lakes has achieved what many centuries of hunting did not: the animal populations associated with the water bodies started to disappear rapidly as a result of habitat degradation and the accumulation of pollutants. Various scholars (Halffter and Reyes-Castillo 1975; Rojas Rabiela 1985; and Niederberger 1987a, 1987b) have described in detail the rich aquatic fauna that existed in the Basin of Mexico, as well as the capture methods that were used by the traditional residents.

The waterfowl species that were found in the basin, and in some cases can still be found in the bowl of Lake Texcoco and other remaining water bodies, are mostly migratory, and use the lakes of the Mexican highlands as a site of winter refuge from November to March. This diverse group of aquatic birds included 22 species of ducks, geese, and swans, 3 species of pelicans and cormorants, 10 species of egrets, bitterns, and herons, 4 species of grebes, 19 species of shorebirds (plovers and snipes), and 9 species of cranes, rails, and coots. The wild ducks or *canauhtli* (*Anas* spp., with 8 species in the basin) and the wild geese or *concanauhtli* (*Anser albifrons*) were the animals most appreciated and sought by hunters.

Within the reptiles and the amphibians of the lakes of Mexico, Niederberger reports five species of toads and frogs, four salamanders or *axólotl*, seven water snakes (*Thamnophis* sp.), and three turtles (*Kinosternon integrum*, *K. pennsylvanicum*, and *Onichotria mexicana*). The salamanders, corresponding to the species *Ambystoma lacustris*, *A. carolinae*, *A. tigrinum*, and *Siredon edule*, were especially appreciated for consumption owing to their delicate flavour, which is similar to that of European eels. In spite of the decline in their populations, even today it is possible to purchase them in the market of Xochimilco, collected from the canals that border the remaining *chinampa* fields.

The lake was also rich in fish, which the early inhabitants of the basin caught with nets. The most abundant taxon was that of the Aterinidae or white fish, called *iztacmichin* in *náhuatl*. This group had three species, all belonging to the genus *Chirostoma* but easily distinguishable by their size. The largest species, *Chirostoma humboldtianum*, called *amílotl* by the Aztecs of the basin (the *mexicas*), measured 25–30 cm in length and was highly regarded as a fresh product. The second species, called *xalmichin* by the *mexicas*, was 15–20 cm long and is known scientifically as *Chirostoma regani*. The smallest species, called *xacapitzahuac* in *náhuatl* and known scientifically as *Chirostoma jordani*, was 5–15 cm long and was usually processed and consumed as sun-dried food, because its small size allows for quick dehydration of the specimens. These small fish are still widely available in Mexican markets under the name of *charales*, but they are now harvested mostly in the lakes of Jalisco and Michoacán.

The other groups of fish that were used by the *mexicas* belong to the families of the Cyprinidae and the Goodeidae. The first, known in *náhuatl* as *xuilin*, live and forage in the muddy lake bottoms, and include four species: *Algancea tincella* (the most abundant one), *Evarra bustamentei*, *E. tlahuaensis*, and *E. eigenmani*. From the family Goodeidae, the *mexicas* harvested only one species (*Girardinichtys viviparus*), known as *cuitlapétotl* or "large-bellied fish."

The early inhabitants of the basin also ate a great number of small aquatic organisms such as arthropods, algae, and fish roe. A species of small lake shrimps (*Cambarellus montezumae*), some 2 cm long, were widely consumed in pre-Hispanic Mexico and even now are frequently sold in the markets near Xochimilco. The *axayácatl*, known as "bird flies" (*mosco para pájaros*) in the city markets, are also important commercial products. The early Mexicans consumed the adult specimens of these insects (which are not really flies but water-bugs, the most important of which is known scientifically as *Ahuautlea mexicana*), and also collected their eggs from the waters of the lakes. These eggs (called *ahuautli*) were collected by submerging grass straws in the water, thus inducing the insects to use them as oviposition sites. In a few days, these stalks were taken from the water covered by *ahuautli*, which were then used for human consumption. Nowadays, the *ahuautli* are produced commercially in the remaining water bodies of Lake Texcoco, and are sold mainly as food for pet birds and fishes. The larvae of other insects were also collected and consumed. Among these, the most important were the larvae of Neuroptera (*aneneztli*), aquatic Coleoptera (*ocuiliztac*), and Diptera (*izcauitli*).

27

The ecological productivity of the Basin of Mexico

The previous descriptions show that the Basin of Mexico was an immensely diverse area in terms of landscapes and natural resources. It had forests, grasslands, and lakes; it was populated by a large number of game species; it attracted millions of migratory birds every year. Maize, chilli, and beans yielded good returns in the *chinampas*, and both the agaves and the *nopales* (prickly-pears) grew almost wild in its drier soils. Care must be taken, however, not to assume that this diversity of resources meant that the *mexicas* had no problems in supplying their populations with their basic needs.

From the ecological point of view, the concept of diversity of natural resources must be distinguished from the concept of productivity and sustainable yield. A high diversity, or biological richness, implies the existence of a wealth of different resources, as well as possibilities of alternative uses between them. The Basin of Mexico was, indeed, a highly diverse system, with a large heterogeneity of landscapes, habitats, and both plant and animal species. Its productivity, measured as the amount of resources that could be harvested per unit area in one year, however, was highly variable. Periodic droughts and winter frosts affected a good part of the basin. To avoid these problems, which basically affected agriculture, the Aztecs fished and hunted in the lake waters, as the large terrestrial herbivores were already scarce in Aztec times. But the collection of wild specimens in the lakes demanded a large hunting effort for relatively small prey. *Chinampa* agriculture, although much more efficient and reliable than dryland farming, also entailed an immense effort in the movement of soil and sediment, in the levelling of the agricultural fields, and in the dredging of the canals.

Thus, although the Basin of Mexico was a system of very high diversity, the pre-Hispanic population growth had surpassed its natural productivity and, therefore, its capacity to sustain its human populations. For reasons we shall discuss in the next section of this chapter, access to an adequate supply of animal protein was a problem for the inhabitants of the Basin of Mexico from very early times. The paucity of large herbivores drove the population to consume waterfowl and small aquatic organisms. It also induced the development of an ingenious system for the use of adventitious plants: the population of the basin started to use the tender seedlings of the weeds from the *chinampas* (known in *náhuatl* as *quilitl*) as vegetables. These seedlings were obtained in great quantities during the weeding of the maize plots and, if collected in the early stages of their life cycle, they had good nutritional value and a relatively high protein content. Aztec agriculture produced *quilitl* (*quelites* in Spanish) from species of many different families. Many of them, such as the *quintoniles, epazote, pápalo, verdolaga*, and *romeritos*, constitute an important part of the diet of modern Mexicans. Niederberger (1987b) mentions the use of 16 species of *quilitl*, from 11 different botanical families (Chenopodiaceae, Amaranthaceae, Compositae, Gramineae, Portulaceae, Oxalidaceae, Scrophulariaceae, Solanaceae, Polygonaceae, Nymphaeaceae, and Umbelliferae). Other weeds served medicinal purposes: the *epazote* (*Chenopodium ambrosioides*) as an effective anti-helminthic, and the marigold or *cempasúchil* (*Tagetes* spp.) as cathartic and anti-fever medication (Ortiz de Montellano 1975). This mixture of the cultivation of domesticated plants with the simultaneous use of wild plants and animals was possibly the most distinctive trait of the pre-Hispanic mode of production in the basin.

As the population in the basin grew, however, the Aztecs perforce resorted to importing into the basin greater and greater amounts of raw materials and products from other regions. At the height of the Aztec empire, Tenochtitlan imported 7,000 tons of maize, 5,000 tons of beans, 4,000 tons of chia, 4,000 tons of amaranth or *huautli*, 40 tons of dried chillis, and 20 tons of cacao seeds from outside the basin every year (López Rosado 1988). It also imported great quantities of dried fish, honey, agave sap (*aguamiel*), cotton, henequen, vanilla, tropical fruits, hides, feathers, wood, rubber, *amate* paper (made from the bark of *Ficus* trees), limestone, *copal* incense (resin from *Bursera* trees), salt, purpura, cochineal, and mushrooms, among many other goods.

Demographic and resource changes in the Basin of Mexico

Natural resources, and the growth and collapse of human settlements

Depletion of natural resources in the Basin of Mexico has been a serious problem in the historical past and has led to massive emigration and sundry socio-cultural collapses. Our discussion delineates some historical periods during which the inappropriate management of natural resources induced the demographic and cultural disintegration of the societies inhabiting the Basin of Mexico. Our analysis

29

relies on the work of Whitmore and Turner (1986; see also Whitmore et al. 1990; and Parsons 1976) on the occurrence of demographic cycles of population and collapse in the Basin of Mexico, coupled with our own studies on environmental change in the area (Ezcurra 1990a, 1990b, 1992). This section examines each of these cycles in relation to natural resource depletion.

Extinctions and the transition to agriculture

Compared with the long human occupancy of the Old World, humans arrived in the American continents in relatively recent times. During the Wisconsin glaciation (between 70,000 and 12,000 BP), towards the end of the Pleistocene period, large masses of ice accumulated at the polar caps and the sea level fell more than 10 m. This fall in the sea level enabled human groups to cross the Behring Strait into the New World. The date of the arrival of the first humans in the American continent is still a matter of disagreement (Lorenzo 1981; MacNeish 1976; Marcus and Berger 1984; Martin 1984). From the available information, however, we can certainly deduce that humans arrived in the New World towards the end of the Wisconsin, after thousands of years of cultural and demographic expansion in the Old World.

The spread of humans in North America and Meso-America co-incided with the simultaneous retreat of the Wisconsin glaciers and the extinction of many species of large mammals such as glyptodonths, antelopes, wild horses, capibaras, deer, various camelids, musk oxen, mastodons, gomphoteres, and mammoths (Halffter and Reyes-Castillo 1975; Martin 1984). The reasons for these massive extinctions are still controversial (see, for example, Diamond 1984, and Martin 1984). A recent theory, known as the "overkill hypothesis," argues that the late Pleistocene extinctions were induced by the arrival of humans, a new predatory species organized in small social groups, culturally evolved, capable of using tools and weapons, and, above all, possessing a deadly efficiency in its hunting methods (Diamond 1984; Martin 1984).

Because of the extinction of the large herbivores (whatever its cause), humans in the New World did not have access to the same array of animals to domesticate as their counterparts in the Old World, especially in regard to herbivores (save, of course, the llama and alpaca of the Andes). The excessive hunting of large herbivores, together with the climatic changes of the end of the Wisconsin period, drove many species to extinction and forced humans in the New

World to survive on plants and small animals, including insects. It is interesting that this same incapacity to domesticate animals accelerated the domestication of crop plants. In a few thousand years, a relatively short period in prehistoric time scales, the hunters who arrived in the New World had become sedentary farmers.

In the Basin of Mexico in particular, archaeological excavations have shown that the proportion of bones in food remains decreased constantly with time. It is estimated that meat formed less than 1 per cent of the diet of the inhabitants of the basin during the Classical period and later (Sanders 1976a; Sanders, Parsons, and Santley 1979). For comparison, it is interesting to note that in the Formative period (1500–800 BC), although most of the large herbivores had already become extinct, meat from white-tailed deer (*Odocoileus virginianus*) still formed an important part of the diet of residents of the Basin of Mexico (Serra Puche 1988; Serra Puche and Valadez Azúa 1989).

The transformation of human groups from nomadic hunters to sedentary farmers was not an easy process. Archaeological evidence suggests that increasing difficulties in securing an adequate food supply, combined with the inferior quality of the game protein, forced this transition. Thus, we can visualize the establishment of the first populations in the Mexican highlands as a long cycle of population expansion that became limited and threatened by an increasing scarcity of game animals. This, in turn, stimulated the rapid development of agriculture and the initiation of a new cycle of expansion under new rules of production and social organization.

Tectonic vulnerability

Given the proximity and direct geological connection of the Basin of Mexico with the Pacific Trench, as well as the numerous faults that exist along the Transversal Volcanic Axis, volcanic processes and tectonic instability in general have long characterized the geological history of the basin (Mosser 1987).

As agriculture took hold in the basin, the human groups became sedentary and organized themselves in small settlements in the lower parts of the valley (Lorenzo 1981; Niederberger 1979). These settlements occupied plains low enough to offer good productive potential, but sufficiently high so as to escape flooding during the rainy season (Niederberger 1979). Between 1700 and 1100 BC, the first large settlements started to develop north-east of the basin. Towards 100 BC,

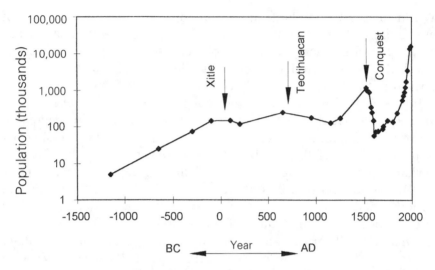

Fig. 2.3 **Population change in the Basin of Mexico (Note: the arrows indicate the approximate time of occurrence of three major events of population collapse: (a) the Xitle volcanic eruption, (b) the downfall of Teotihuacan, and (c) the conquest of the Aztec empire by Hernán Cortés; population numbers are plotted on a logarithmic scale. Source: various sources – see Ezcurra 1992, 1995)**

the population of the basin was around 150,000 (fig. 2.3). Three large settlements developed during this period: Texcoco, north-east of the Lake of Mexico, Teotihuacan to the north, and Cuicuilco to the south-west.

Cuicuilco developed in a region with more rainfall than the semi-arid settlements of the north, and which also received water from the rivers that descended from the Ajusco range. Thus, towards the beginning of the Christian era, Cuicuilco was a flourishing culture, as important as or more so than Teotihuacan. But the eruption of the Xitle volcano around AD 100 generated an immense flow of lava that completely buried this large urban and ceremonial centre. Worse still, the lava buried the best agricultural soils of the region under its basalt mantle and wiped out the Cuicuilco culture. This catastrophe decisively marked the physical hazards that the volcanic geology of the Mexican highlands can impose on human development. The Xitle eruption produced a demographic collapse and induced massive migration northward. This sole event consolidated the future political pre-eminence of Teotihuacan, a city-state that would forever mark the basin as the population and urban centre of Mexico.

Temples and desertification

Towards AD 100, Teotihuacan, situated in the north-east of the basin, had some 30,000 inhabitants. Five centuries later, in AD 650, its population of 150,000 made it one of the largest cities in the world (Parsons 1976; Millon 1970). A century later, the population of Teotihuacan had collapsed to fewer than 10,000. The cause of this decline is not well known. Some researchers attribute it to the rebellion of subjugated groups; others, to the exhaustion of the natural resources exploited by the Teotihuacans. Even if the first hypothesis were true, the ecological significance of war tribute was the importing of natural resources that served to subsidize the local economy. In either case, the exhaustion of local resources and conflicts over the appropriation of foreign commodities appear to be the driving forces of the collapse. According to Sanders (1976a; see also Sanders, Parsons, and Santley 1979), the overexploitation of the natural resources in the semi-arid environment surrounding Teotihuacan and the lack of a sufficiently developed technology to exploit the fertile but flood-prone terrains of the basin lake beds were decisive determinants in the sudden collapse of this civilization.

Good evidence shows that the Teotihuacan area was severely disturbed at the time of the decline and remains so today. The area is strongly desertified and completely lacks native woody vegetation. It is possible to calculate, for example, the amount of wood needed to calcinate the mortar and stucco used to construct the gigantic pyramids of the city as being in the order of tens of thousands of tons (Cook 1947). Adding to this the amount of wood necessary to satisfy the domestic needs of 150,000 persons (a conservative estimate is 30,000 tons per year), it becomes clear that the development of Teotihuacan brought a large-scale process of deforestation in the north of the basin, with erosion and loss of good agricultural soils as consequences. The total amount of wood used by Teotihuacan during its last century implies the cutting of 30,000–60,000 ha of dry pine and oak forests (Ezcurra 1992). Everything seems to indicate that resource exhaustion was a key determinant of the decline of Teotihuacan.

The rise and fall of Tenochtitlan

After a brief hiatus during which the dominant city-state moved to the northern edge of the basin, populations and polities flourished anew around the lakes. This settlement was substantial by the time the Aztec tribes entered the basin, especially in southern areas. The occupation of the basin was becoming increasingly lacustrine, particularly with the development of *chinampa* cultivation (Calneck 1972). Around AD 1325, the Aztecs, or *mexicas*, founded their city, Tenochtitlan, on a low, floodable island that became in a few centuries the capital of the powerful Aztec empire and the political, economic, and religious centre of Meso-America. To fuel this empire, the state undertook impressive feats of hydro-engineering to control flooding and arrest salinization of water in southern sections of the basin (Palerm 1973).

So supported, during the late fifteenth century the population of the basin reached an estimated 1.5 million inhabitants, distributed in more than 100 towns. The Basin of Mexico was probably the largest and most densely settled urban area in the world at that time. When the Spaniards arrived in 1519, the basin was the centre of a Meso-American civilization, founded on the cultivation of the state-controlled *chinampa* fields, especially in the southernmost lakes of Chalco and Xochimilco.

Care must be taken, however, not to interpret the success of Tenochtitlan and the Aztec empire as resulting from sustainable use of the basin's natural resources. As discussed above, although the basin was a system of high environmental diversity, various hazards threatened its productivity.

In spite of innovations and adjustments to counter a dwindling food supply, mounting population growth prompted the Aztecs to wage war on surrounding groups and to force them to pay tributes to Tenochtitlan. Some cruel rituals such as cannibalism have been interpreted as a way of imposing Aztec rule by terrorizing the subdued groups (see Anawalt 1986; Duverger 1983; Harner 1977). Matos Moctezuma (1987) has shown that the two pillars of Aztec power were symbolized in the sanctuary of the Great Temple of Tenochtitlan: Tlaloc, the god of water, rain, and agriculture, and Huitzilopochtli, the goddess of sun, fire, and war. Thus, the Aztec empire rested both on *chinampa* agriculture and on war tribute. As discussed above, the appropriation of essential food products, such as maize, beans, chia, and amaranth, from subjugated groups became more and more important as the Aztec ruling system evolved.

In 1519, after a siege of 90 days, the soldiers of Cortés, backed by a large army of local allies who wanted to get rid of the Aztec rule, took over Tenochtitlan, and in a very short time dismantled the Aztec dominion. The support that Cortés received from other groups was largely the result of hostility toward the war-tribute system imposed by the Aztecs. In a way, the lack of self-sufficiency of Tenochtitlan and the Aztec state figured prominently in their downfall.

With the Spanish Conquest, horses and cattle were introduced to Mexico, and both transportation and the agricultural structure changed accordingly (Whitmore and Turner 1992; Turner and Butzer 1992). Many of the Aztec canals were filled in to create roads for horses and carts. Thus, the *chinampas* were displaced from the centre of the city. Cattle, sheep, goats, pigs, and chickens provided new sources of protein. The land use and physiognomy of the surrounding mountains started to change, mostly through cattle grazing and timber logging. The Spanish Conquest also triggered a tremendous population decline in the basin, largely through the introduction of new diseases (León Portilla, Garibay, and Beltrán 1972). A century after the Conquest, the population of the basin had fallen below 100,000 (Whitmore and Turner 1986; Whitmore et al. 1990).

The colonial period

The Spaniards were also changed by the indigenous culture, in perhaps a more subtle but equally irreversible manner. The Mexican colony became a synthesis of both Aztec and Spanish traditions (DDF 1983). Some persistent cultural differences, however, led to further transformations of the landscape. From early colonial times, it became clear that the new city plan was not compatible with the lacustrine landscape of the basin (Sala Catalá 1986). The filling of the Aztec canals and the *chinampas* to build elevated roads obstructed the surface drainage of the city and created large expanses of stagnant water, while the grazing and logging of the slopes surrounding the basin resulted in increased surface runoff and silting during the rainy season. The first severe flood occurred in 1553; floods recurred in 1580, 1604, and 1629, and thereafter at shorter intervals. The low altitude of the northern ranges, and the existence of nearly level passes between them, encouraged the colonial government to plan the drainage of the basin towards the north, from Lake Zumpango. The first drainage canal, El Tajo de Nochistongo, was 15 km long and opened the basin towards the Tula basin in 1608 (Lara 1988). The larger works of the Canal de Huehuetoca began in the late sixteenth century and continued until the early twentieth century. At first the canal served only as a spillover system but, with the construction of the auxiliary Canal de Guadalupe in 1796, the lacustrine area in the Basin of Mexico began to shrink rapidly (Trabulse 1983). In spite of the drainage works, navigation by canals was still very popular towards the end of the colonial period. Boats departed regularly to Xochimilco and Chalco from a pier near the old market of La Merced, east of the Central Plaza known as El Zocalo (Sierra 1984). The Canal de La Viga, among many others, remained active throughout the colonial period and represented an important trading route for agricultural products between the *chinampas* of Xochimilco and the city.

Independence

The war of Independence (1810–1821) brought little change to the general physiognomy of the city (González Angulo and Terán Trillo 1976). Drainage works in the Canal de Huehuetoca were greatly extended during the nineteenth century. During the long dictatorship of Porfirio Díaz, in the late nineteenth and early twentieth centuries, the Industrial Revolution brought factories and railroads. The city was modernized for the benefit of a small, centralist, and powerful bourgeoisie whose aim was to transform the wealthier quarters of Mexico, copying the layout of European cities. The basin, once regarded as a series of separate towns linked more by commerce than by a central administration, now came to be considered as a single unit. The newly laid railroads brought peasants looking for employment in the new industries, and some of the smaller towns near the centre of the city – e.g. Tacuba, Tacubaya, and Azcapotzalco – were engulfed by the urban perimeter.

The Revolution

Between 1910 and 1920 the Mexican Revolution brought a decade of ruthless confrontation between the old Porfirian bourgeoisie, which defended its privileges, and other social sectors demanding more participation in the distribution of the national wealth. Mexico City had at that time approximately 700,000 inhabitants and, unexpectedly, suffered little damage. The Revolution was mostly a rural movement, and the city became a haven for middle-class provincial

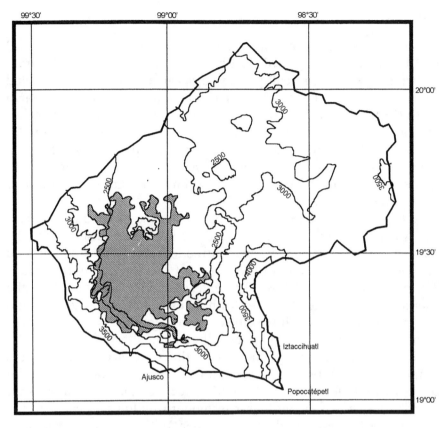

Fig. 2.4 **The urban area of Mexico City, 1990 (cf. fig. 2.2)**

families, who flocked into the Basin of Mexico seeking shelter under the new bureaucracy and the rising industries.

The Revolution became institutionalized in 1924 and peace returned to Mexico City, which proceeded to grow rapidly. Realizing the environmental importance of the surrounding forests, President Lázaro Cárdenas (1934–1940) created various national parks in the mountains enclosing the basin. Two, Desierto de los Leones and Cumbres del Ajusco, were created to the west and south as a way of restricting the deforestation of the basin slopes. Unfortunately, during the presidency of Miguel Alemán (1946–1952) a large part of the Ajusco park was given to a paper mill, which embarked on an ambitious timber-logging programme (DDF 1986). The consequent elimination of the park and the ensuing deforestation of neighbouring areas opened the way for urban expansion.

37

Modern Mexico

During the post-revolutionary period, and particularly after World War II, the industrial growth that had been heralded by the Porfirian government became a reality. Mexico became an industrial city, and massive migration occurred from the country into the city (Garza 1986). In fewer than 80 years, the population of the urban conglomeration jumped from 700,000 to nearly 16 million in 1987 (Aguilar 1986). Peripheral cities, such as Coyoacán, Tlalpan, and Xochimilco, were incorporated into the urban perimeter (fig. 2.4). The urban area of Mexico City now covers some 1,200 km^2, and has expanded over most of the former lake beds.

To divert the torrential urban runoff from the basin, a deep drainage system was built and most of the old lake beds became dry. The drainage of the lake beds and extraction from the underground aquifer led to a lowering of the centre of the city by approximately 9 m between 1910 and 1987. The extremely low wind speeds in the high-altitude plateau, together with intense industrial activity and the emissions from 4 million vehicles, have degraded air quality in the basin to levels that are dangerous to human health.

The tectonic instability that ended the Cuicuilco culture in the south of the basin two millennia ago remains an important cause for concern. In spite of new engineering technologies for anti-seismic foundations, many of the high-rise modern buildings located in the lacustrine plain collapsed in September 1985, with an earthquake registering 7.6 on the Richter scale. Although no official figures have been released, it is estimated that the final death toll numbered some 30,000 (see Pradilla Cobos 1993). Many engineers have insisted since then that the clayey sediments of the old lake beds, weakened by the pumping of water, are capable of amplifying the tremors' vibrational waves and were partly responsible for the concentration of damage in the lower parts of the basin. Should this be true, then we should conclude that, new engineering technologies notwithstanding, earth tremors can still threaten the sustainability of the basin and could pose a real risk for the future.

3

The socio-economy of the Basin of Mexico

Mexico City is a massive urban area. Originally contained within the boundaries of the Federal District, during the 1950s it spilled beyond these borders into the adjacent municipalities of the State of Mexico. Mexico City contains 16 sub-units, called *delegaciones*, of the Federal District as well as 29 municipalities (*municipios*) in the neighbouring State of Mexico (henceforth we shall use the general term "municipalities"when referring to both *delegaciones* and *municipios*). Thus, the limit of the urban physical unit does not coincide with political administrative divisions. This urban expanse is referred to as the Metropolitan Area of Mexico City (hereafter Mexico City; Negrete and Salazar 1986).

Larger, of course, is the Basin of Mexico, a hydrologically defined unit that encompasses 84 municipalities of four different states: the Federal District and the states of Mexico, Hidalgo, and Puebla. Mexico City, concentrating 95 per cent of the total population of the basin, represents the most important socio-economic unit within the basin. Thus, the Basin of Mexico and Mexico City are almost synonymous in demographic terms, but the latter is a subset of the former in geographical terms (Valverde and Aguilar 1987).

Urban growth and social distribution

Urban growth

In the twentieth century Mexico City experienced remarkable growth, characterized by a great centralization of economic activities, notably industry, and high rates of population growth, driven to a large extent by migration from rural areas into the city. With more than 15 million inhabitants in 1990, Mexico City is at present one of the largest cities in the world (Soms García 1986a, 1986b).

The urban growth of Mexico City during the twentieth century can be divided (following Unikel, Ruiz Chiapetto, and Garza 1976: 136–137) into three different periods: 1900–1930, 1930–1950, and post-1950. In the last period, a division can be made between the periods 1950–1970, and 1970 to the present.

1900–1930
Throughout the first period the city had a relatively high annual growth rate of 3.4 per cent, almost three times the national rate. Much of this increase derived from immigration, which Garza and Schteingart (1978: 53) argue was a product of the 1910 revolution and subsequent efforts of agrarian reforms that failed to retain rural population. Mexico City offered physical shelter and a source of employment. In these three decades the city grew from half a million to 1.3 million and its primacy within the nation increased – it became 5.7 times the size of Guadalajara, the second-largest city in Mexico.

1930–1950
During 1930–1950 the city continued to experience steady growth. Between 1940 and 1950 it reached an annual growth rate of 5.5 per cent, the highest in the twentieth century. Suburbanization and continued industrial location around the city brought about a wide spatial expansion, though this was still contained within the limits of the Federal District. The process of metropolitanization began to spread and in 1950 Mexico City comprised some 3.0 million inhabitants (table 3.1). It is important to emphasize that during the 1940s migration from impoverished rural areas into the Basin of Mexico accounted for 73.3 per cent of the city's growth. Natural increase acquired greater importance only in following decades (Stern 1977a, 1977b).

Table 3.1 **Population in the Basin of Mexico, 1940–1990**

	1940	1950	1960	1970	1980	1990
Basin of Mexico (1)	2,217,250	3,624,772	5,816,936	9,451,726	14,682,679	15,887,991
Mexico City (2)	1,979,235	3,360,729	5,487,852	9,029,928	14,074,683	15,079,628
Rest of the Basin of Mexico	238,015	264,043	329,084	421,798	607,996	808,363
% urban population [(2)/(1)]	89.27	92.72	94.34	95.54	95.86	94.91

Source: DGE (1990).
Note: Because of variations in population estimates between different sources, the figures given in the tables in this chapter may differ slightly from those given in chapters 4 and 5.

1950–1970

After 1950 the city underwent rapid and enormous physical expansion, notably in the form of industrial areas beyond the north and north-eastern borders of the Federal District (DF, for the Spanish *Distrito Federal*). The urban area began to invade the municipalities of the State of Mexico, which had annual growth rates more than double those of the DF. Whereas the city as a whole grew at 5.1 per cent during 1960–1970 and at 4.6 per cent in 1970–1980 (table 3.2) several surrounding municipalities had annual growth rates of 12, 16, and 18 per cent over those two decades. The Metropolitan Area increased from 5.5 million in 1960 to some 14 million in 1980, with migration still accounting for approximately 45 per cent of the city's growth (DDF 1982; Goldani 1976). Since the 1960s the city has become six times larger than Guadalajara and contains around 20 per cent of the country's total population (Unikel, Ruiz Chiapetto, and Garza 1976; Negrete and Salazar 1987).

1970 to the present

During the 1970s the city entered a new phase in its urban growth. A slight decline in the population growth rate during this decade became during the 1980s a significant decrease. The contribution of migration to urban growth also declined, from 38.2 per cent in 1970 to 25 per cent in 1980 (Partida 1987). The lure of the capital, a favourite destination for immigrants from rural or urban areas alike in 1940, lost its appeal as the concentration of economic, cultural, and political decisions abetted a deterioration in the overall quality of life. In fact, the migration flows formerly destined for Mexico City now head for smaller metropolitan areas where they represent an important component of rapid growth. Concomitantly, the capital city is tending to lose population, particularly from the middle class, to other cities in the central region of the country where the quality of life is perceived as more agreeable. For example, Izazola and Marquette (1995) report that women play an active role in the decision of a growing number of middle-class families to migrate away from Mexico City as a survival strategy in response to the perceived negative health impacts of the environment on their children.

Even so, the urban area still presents an active process of metropolitanization, especially in the neighbouring territory of the State of Mexico. Although the growth rate for the Federal District, and especially for the central city, was negative during 1980–1990, the municipalities in the neighbouring State of Mexico are still growing at high

Table 3.2 **Population growth rates in the Basin of Mexico, 1940–1990 (%)**

	1940–50	1950–60	1960–70	1970–80	1980–90	1970–90
Basin of Mexico	5.04	4.84	4.97	4.50	0.79	2.63
Mexico City	5.44	5.03	5.11	4.54	0.69	2.60
Rest of Basin of Mexico	1.04	2.23	2.51	3.72	2.89	3.31

Source: DGE (1990).
Note: Because of variations in population estimates between different sources, the growth rates calculated in this table differ slightly from those presented in chapter 5.

rates (2.6 per cent on average), and some of them, such as Chimalhuacan and Chalco, show rates higher than 10 per cent. It is in these areas where urban growth is currently causing the stronger impacts in terms of land occupation (fig. 3.1; table 3.3).

Recent projections suggest that the total population at the beginning of the twenty-first century (year 2010) will be of the order of 26 million for the whole Metropolitan Area. And, if other near-metropolitan areas such as Cuernavaca-Cuautla, Puebla-Tlaxcala, Pachuca-Tulancingo, and Queretaro-San Juan del Río consolidate their functional integration with the country's capital, the Metropolitan Area of Mexico City will probably comprise a population of 35 million people in 2010 (Garza 1987b).

Meanwhile, the population in the rest of the basin is growing at more than 3 per cent, a rate that exceeds that for Mexico City itself. Should this pattern persist, it may lead to a future characterized by more dispersed settlements throughout the basin (see tables 3.1 and 3.2 and fig. 3.1).

The pattern of physical expansion

The spatial development of Mexico City until 1950 was characterized by concentration in the four central *delegaciones* of the DF, which contained around 70 per cent of the urban area at that time. Thereafter the expansion of the city underwent a rapid suburbanization that affected the surrounding *delegaciones* and finally produced a spillover of population into the adjacent municipalities of other states. In this process, the city converted agricultural land or land unsuitable for urbanization, such as the desiccated lake bed of Texcoco to the east, a group of abandoned sand quarries and open-cast mines to the west, and the forested mountain slopes of the south of the basin. To some extent, physical barriers in the south and west have contributed to the restriction of urban growth: the large and flat valley of the basin (approximately 2,250 m above sea level) is surrounded by volcanic mountain ranges that open only to the north and the south-east.

The Spanish established the colonial spatial structure of the city with their grid-iron layout for the central urban area organized around a central square (the *Zocalo*), which in turn had been the ceremonial centre of the Aztec city. During colonial times, and even through most of the nineteenth century, this basic structure suffered only minor alterations. The nationalization of the large church land-

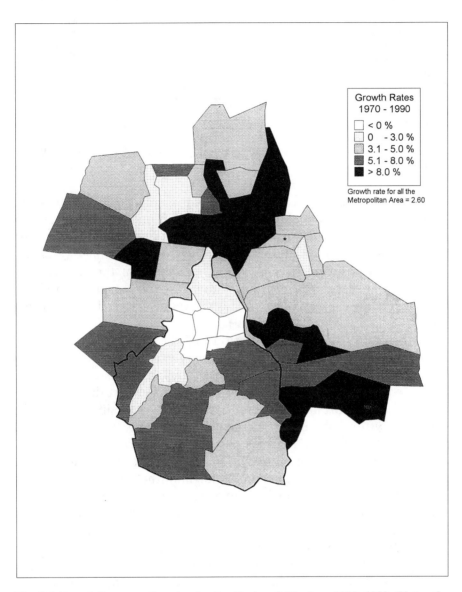

Fig. 3.1 **Population growth rates in the Basin of Mexico, 1970–1990 (Note: the Metropolitan Area is taken as defined by INEGI (1990) in the 1990 population census. The values for the municipality of Tezoyuca, indicated by an asterisk, were estimated from neighbouring municipalities for lack of adequate data. Source: DGE 1990)**

Table 3.3 **Population growth in the Metropolitan Area of Mexico City, 1970–1990**

	1970	1990	Growth rate (%)
Metropolitan Area[a]	9,029,928	15,079,628	2.56
Federal District	6,874,165	8,235,744	0.90
Peripheral municipalities	2,155,763	6,843,884	5.77
Central city[b]	2,902,969	1,930,267	−2.04

Source: DGE (1990).

a. The Metropolitan Area comprises the whole of greater Mexico City, including the Federal District and the peripheral municipalities of the State of Mexico.

b. The central city comprises the *delegaciones* of Benito Juárez, Cuauhtémoc, Miguel Hidalgo, and Venustiano Carranza.

holdings in 1856, however, set important changes in motion. Land around the city was subdivided and sold off and the upper classes moved to the periphery from their mansions in the city centre. The central area, in turn, gradually deteriorated and dwellings were subdivided for low-income groups. This movement of the rich classes, largely towards the west, was accelerated by the construction in the late nineteenth century of the majestic avenue Paseo de la Reforma (Bataillon and Rivière d'Arc 1973).

By the end of the Porfirian period in 1911 clear signs of a spatial segregation along social class lines already existed. To the north and east, new neighbourhoods were occupied by lower classes, commonly employed in factories and railroads and as artisans. At the same time, the west saw important urban improvements (e.g. the installation of a sewerage system) and expensive new developments that allotted land for the affluent sectors. By the 1920s the urban structure was mainly characterized by the concentration of commercial activity in a single centre, the emergence of residential neighbourhoods to the west (e.g. Lomas de Chapultepec), and the expansion of outlying small villages such as Tacuba, Tacubaya, and San Angel, primarily for weekend homes (Garza and Schteingart 1978).

The 1930–1950 period witnessed important improvements in the central road system and a further decentralization of urban activities southward along two main avenues, Insurgentes and Calzada de Tlalpan. This process set in motion the development of commercial concerns with the establishment of services and institutions along these thoroughfares. The commercial development in turn stimulated the appearance of low-density neighbourhoods to the south and west, such as Polanco, Del Valle, and Chapultepec-Morales, mainly occupied by the upper social classes (Unikel 1974). The price per square metre in some of these developments increased by 500–600 per cent in the 1930–1950 period (Flores 1959). However, the most impressive impact was undoubtedly that of the expansion of low-income neighbourhoods spawned by the location of industry in the north of the basin. The demand for labour attracted migrants particularly to *delegaciones* such as Azcapotzalco and Gustavo A. Madero; between 70 and 80 per cent of the growth of these municipalities in the 1940–1950 decade was due to migration. The central city also absorbed some of the migrants, who found accommodation in the old and dilapidated dwellings (*vecindades*) that had been long abandoned by the wealthy (Garza and Schteingart 1978).

Government bans on new housing developments within the DF stimulated the process of suburbanization at the beginning of the 1950s. Tax incentives in the State of Mexico encouraged industrial zones to expand around the railheads, especially to the north-east (Ecatepec) and north-west (Tlanepantla, Naucalpan). This expansion was accompanied by new housing developments and supported by significant improvements in the road system, such as the Mexico–Querétaro freeway, which reduced travel time from the new suburban areas to both the city centre and the industrial zones. The process encouraged the middle and upper classes to settle towards the north-west in suburban developments around Ciudad Satélite, which opened in 1957 (Unikel 1974). In contrast, the low-income groups were segregated to the east on the inhospitable land of the dry and salty lake bed of Lake Texcoco in settlements lacking many basic services and also vulnerable to seasonal flooding and dust storms. The increasing arrival of migrants and the flight of poorer residents from the city centre induced the proliferation of settlements, most of them the product of illegal subdivision of the land. Perhaps the most impressive example was that of Ciudad Nezahualcóyotl, established in large part on the dry lake bed, which increased its population from 65,000 in 1960 to 650,000 in 1970 and today contains a population of about 2 million (see Ferras 1977). These developments account for the extremely rapid growth of the urban area within the State of Mexico during the 1950s and 1960s, compared with the urban areas of the DF.

The urban area of the basin expanded dramatically from around 380 km^2 in 1960 to some 650 km^2 in 1970 (a 57 per cent increase), and to almost 1,000 km^2 in 1980 (an additional increase of 70 per cent; Graizbord and Salazar 1987). Exacerbating the problems induced by explosive city growth was the increasing complexity of the urban structure. The city centre continued to accommodate the head offices of financial institutions, the most important supply market, and some light industries, though new peripheral residential developments induced the creation of important new business and commercial sub-nuclei. Some of the commercial decentralization took a linear path along commercial streets such as Insurgentes. In other cases, the emergence of malls and shopping centres dominated by department stores characterized the middle-class sectors to the south and north-west (Plaza Universidad, Plaza Satélite, and more recently Perisur). Very quickly, previously outlying towns, such as Azcapotzalco and Tacuba, suffered economic diversification and many lost their traditional residential and rural character, giving way to a physical mixture of commerce and industry. Others, such as Coyoacán, San Angel, and Tlalpan, underwent renewal of their "colonial" style and continued to be favoured by the upper middle classes (Bataillon and Rivière d'Arc 1973).

Accelerated urban growth led to the proliferation of illegal, usually poorly urbanized, settlements either in the State of Mexico or in the DF, where the ban upon new developments provoked an increase in squatting (Ward 1981). In 1968, the prohibition on new housing developments in the DF was lifted, and this stimulated the growth of new residential neighbourhoods, particularly in the south. Between 1970 and 1975 some southern *delegaciones*, such as Tlalpan and Xochimilco, almost doubled their urban area, while Cuajimalpa tripled in size (DDF 1976). In the east and west of the DF, light industry was established in *delegaciones* such as Iztapalapa, Iztacalco, and Álvaro Obregón (DDF 1976; Ward 1981).

Throughout the second half of the 1970s this suburbanization continued and reinforced previous patterns, such as the middle-class corridor in the north-west, along the Mexico–Querétaro highway, accompanied by the establishment of more heavy industry. In the inhospitable lands of the east and north-east, low-income populations concentrated in Nezahualcóyotl and Ecatepec, while to the south a boom in residential development occurred and diverse social groups occupied the mountain slopes in an uncontrolled fashion. It is worth noting that this expansion has been in part stimulated by governmental decisions such as the construction of a paved highway to the Ajusco mountain range and the massive construction of large lower-middle-income housing units (mostly for governmental workers) that have emerged in peripheral locations (DDF 1976; see figs. 3.2 and 3.3).

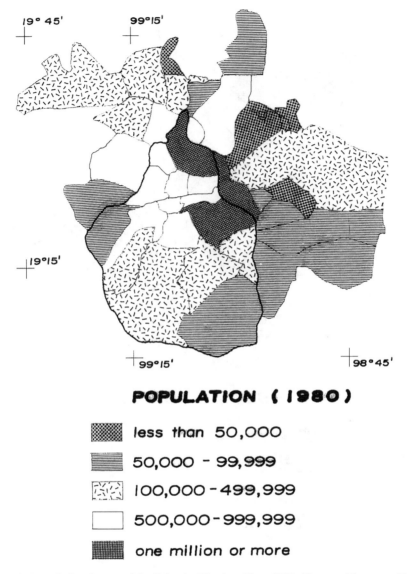

POPULATION (1980)

less than 50,000

50,000 - 99,999

100,000 - 499,999

500,000 - 999,999

one million or more

Fig. 3.2 **Population by municipalities in Mexico City, 1980 (Source: Tamayo, Valverde, and Aguilar 1990)**

In the late 1980s and early 1990s, Mexico's national economic
policy changed radically from governmental intervention and state-
owned industries to the "neo-liberal" approach of a free-market
economy open to foreign investment. This change brought a significant increase in foreign investment in the basin's urban space. The

49

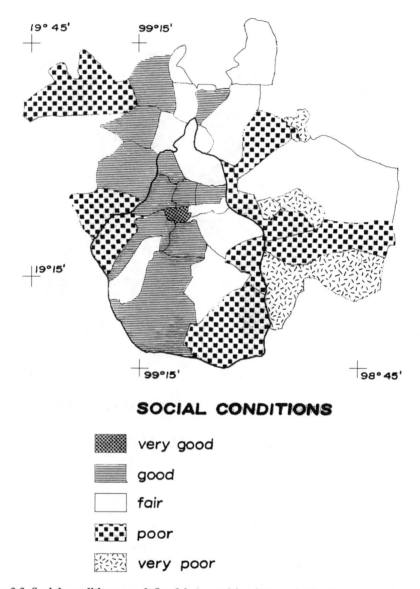

Fig. 3.3 **Social conditions, as defined by a multivariate social indicator, by munici-palities in Mexico City, 1980 (Source: Tamayo, Valverde, and Aguilar 1990)**

neo-liberal process was reflected in the construction of buildings, urban centres, and malls dedicated to commercial and business activities, first-class hotels, and other attractions. These novel land uses emerged especially towards the south and the west of the city and along Paseo de la Reforma, the historical commercial street of central Mexico City. The most prominent example of the new trend is the Santa Fe centre, west of Mexico City, an urban complex of commercial offices, educational institutions, and miscellaneous "clean" industries that runs along the highway to Toluca.

At present the expansion of Mexico City is taking three main directions – to the north, the east, and the west. Expansion to the north, which started in the 1950s, is maintaining its pace; after the city spread beyond the Sierra of Guadalupe, it started to occupy the plain of the former lake of Zumpango with new and important industrial and housing developments. Expansion towards the east has acquired importance in recent years, incorporating land from the former Lake Chalco and consolidating occupation around the Sierra of Santa Catarina in areas such as Ayotla and Ixtapaluca. At the same time, new urban areas are emerging along a corridor in the direction of Texcoco. The westward trend will consolidate the development of the Santa Fe centre and surrounding areas, where higher population densities tend to occur along the highway to the neighbouring city of Toluca, although the slopes of the Sierra de las Cruces represent an imposing limit to this expansion.

With all these new urban expansions, the city has for the first time initiated relations, in terms of land use, with the states of Puebla and Hidalgo through the municipalities of Ixtapaluca and Tecamac, respectively. It is likely that the ongoing expansion of Mexico City will incorporate some municipalities of the State of Hidalgo, especially those situated in the direction of Tizayuca, where the flat terrain is a favourable factor.

The process of metropolitanization

From the 1950s onwards, the process of metropolitanization that has dominated the growth of Mexico City has resulted in a massive suburbanization of both population (housing developments) and employment (industrial and commercial zones). In the 1950s, metropolitanization entailed the physical and functional integration of contiguous political-administrative units from the Federal District and the State of Mexico to form the Metropolitan Area of Mexico City (see table 3.4). Whereas only one *municipio* of the State of Mexico formed part of the conurbation in 1950, 11 *municipios* had been engulfed by the growth of the city by 1970, and the number had risen to 21 by 1980. At present, the Metropolitan Area of Mexico

Table 3.4 **Evolution of the Metropolitan Area of Mexico City, by municipality, 1950–1990**

Delegaciones and *municipios*	Population				
	1950	1960	1970	1980	1990
Metropolitan Area[a]	**2,952,199**	**5,125,447**	**8,623,157**	**13,878,912**	**15,079,628**
Federal District	**2,923,194**	**4,816,617**	**6,840,471**	**8,831,079**	**8,235,744**
Alvaro Obregón	93,176	220,011	456,709	639,213	642,753
Azcapotzalco	187,864	370,724	534,554	601,524	474,688
Benito Juárez				544,882	407,811
Coyoacán	70,005	169,811	339,446	597,129	640,066
Cuajimalpa		19,199	36,200	91,200	119,669
Cuauhtémoc				814,983	595,960
Gustavo A. Madero	204,833	579,180	1,186,107	1,513,360	1,268,068
Iztacalco	33,945	198,904	477,331	570,377	448,322
Iztapalapa	76,621	254,355	522,095	1,262,354	1,490,499
Magdalena Contreras	21,955	40,724	75,429	173,105	195,041
Miguel Hidalgo				543,062	406,868
Milpa Alta				53,616	63,654
Tláhuac			62,419	146,923	206,700
Tlalpan		61,195	130,719	368,974	484,866
Venustiano Carranza				692,896	519,628
Xochimilco		70,381	116,493	217,481	271,151
State of Mexico	**29,005**	**308,830**	**1,782,686**	**5,047,833**	**6,843,884**
Acolman					43,276
Atenco				16,418	21,219
Atizapán de Zaragoza			44,322	202,248	315,192
Chalco				78,393	282,940
Chiautla				10,618	17,764
Chicoloapan				27,354	57,306
Chiconcuac				11,371	14,179
Chimalhuacán		76,740	19,946	61,816	242,317
Coacalco			13,197	97,353	152,082
Cuautitlán			41,156	39,527	48,858
Cuautitlán lzcalli				173,754	326,750
Ecatepec		40,815	216,408	784,507	1,218,135
Huixquilucan			33,527	78,149	131,926
Ixtapaluca				77,862	137,357
Jaltenco					22,803
Melchor Ocampo					26,154
Naucalpan de Juárez		85,828	382,184	730,170	786,551

Table 3.4 **(cont.)**

Delegaciones and *municipios*	Population				
	1950	1960	1970	1980	1990
Nextlalpan					10,840
Nezahualcóyotl			580,436	1,341,230	1,256,115
Nicolás Romero				112,645	184,134
La Paz			32,258	99,436	134,782
Tecamac				84,129	123,218
Teoloyucan					41,964
Tepotzotlán					39,647
Texcoco				105,851	140,368
Tlalnepantla	29,005	105,447	366,935	778,173	702,807
Tultepec					47,323
Tultitlán			52,317	136,829	246,464
Zumpango					71,413

Source: INEGI (1990).

a. The 1950–1970 limits for the Metropolitan Area follow Unikel, Ruiz Chiapetto, and Garza (1976); the 1980 limits are based on Negrete and Salazar (1986); and those for 1990 follow INEGI (1990).

Table 3.5 **The municipalization of the Metropolitan Area of Mexico City, 1950–1990**

Delegaciones and *municipios*	No. of municipalities				
	1950	1960	1970	1980	1990
Delegaciones in the Federal District	7	10	11	16	16
Municipios in the State of Mexico	1	4	11	21	29
Total	8	14	22	37	45

Source: INEGI (1990).

City includes 16 municipalities of the Federal District and 29 munici-palities of the State of Mexico (table 3.5).

Not only has the metropolitanization process generated an increas-ing aggregation of political-administrative units, but it also implies a population redistribution in the whole Metropolitan Area, accom-panied by processes such as land-use changes, higher population densities, and modifications in the urban structure (Garza 1990). Two factors have been very influential in this suburban expansion: low transport costs and the availability of less expensive land in the periphery compared with central locations.

The gradual occupation of territory can be best observed through the evolution of population growth within the different metropolitan

53

Table 3.6 **Population distribution in the Metropolitan Area of Mexico City, by metropolitan rings, 1940–1990 (%)**

	1940	1950	1960	1970	1980	1990[a]
Central area	73.18	66.50	51.61	32.15	18.44	12.80
Inner ring	12.90	22.27	36.80	54.44	58.28	52.80
Intermediate ring	6.49	5.63	6.98	9.03	17.89	25.62
Outer ring	7.43	5.60	4.61	4.39	5.38	8.78

Sources: DGE (1990) and INEGI (1990).
a. The Metropolitan Area in 1990 was defined according to INEGI (1990).

Table 3.7 **Population growth rates in the Metropolitan Area of Mexico City, by metropolitan rings, 1940–1990 (%)**

	1940–50	1950–60	1960–70	1970–80	1980–90
Metropolitan Area[a]	5.44	5.03	5.11	4.54	0.69
Central area	4.43	2.40	0.25	−1.11	−2.92
Inner ring	11.36	10.44	9.30	5.25	−0.30
Intermediate ring	3.94	7.31	7.85	11.94	4.37
Outer ring	2.50	3.00	4.58	6.70	5.74

Sources: DGE (1990) and INEGI (1990).
a. The Metropolitan Area in 1990 was defined according to INEGI (1990).

rings that surround the central city. The current Metropolitan Area includes a central city and three metropolitan rings, and each of these areas possesses distinctive characteristics. Both population distribution and population growth show marked differences between rings (tables 3.6 and 3.7). Whereas in 1940 the central city contained 73 per cent of the total urban population of the basin, by 1960 this proportion had declined to 52 per cent, and by 1990 it represented only 13 per cent (table 3.6). By contrast, the inner ring had only 13 per cent of the total population in 1940, but by 1990 the proportion had increased to 53 per cent, making it the most densely populated zone in the city. The intermediate and outer rings together accounted for 14 per cent of the metropolitan population in 1940, but by 1990 their proportion had increased to 34 per cent

Data on growth rates (table 3.7) reveal that the central city is experiencing a depopulation process that started slowly in the 1970s and is progressively speeding up. In a similar way, the inner ring, after considerable population increases in the 1940–1970 period, started to show the first signs of a depopulation process with negative growth rates after 1980. The 1970s were a period of particularly high growth rates in the intermediate and outer rings (12 per cent and 7 per cent, respectively). Although these high rates decreased to between 4 and 6 per cent in the 1980s, the peripheral municipalities still had the fastest-growing population of the megalopolis, enhancing the trend to incorporate contiguous municipalities.

The economy of the basin

Demographically, the Basin of Mexico contains almost 25 per cent of Mexico's population, but its economic importance is even greater. In the 1940s, Mexico City constituted an economically optimal location for industrial development. Its extensive urban infrastructure, a concentrated market for industrial products, a variety of professional and financial services, and its abundant facilities for administrative transactions (as the seat of the federal government) were all reinforced by a flow of government investments and fiscal incentives that stimulated and enhanced the concentration of economic development in the area. At the time, the basin contained 8 per cent of the nation's total population and its share of national industrial output was 32 per cent.

In the early 1950s, industrial activity in the basin became especially dynamic and, at a national level, a clear trend appeared towards concentration in the capital city. In 1940, 8.7 per cent of the country's industrial establishments were located in Mexico City. This proportion rose steadily to 28 per cent in 1970 and 30 per cent in 1980. During the 1970s the number of industries increased by 10–15 per cent, and the investment of industrial capital also went up. This dramatic industrial concentration in the capital during the twentieth century has generated a situation in which the capital city accounts for about one-third of national industrial production.

The industrial expansion during the 1940s and 1950s contributed to the absorption of an expanding workforce, whose growth was fuelled both by migration and by rapid natural increase. Data show, however, that in recent years industrial concentration has decreased in the capital and currently favours middle-sized industrial cities elsewhere in the country. Both the number of firms and the size of the labour force occupied in industrial activities have decreased in the capital city relative to national totals. Between 1980 and 1989, although the economically active population employed in the industrial and services sectors combined increased by 9.4 per cent (from 1,739,066 to 1,902,787 jobs), industrial employment fell by 10.5 per cent and the number of industrial establishments in the capital city decreased by

Table 3.8 **Mexico City's contribution to the country's gross domestic product, by economic sector, 1970–1990 (%)**

Sector	1970	1990
Manufacturing	37.54	33.71
Commerce	32.11	34.18
Services	34.05	43.23
Other	12.52	12.96
Total GDP	28.60	30.62

Source: Garza and Rivera (1994).

9 per cent. The labour force has turned progressively to the service sector, which experienced growth of 31.0 per cent (Aguilar 1997). In fact, in the 1970–1990 period, the contribution of the industrial sector to Mexico City's gross domestic product (GDP) fell from 37.5 to 33.7 per cent, while the contribution of its service sector rose from 34.0 to 43.2 per cent, and that of the commerce sector increased from 32.1 per cent to 34.2 per cent. By 1990, Mexico City's contribution to the total gross domestic product of the country was 31.0 per cent (table 3.8)

Despite the emigration of some industries away from the basin, the economic dynamics of Mexico City are still the highest of the nation. In 1985, the large conurbation of Mexico City contained 38 per cent of the industrial labour force of the nation (13 per cent in the municipalities of the State of Mexico and 25 per cent in the Federal District). The second most industrialized state, Nuevo León, accounted for 8 per cent of the nation's industrial labour force, followed by Jalisco with 6 per cent and Veracruz with 5 per cent (see Icazuriaga 1992).

To understand the economic dynamics of the basin, it is important to analyse the diversification and internal structure of industry in Mexico City. This structure falls into two broad sectors: means of production and consumer goods (table 3.9). The first sector represented 27.4 per cent of all industry in 1970, divided between capital goods (11.1 per cent), such as machinery and tools, and intermediate goods (16.3 per cent), which are basically raw materials for other industries. Consumer goods industries, in contrast, represented 73.0 per cent of the total. This sector is in turn divided into two groups: immediate consumption goods (56.0 per cent; e.g. food, beverages, tobacco, clothing) and durable goods (16.5 per cent; e.g. electrical

Table 3.9 **The industrial structure of Mexico City according to aggregated value, 1950–1970**

Industrial groups and sectors	Percentage of total aggregated value			Growth rate 1960–70 (%)
	1950	1960	1970	
Production goods	**25.25**	**22.61**	**27.37**	**12.2**
Capital goods	*7.35*	*5.58*	*11.06*	*17.2*
Metallic products	6.02	4.22	7.85	16.5
Non-electric machinery	1.35	1.36	3.21	18.9
Intermediate goods	*17.88*	*17.03*	*16.31*	*9.9*
Wood	3.58	0.31	0.32	10.4
Cellulose and paper	2.78	3.35	3.20	9.9
Oil and coal products	3.84	3.61	3.55	10.2
Non-metallic minerals	4.47	4.68	4.25	9.4
Basic metals	3.21	5.08	4.99	10.2
Consumer goods	**74.75**	**77.39**	**72.63**	**9.7**
Immediate consumption goods	*64.52*	*61.31*	*56.09*	*9.4*
Foods	11.14	10.68	9.77	9.4
Beverages	8.67	8.43	4.48	4.0
Tobacco	2.27	0.99	0.90	9.3
Textiles	11.13	8.67	6.41	7.3
Shoes and clothing	5.38	3.24	4.60	13.8
Printers	3.91	5.35	4.38	8.8
Leathers	1.12	0.70	0.56	8.0
Rubber products	4.77	3.55	3.63	10.5
Chemicals	15.93	19.70	21.16	11.0
Durable consumption goods	*10.43*	*16.08*	*16.54*	*10.6*
Furniture	1.63	0.81	1.34	15.7
Electric appliances	2.18	6.01	8.02	13.2
Automobiles and parts	3.49	6.31	5.47	8.9
Other industries	3.13	2.95	1.71	4.9

Source: Garza (1984).

appliances, automobiles, furniture). The durable goods and the capital goods sectors showed the highest increases in the 1950–1970 period (Garza 1984).

The spatial distribution of industry within the basin is another important factor explaining the geographical growth of the megalopolis and the distribution of various social groups (see fig. 3.4). In 1960, a time when small and intermediate industries were located in central areas and big firms on the periphery, the Federal District contained 96 per cent of all industrial establishments in the city. In the 1970s and 1980s, however, the spatial distribution of industry changed sig-

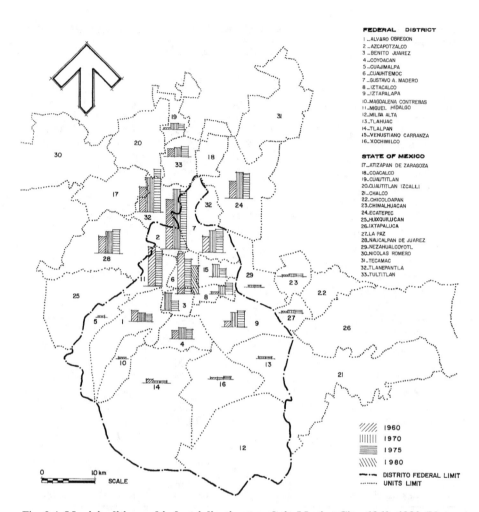

Fig. 3.4 **Municipalities and industrialization trends in Mexico City, 1960–1980 (Note: the height of the bars is proportional to the number of industries in each municipality. Industries are located principally in Azcapotzalco, in the north of the Federal District, and in the surrounding municipalities of the State of Mexico. Source: Garza 1987b: 103)**

nificantly, growing more rapidly in the municipalities of the State of Mexico, north of the city, than in the DF. By 1980 the Federal District had reduced its proportion of firms to 74.7 per cent, while the share of the metropolitan municipalities in the State of Mexico had increased to 25 per cent. The first to develop industrially were Tlalnepantla, Naucalpan, and Ecatepec. The industrial consolidation continued in conurbations such as Tultitlán, Cuautitlán, and Cuautitlán-

Izcalli; more recently it has spread into some eastern municipalities such as La Paz and Chimalhuacán, which still present an incipient degree of industrialization (Garza 1987a).

In this latest pattern of spatial distribution, the Federal District is becoming more and more an area of services than of industrial activity, although its central areas still specialize in the production of immediate consumption goods (food, beverages, tobacco, and clothing, among others). At the same time, the municipalities in the State of Mexico that are gradually becoming important industrial zones house those companies that require a lot of space for their installations, many of them dedicated to the production of intermediate and capital goods (including machinery and tools, metallic products, and non-metallic minerals) (Villegas Tovar 1988).

The economic predominance of Mexico City over the rest of the country also surfaces in other economic sectors. The city contains an enormous share of the major financial exchanges, private businesses, and central offices in Mexico; it also has the largest number of institutions of higher education and centres of culture. Indeed, compared with industry, services show an even higher trend to concentrate in Mexico City. Many industrial firms that have relocated their manufacturing operations to outlying cities have kept their administrative headquarters in the capital. In general and aggregate terms, the economic base of the city relies mainly on industry, construction, commerce, restaurants and hotels, and financial services. In 1980, 4.9 per cent of the active population was employed in the primary sector, 41.4 per cent in industrial activities, and 53.7 per cent in services.

Socio-economic pre-eminence

Despite its enormous environmental problems, the Basin of Mexico remains the main economic conglomeration in the country. Mexico City accounts for an enormous share of the major financial and industrial enterprises, and the highest concentration of services. With approximately 20 per cent of the population of the country, the basin contributes almost one-third of the gross domestic product.

Along with its economic and political-administrative advantages, Mexico City's sheer size means that it can offer "social opportunities" that are not so readily available elsewhere. These include the accessibility of the most varied and up-to-date information, specialized education and training, multiple and high-level social services, and diverse forms of recreation. All of these services, together with the

59

existence of a large consumer market, a large labour force, the avail-ability of credit, and a high return on investments, represent addi-tional benefits for corporations and business firms. These direct and indirect advantages have stimulated the construction of additional infrastructure and developments, which in turn have had a positive feedback on the process of growth and concentration of resources in Mexico City.

Strong changes in the pattern of urbanization, however, are occur-ring inside the megalopolis itself. The central city is experiencing a marked depopulation process. The peripheral municipalities, in contrast, are growing very rapidly, and the expanding conurbation is constantly incorporating new municipalities. Apart from the 29 *municipios* of the State of Mexico that have been engulfed by the conurbation, Mexico City is now also establishing urban links with the states of Puebla and Hidalgo. In short, despite the negative growth rates in the central city, the trend to expand the urban area into neighbouring municipalities is likely to continue, increasing the areal extent of the megacity during the first decades of the twenty-first century.

4

Recent changes in the environmental situation of the basin

As discussed in chapter 2, during more than 7,000 years of human habitation, the environment of the Basin of Mexico has changed drastically (Niederberger 1987a, 1987b), and probably irreversibly in many instances. Changes have ranged from transformations of the natural systems, without fundamentally altering their main ecological structure, to elimination of whole ecosystems, with the concomitant extinction of species and degradation of the surroundings. The transformation of the natural environment by human societies dates back to pre-Aztec times and has had profound environmental consequences.

Vegetation changes in the Basin of Mexico

The first human settlements were established in the lower parts of the basin after agriculture started in this region. The reconstruction of the natural vegetation of the basin is a difficult task (see chap. 2), given that at least 4,000 years of agriculture, not to mention more than five centuries of urban development, have completely changed the physical environment (Sanders 1976a). This region used to be rich in plant species and vegetation types. According to Sanders (1976b), by the time humans colonized the Basin of Mexico, particularly in the Texcoco region, a conifer forest covered the mountain ridges and the higher piedmont, while a moist broadleafed (meso-phyllous) forest, rich in oaks, probably covered the lower piedmont. Rzedowski (1969) reports that many of the moist ravines in the south and south-eastern parts of the basin might have been occupied by this type of forest.

Pressures on the natural vegetation

Mesophyllous forest

Nowadays, the mesophyllous forest is best represented on the lower western slopes of Iztaccíhuatl, as well as on some of the eastern slopes of the Sierra de las Cruces, between 2,500 and 3,000 m, but not more than 2 km^2 are occupied by this type of vegetation (Ezcurra 1990b). Near Amecameca, a relatively large town in the lower part of the Sierra Nevada, a small forested slope known as Sacromonte (the "Sacred Mount") rises from the alluvial plain. The presence of the church and religious practices might have played an important role in the relative preservation of this place. Though it has been deeply disturbed, some elements (e.g. *Quercus rugosa* and *Cupressus lindleyi*) of the original mesophyllous forest still grow on the slope. Contrasting with most forests in the Basin of Mexico, this one is rich in epiphytes and ferns. Rzedowski (1969) considers that this type of vegetation must have been better represented and more continuously distributed in the Basin of Mexico in the past. As a consequence of the deep disturbance it has suffered, many of the original elements have prob-ably been lost.

Fir, pine, and oak forests

Since the first settlements appeared in the basin, conifer and oak forests have been used as sources of wood for building and burning. Oak trees were also a main source for charcoal. Although oaks (*Quercus* spp.) now cover only dispersed patches of different sizes, they used to be very abundant in the basin. Communities charac-terized by different species of *Quercus* covered the lower parts of the mountains and some patches of the volcanic substrate formed after the eruption of the Xitle volcano (Álvarez del Villar 1971; Rzedowski 1975, 1979). According to Rzedowski (1979) and Domínguez (1975), it is probable that many of the pine communities present in the basin are of secondary origin, and the characteristic abundance of the tussocky grass known as *"zacatón"* (*Muhlembergia* sp.) is a symptom of disturbance.

Wood extraction had already been going on for a long time when the Spaniards arrived in the Basin of Mexico. During the colonial period, however, the rate of extraction increased significantly, as more and more wood was needed to build the new, European-style houses of the conquerors. In the first half of the twentieth century, these forests were intensively utilized by three paper factories: San Rafael, Loreto, and Peña Pobre. Even zones officially designated as protected areas were given as concessions to the paper factories, as happened in San Rafael.

Chapultepec, located in the western part of the basin on an elevation of the Sierra de las Cruces, harboured an important conifer forest dominated by *Taxodium mucronatum* (*ahuehete*), a species of swamp cypress. Chapultepec, a recreational area as early as 1280, also had a temple to the god Hutzilopochtli. Aztec emperors used to visit the area for its dense forest and its natural springs, which the ruling class used for bathing. At that time, the Chapultepec forest already contained introduced, non-indigenous species of plants. During the early colonial period, Cortés owned Chapultepec, but in 1530 the Spanish government designated it the public property of Mexico City and granted free entrance to everyone. Today, only 230 of the 438 hectares occupied by the original forest remain as a park, and a large proportion has been invaded by exogenous species such as *Eucalyptus* spp. (Martinez González and Chacalo Hilu 1994).

The zone that surrounds what is now Chapultepec gained economic value towards the end of the Revolution (*c.* 1920), as people from the rural estates (*haciendas*) of the Mexican highlands fled from the violent struggle dominating the countryside and sought security in the Basin of Mexico. Many of the workers from the *haciendas* also fled the Revolution and crowded into the centre of the city, prompting the upper classes to seek out relatively secluded places to retreat to. In fact, these migratory forces were one of the major factors giving rise to the incorporation into Mexico City of towns such as Coyoacán, Tacubaya, San Angel, Tizapán, and Tlalpan. By 1930, the search for suburban plots in Mexico City had driven people into the green, mild zones of the west and south. One of the first manifestations of this preference was a trendy district developed by the new and wealthy post-revolutionary classes, built on land surrounded or still occupied by the conifer forests that originally characterized Chapultepec. Lomas de Chapultepec, as its name indicates, emerged in the gently sloping hills where conifers such as firs and the typical *ahuehuetes* originally grew (Suárez 1974).

Grasslands
Grasslands above the timberline are among the least-altered plant communities in the basin.

Xerophytic scrub
Until the beginning of the twentieth century, the lava badlands of El Pedregal and their shrubby plant communities were considered a hostile environment and no urban developments were attempted in them for many years. The lack of water flows or lakes, the high permeability of the rocky and uneven substrate, and the abundance of dangerous animals, especially snakes, kept people away for centuries. During colonial times, a few large *haciendas* were established in the areas where some soil had developed. The most important *haciendas* were located in zones with oaks and pines. The surrounding zones, such as Coyoacán and San Angel, became wheat producers during the colonial period, and the occupation of these lands by large tenants forced the original inhabitants to move to the less favourable environments of El Pedregal (Carrillo 1995).

In the early 1950s, an affluent residential district, characterized by large houses of modern architecture with big gardens, began to emerge in El Pedregal, which still enjoyed a reputation as a secluded urban district, removed from the turmoil of the growing city. In fewer than 20 years the original vegetative cover of the lava flow almost disappeared. Today, less than 3 km^2 of the original *pedregal* remain. Small patches can be found on some slopes and even in some gardens, but most of what is left is in the grounds of the campus of the National Autonomous University of Mexico (UNAM), built directly on El Pedregal, despite the protests of a small group of citizens already aware of the biological importance of this ecosystem. Paradoxically, the fact that the remnants of El Pedregal are on university ground has proven crucial: in 1983 a group of students and professors reacted strongly to a proposed urban development of this zone and succeeded in having it declared a protected area, which may be used only for education and research (Rojo 1994). This is one of the few cases in the Basin of Mexico in which the construction of streets and commercial centres has been stopped or redesigned in order to protect a natural zone. Today, the natural reserve harboured by UNAM is the largest natural protected area within an urban area in Mexico.

Though small and insufficient as a formal natural reserve, this area has become extremely important for the conservation and protection of the diversity that evolved around the Xitle lava flows (Rojo 1994). Six years later, in 1989, a higher part of El Pedregal in which deep disturbance had already taken place was declared a protected area (the Parque Ecológico de la Ciudad de México). As a result, patches of open and dense oak forests, as well as some well-preserved patches of the characteristic *Sedum* shrubs, enjoy protection. Other patches colonized by *Buddleia*, or naked basalt covered only by some rare rock vegetation, are also frequent in this region.

In the Sierra de Guadalupe, a small representation of the natural xerophyllous shrublands and some patches of *Eysenhardtia poly-stachia*, once an abundant dominant species, are still present. As in El Pedregal, this shrubby vegetation is rapidly disappearing as urban and industrial settlements appropriate the land.

Pressures on cultivated land and the lacustrine system

Agricultural land

The pressure on land after the Revolution affected not only places with natural vegetation, but also important farming and agricultural areas. The owners of *haciendas* in the Basin of Mexico, who were sometimes very wealthy, subdivided their possessions and sold them. An example is the *hacienda* that belonged to the wealthy Escandón family, which sold off this huge agricultural zone in plots. It is now a crowded, middle- to lower-class district, named Escandón after the former landowners. In the western region of the basin, wood was collected in the forests surrounding Tacubaya until the late 1920s. Shortly after, the forest lands were sold for urban development and the town became incorporated into the urban perimeter as another densely populated district with few green areas. The eastern agricultural lands were also sold as part of a fever of speculation that has been ongoing since the 1930s. In the southern part of the basin, new housing districts continue to spring up in places that were still active in agriculture until a short time ago. Haciendas de Coapa, in the south-eastern part of the basin, is among the most dramatic examples. Until the late 1960s and early 1970s, this region of the basin had witnessed little construction other than the lodging halls to house athletes during the 16th Pan-American Games. This event marked the beginning of numerous land divisions for urban developments, in conjunction with intensive speculation in land values in this zone, a process that completely transformed it from an agricultural region to a densely urbanized area in less than a decade.

The lacustrine area
The lower regions of the basin were covered by discontinuous vegetation types, including moisture-loving trees along the borders of the lake and oak forests in the well-drained soils, which alternated with seasonally flooded patches occupied by aquatic species. Aquatic vegetation was once extremely abundant in the Basin of Mexico. Rzedowzki (1975) presumes the existence of several endemic species that are now extinct. Sanders, Parsons, and Santley (1979) report on Kovac's pollen profiles for the Teotihuacan Valley, where the first big Meso-American urban settlement was established, developed, and survived for several centuries (Niederberger 1987b). In these profiles, pollen of arboreal genera such as *Pinus, Abies, Quercus, Alnus,* and *Salix* was found together with herbaceous species of the families Compositae, Amaranthaceae, and Gramineae, among others. The presence of the pollen of members of the sedge family (Cyperaceae) is especially important, because it indicates the original extent of Lake Texcoco, which seems formerly to have stretched all the way to the slopes of Chapultepec.

Equally important is the fact that the abundance of the pollen of these species tends to diminish as corn registers increase. In other words, the shores of Lake Texcoco were gradually occupied by cornfields, which replaced the natural vegetation of the periodically flooded shores. The forests and the aquatic vegetation that characterized this region of the basin were gradually displaced as a consequence of agriculture. The springs and water flows upon which the Teotihuacan empire depended allowed intensive cultivation of these lands (Millon 1970; Sanders 1976a); their loss was probably related to the environmental impoverishment that resulted from human overuse of the natural resources, and which seems to have played an important role in the fall of the Teotihuacan empire (Sanders 1976a; Ezcurra 1992, 1995).

Climate was a limiting factor for human settlements in the temperate zones of Mexico, where the dry season, starting in October and ending in May or June, allowed only one harvest for most crops. Many of the early inhabitants regarded the muddy bottom of the lacustrine system of the basin as unsuitable for settlement. When the Aztec immigrants arrived in the basin, they were apparently displaced into the lowlands by established, dominant peoples of the basin. The lakes, however, proved to be the solution for coping with the seasonal droughts. The Aztecs developed the unique *chinampa* agricultural system, which consisted of artificial islands built with the rich silt of the swampy lakes. The soil was never exhausted because, as soon as soil fertility was reduced by the crops, the silt was replaced by a new layer of rich lake-bottom sediment. Water was also available throughout the year, since the shallow soil of the artificial islands absorbed water directly from the water table of the lakes. Nor were the *chinampas* washed away by water because trees with large root systems, mainly willow (*Salix bomplandiana*), were planted along their edges to protect the plots from the eroding effects of water. Although this system required a large amount of work (building the *chinampas*, cleaning the canals, protecting seedbeds from freezing during cold winter mornings), it turned out to be one of the most productive Meso-American agricultural systems (Armillas 1971; Coe 1964; Sanders 1976a; Whitmore and Turner 1992).

Despite its productivity, *chinampa* agriculture was not able to satisfy all the needs of Tenochtitlan, the capital of the Aztec empire, which imported many agricultural goods from outside the basin. Imported products included corn, beans, and other vegetables, which were also produced in *chinampas*, as well as ritual objects (Ezcurra 1990a; Logan and Sanders 1976). Palerm (1973) alleged that the *chinampa* system was the most appropriate agricultural means of dealing with the environmental problems attendant on the climate and the lake system of the basin. *Chinampas* expanded to the northern parts of the basin, particularly into Zumpango, Xaltocan, and Texcoco. Additionally, Palerm hypothesizes that "inland *chinampas*" also developed on the shores, according to the same principles used to build the first *chinampas*.

The Conquest of Mexico by the Spaniards brought, among many other things, an introduction of alien plant and animal species as well as unfamiliar techniques for the use of natural resources. With the introduction of cattle came the first use of animals for labour and transportation. A dramatic increase in the demand for wood for building resulted in the cutting of some 25,000 trees yearly from the lower piedmont and the mountain slopes of the basin. The need for charcoal also increased the logging of the local forests, especially the oak woodlands. Carriages, seen for the first time (wheels were not used by Meso-American cultures), prompted the drainage of the lakes and rivers to allow land transportation to substitute for the traditional canoes (*trajineras*) used before the Conquest. These changes did not alter the main *chinampa* region, however, for the Spaniards concentrated in the centre of urban Tenochtitlan and somehow overlooked this agricultural system. Ignored and lacking the support of the Spanish colonial governments, *chinampas* escaped destruction by the new rulers, and the agricultural landscape probably remained unaltered for many years. The lakes gradually dried up during the following centuries, owing to the artificial drainage of the basin, the extraction of ground water for the city, the change in runoff patterns caused by the deforestation of the basin's slopes, and the evaporation of the shallow waters.

Although some emergent and floating aquatic plant species still remain in the southern *chinampas* of the basin, submerged species (i.e. rooted in the lake bottom and with underwater leaves) have almost completely disappeared as lakes and canals have dried out or filled with turbid water through which light cannot penetrate. During the warm season, the introduced and invasive water hyacinth can completely cover canals in the Xochimilco region, which requires substantial efforts to clean them, even partially. The clonal growth of this water weed facilitates its dispersion and complicates its elimination. Obviously, the disappearance of the lakes and their plants has had a drastic effect on species of migratory bird, many of which have disappeared from the basin and some of which are even believed to be locally extinct (Rzedowski 1975). The desiccation of the lakes, especially Zumpango and Chalco, and the subsequent induction of soil salinization, allowed the establishment of halophilous plant communities in many parts of the basin. These communities form dense grasslands with low shrubs.

In spite of major environmental change, the lakes Chalco and Xochimilco did not completely disappear. The waters of Lake Chalco were not directly exposed to the sun because a thick mat of aquatic vegetation covered its surface. This vegetation provided a source of food for the inhabitants of this zone, who harvested both wild plants and aquatic organisms (Rojas Rabiela 1985). Unfortunately, this region has undergone drastic change during the past 50 years, and at an unprecedented rate. The remnants of Lake Chalco were drained in 1945 during the search for new agricultural land. As could have been expected, the thin soil layer that remained after desiccation soon accumulated high concentrations of salt, and few crops – with the exception of a few salt-tolerant species such as sugar beet – are now harvested in this part of the basin. With the loss of the agricultural value of the land, irregular settlements proliferated. In the late 1980s, a new lake started to form owing to subsidence induced by groundwater extraction in the area of the old lake bed (Ortega-Guerrero, Cherry, and Rudolph 1993).

Lake Xochimilco has conserved some of its pre-Hispanic physiognomy. Traditional agriculture is still practised, though less intensively; it is mostly directed to the cultivation of traditional crops such as amaranth and *romeritos* (*Suaeda mexicana*), vegetables, and flowers for the markets of Mexico City. A recently inaugurated protection programme includes restoration of the water canals and the surrounding vegetation, as well as cultural and recreational activities. The long-term impacts of this programme are still to be seen and evaluated, but it certainly implies a change of attitude among governmental authorities towards this important agricultural zone.

Other efforts to restore what is left of the lacustrine system are found in the dry bottom of the former Lake Texcoco. Since the 1970s the National Water Commission has developed a programme to stimulate the establishment of halophytes in the old lake beds, with the purpose of covering the formerly bare clayey soils and warding off the dust storms that troubled the city during the dry season. An artificial reservoir has also been built. This programme has been very successful, and at present the halophytic plant communities are one of the few vegetation types of the basin that have actually increased their cover during the past 20 years. In addition, some migrating bird species that had not been seen for decades in the Basin of Mexico are now again visiting this area as part of their migratory route.

Environmental transformation

Mexico City inherited one of Tenochtitlan's main traits: the high density of its human population. The Basin of Mexico is, and has been for centuries, a region with dense human settlements. Since 1920 and particularly after 1940, growth has increased constantly, so peripheral towns such as Coyoacán, San Angel, Atizapan, and Tlatelolco have become an integrated part of the megalopolis. The forests and agricultural lands that once separated them have completely disappeared. Only a small proportion of the lakes has survived, and only Xochimilco and Tláhuac subsist as *chinampa* regions, although they are at risk owing to the excessive use of water for urban consumption. Many aquatic, subaquatic, and halophilous species have become extinct.

Other vegetation types are on the verge of extinction, as is the case with the moist mesophyllous forests. The forest communities in general have been profoundly disturbed. More than 9,000 hectares of trees have disappeared since 1985 alone, and some insect pests that thrive on the trees debilitated by air pollution are attacking the protected forests. The widespread use of introduced species to reforest the basin has resulted in the loss of animal species that relied on the native plants for food or shelter. In particular, eucalyptus were introduced extensively throughout the basin to increase evaporation and hasten the drying-up of the lake system. Several communities were reforested with these trees, which were also used to protect eroded soils. In this and other ways, the floristic diversity of the basin has suffered significantly. Segura Burciaga and Martínez Ramos (1994) report that some eucalyptus, planted as a barrier on the borders of the reserve of El Pedregal, quickly proliferated, invading the reserve and disrupting the life-cycles of the endangered native species.

When Miguel Ángel de Quevedo, an eminent Mexican forester, intensively introduced eucalyptus trees to desiccate and reforest different parts of the city he probably never anticipated that the high rates of reproduction and growth would allow eucalyptus to reach the point where they posed a threat to the native vegetation. Similarly, those who drained the lakes in search of fertile soils did not understand that the fertility of the flooded areas was due to the presence of the lake itself, and they proceeded unwittingly to generate large expanses of unproductive soils where previously soils were fertile and biological diversity was high. The history of the environmental transformation of the basin abounds with ill-informed decisions that have conspired with intensive historical, economic, and social factors to produce disastrous effects on ecological systems.

The environmental impact of urbanization patterns

The growth rate of the urban area of Mexico City between 1953 and 1980, estimated from aerial photographs (IGUNAM 1989; Ezcurra 1990a), was 5.2 per cent (table 4.1), slightly higher than that of the population (4.8 per cent for the same period). In 1953, the urban area covered 240 km² (3 per cent of the basin), whereas by 1980 it had increased to 980 km² (14 per cent of the basin), and by 1990 it covered 1,161 km² (figs. 4.1 and 4.2). At present the metropolis occupies

Table 4.1 **Total urban area of Mexico City estimated from aerial photographs, 1953–1990, and estimated rates of growth of the city**

Year	Area (km^2)	Annual growth rate (%)
1953	240.6	–
1980	980.0	5.2
1990	1,160.9	1.7

Sources: DDF (1986) and Instituto de Geografía (1990).

more than 17 per cent of the area of the Basin of Mexico (IGUNAM 1989). In a few decades, it changed from a small city to an emerging megalopolis.

In 1980, several metropolitan areas in Central Mexico started to become united in a single very large conurbation merging Mexico City (constituted by 16 *delegaciones* in the Federal District and 21 *municipios* in the State of Mexico), the metropolitan area of Toluca (comprising 6 *municipios*), the metropolitan zone of Puebla (which includes the neighbouring State of Tlaxcala and is composed of 8 *municipios*), and Cuernavaca-Temixco-Jiutepec and Cuautla-Yautepec (which formed small metropolitan areas in the State of Morelos, south of Mexico City) (Negrete and Salazar 1986; Garza and Damián 1991).

Mexico City established regional associations with the states of Puebla, Hidalgo, Mexico, and Morelos in the 1980s. The conurbation process between Mexico and Toluca, for example, involves the *municipio* of Huixquilucan in the State of Mexico, which has grown rapidly in recent years. The two cities are now linked by the urban area of Huixquilucan, which acts as a metropolitan "bridge" and has helped to form a large urban conglomeration that started to emerge in 1980 as the first Latin American megalopolis (Garza and Schteingart 1984). According to Brambilia (1987), Mexico City differs from other megacities in developed countries – such as New York–New Jersey, or Tokyo–Yokohama – because it is a single contiguous conglomeration, whereas the other megalopolises are formed by two or more distinct urban centres joined by highways and transportation.

This rapid expansion of Mexico City has not kept the old style of urbanization that still prevails in the traditional areas of the colonial city. New developments are more dense and less planned, and generally include fewer open spaces. Many developments are now built

71

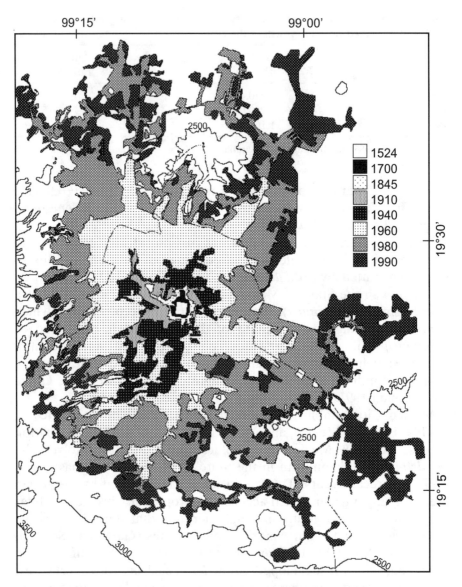

Fig. 4.1 **Areal growth of Mexico City, 1524–1990 (Note: the numbered lines correspond to elevation contours in metres. Source: MacGregor et al. 1989, digitized from a map edited by the Instituto de Geografía, UNAM)**

on hillsides, generating a considerable amount of soil erosion and a significant increase in flash floods after rainstorms (Galindo and Morales 1987). In 1950, the urban area included a large proportion of agro-pastoral fields, together with numerous empty lots, parks, and

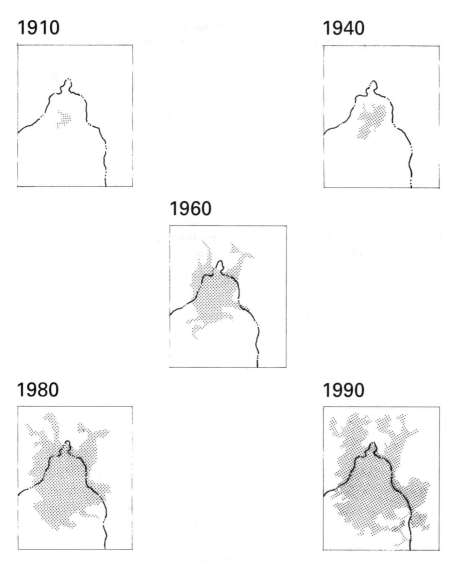

Fig. 4.2 **Growth of the urban area of Mexico City, 1910–1990 (Source: MacGregor et al. 1989, simplified from fig. 4.1)**

public spaces. The relative abundance of these open spaces within the city has decreased considerably with the new industrial style of urbanization. All kinds of open space within Mexico City are decreasing, but at different rates. Agro-pastoral fields, previously very important within the city as dairy farms, and domestic maize fields (*milpas*) have been disappearing at an annual rate of 7.4 per

73

Table 4.2 **Rate of change of green areas within the Metropolitan Area of Mexico City, 1950–1980 (estimated from aerial photograph samples)**

Green area	As % of total city area		Yearly change (%)
	1950	1980	
Parks, gardens, and public spaces	13.1	8.3	−1.5
Empty lots	8.1	3.2	−3.1
Agro-pastoral fields	21.2	2.3	−7.4
Total	42.4	13.8	−3.7

Source: Lavín (1983).

Table 4.3 **Rate of change of green areas within different sectors of the Metropolitan Area of Mexico City, 1950–1980 (estimated from aerial photograph samples)**

Sector	Green areas as % of area of sector		Yearly change (%)
	1950	1980	
North	52.6	21.8	−2.9
South	41.6	14.7	−3.5
East	23.5	4.0	−5.9
West	62.5	28.1	−2.7
Centre	5.0	3.7	−1.0

Source: Lavín (1983).

cent and are now practically non-existent within the city. Industrial buildings and housing developments now occupy most of these areas. Parks, private gardens, and public spaces have been somewhat better conserved, disappearing from the city at an average annual rate of 1.5 per cent. New roads have accounted for most of the loss. Overall, vegetated areas have been decreasing at an annual rate of 3.7 per cent (table 4.2; Lavín 1983).

The total rate of change of open spaces and green areas varies considerably from one sector of the city to another (Lavín 1983). The east of Mexico City, where the larger proletarian settlements lie (in particular, Ciudad Nezahualcóyotl, with some 5 million inhabitants, and Chalco, with some 2 million), is the area changing most rapidly: nearly 6 per cent of its open space disappeared each year between 1950 and 1980 (table 4.3). Open spaces are disappearing most slowly in the old centre of the city (−1.0 per cent). The rate of change within urbanized areas depends on the social position of their inhabitants and on the time of their establishment. In the poorer and more recently established areas, vacant land is quickly taken over for new houses, leaving fewer vegetated areas per person. The distribution of green areas, like the distribution of wealth, is very uneven at present and varies considerably from one part of the city to another. Although some districts have more than 10 m^2 of green land per person, others have much less. Azcapotzalco, an industrial district with a population of some 700,000, has 0.9 m^2 of green areas per inhabitant (Calvillo Ortega 1978; Barradas and J-Seres 1987).

The draining and drying-up of the lake beds and the lack of vegetated areas have produced a seasonal phenomenon of dust storms between February and May. The midday air temperatures during the dry season generate strong advective currents that suspend salt and clay particles from the former lake bottom in the atmosphere. These particles are later blown into the city by the prevailing easterly winds. The problem of dust storms, however, peaked in the 1970s and has declined slightly since (Jáuregui 1983). The decline (or at least the lack of increase) in soil particles in the atmosphere during the dry season seems to be associated with successful government efforts to vegetate the dry mud-bed of the former Lake Texcoco (Jáuregui 1971, 1983), which has now become a pasture of halophilous grasses and small herbaceous shrubs.

The development of the modern city has affected the local climate in other ways. The city has become significantly hotter during the day, because the dry pavements can absorb a lot of heat from direct solar radiation, and the lack of plants and moist soil in the urban environment does not allow evaporative cooling. This so-called "thermal island effect" that results from massive urbanization renders large cities more variable in their temperature than equivalent vegetated areas (Jáuregui 1990). Most of the precipitation falling in Mexico City is of convective origin; that is, it is mainly formed by summer rains that precipitate during the day, when the warming of the earth's surface generates strong upward thermal currents (Barry and Chorley 1980; Miller 1975). Thus, the development of the urban mass of Mexico City can significantly increase the afternoon temperatures in summer, thereby increasing the intensity of the summer rain showers, which can produce as much as 50 mm of precipitation in 24 hours (fig. 4.3). Indeed, the very existence of the city is in itself

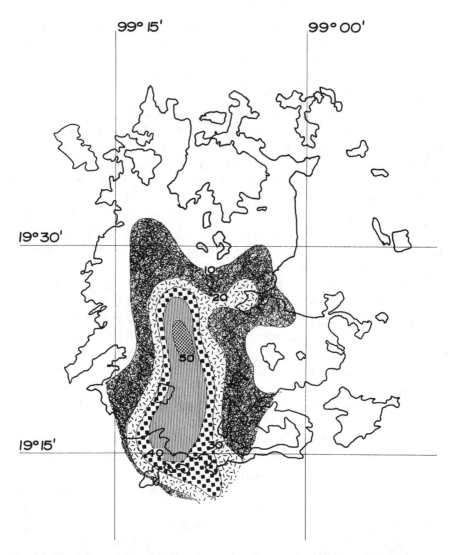

Fig. 4.3 **The "thermal island" effect (measured in mm of rainfall per 24 hours) above Mexico City (Note: the highest increases above the normal rainfall values are observed in the central part of the city, where the accumulation of heat by the city's pavements and buildings is maximal. Source: Jáuregui 1990)**

capable of adding an extra factor of risk and criticality to the already overburdened hydrological system of the Basin of Mexico. More intense rain showers generate massive surface runoff that floods the city and eventually flows into its gutters, inundating the deep drainage system and failing to infiltrate into the soil and recharge the aquifers.

76

Water resources

Water systems

Water has played a fundamental role in the Basin of Mexico from the social, economic, and environmental perspective during different historical periods (Lara 1988; Serra Puche 1990). Despite the construction of dykes and *chinampas*, at the time of the Spanish Conquest in 1519 the lacustrine system on the floor of the basin still covered approximately 1,500 km^2 (fig. 4.4). Lake Texcoco was the lowest in altitude and also the largest of the lakes, and the entire system drained towards it. During high precipitation, the lakes formed a connected surface system, but during extreme drought they may have dried up sufficiently to be separated. The three northern lakes were briny, whereas the two southern lakes contained fresh water, owing to the greater volume of precipitation and the number of freshwater springs that occur in the south of the basin. The connections between these bodies of water were altered during the fifteenth century by the Aztecs, who first dyked the connection between lakes Xochimilco and Texcoco and then also divided Lake Texcoco to protect the south-western portion of the lake in which the island capital of Tenochtitlan was situated (Bribiesca 1960; Palerm 1973). This system has been destroyed and transformed into a highly urbanized plain built on top of the lacustrine sediments and extending into the surrounding mountains. The natural water bodies have almost disappeared. All that remains is a small section of Lake Texcoco, which is mainly an artificially constructed reservoir (Lago Nabor Carrillo), some of the old *chinampa* canals in Xochimilco and Chalco, and an artificial reservoir near Zumpango.

The Basin of Mexico includes three geotechnical zones: the lacustrine, the transition, and the mountainous zone (Marsal and Mazari 1969, 1987, 1990; DDF 1988a; Mazari-Hiriart and Mackay 1993). The lacustrine clay deposits, originated from the lake system, are characterized by extremely high compressibility (mean values 0.745 cm^2/kg recompression, 2.285 cm^2/kg virgin) and high porosity (80–90 per cent; Marsal and Mazari 1969). The clayey zone is considered an aquitard, a layer of less permeable strata in the stratigraphic sequence as compared with the aquifer. Although these clayey layers are not sufficiently permeable to allow extraction of significant amounts of water by wells, they do allow some water movement. The fringe area between the lacustrine and the mountainous areas is

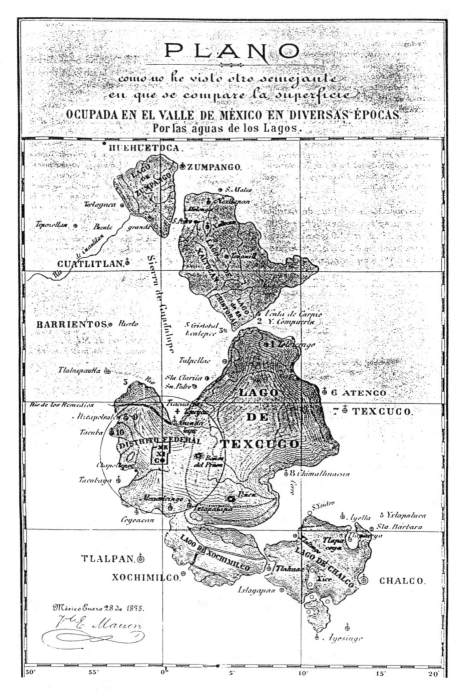

Fig. 4.4 **The lacustrine system in the south-western part of the Basin of Mexico in 1875 (Source: DDF 1975)**

78

known as the transition zone. The main recharge to the aquifers occurs by infiltration through the transition zone, primarily during the rainy season (DDF 1988a; Marsal and Mazari 1969). The mountainous areas serve primarily to direct precipitation towards the central part of the basin, either in surface runoff or in subsurface flows through the more permeable soils of the mountainous areas.

The main aquifer system in the basin is composed of alluvial and volcanic sediments ranging from 100 to 500 m in thickness, directly overlain by the lacustrine clays (Marsal and Mazari 1969; Ortega and Farvolden 1989). The system can be divided into several interconnected subsystems (hereafter called the aquifers) from which most of the water is supplied to the Metropolitan Area: Xochimilco–Tláhuac–Chalco to the south, Zona Metropolitana mainly to the west, Lago de Texcoco to the east, and Teoloyucan–Tizayuca–Los Reyes–Chiconautla to the north (DDF 1987b; Mazari-Hiriart and Mackay 1993). Birkle, Torres, and González (1995) have evaluated the potential existence of deep aquifers in the Basin of Mexico that have not yet been tapped for the extraction of underground water, but this hypothesis is still under investigation.

Water demand, use, and recharge

Water management has been fundamental in the establishment and evolution of various cultures in the basin. In pre-Hispanic times, the Aztecs used water from artesian wells located within the lacustrine zone and aqueducts in the west, and were completely self-sufficient in the use of this resource (Mazari and Alberro 1990). Groundwater extraction began in 1847, expanding significantly in the 1940s, and providing enough water to supply the inhabitants of Mexico City until the mid-1960s (Ramírez 1990a). Since that time, additional water has been pumped from two external watersheds, the Lerma basin located in the state of Mexico, and the Cutzamala basin located in the states of Mexico, Guerrero, and Michoacán. During the twentieth century, the basin has gone from a high level of self-sufficiency in water resources to a strong dependence on imports from other parts of Mexico (Ezcurra and Mazari-Hiriart 1996).

In 1990, water use in Mexico City, including the conurbation formed by the Federal District and the State of Mexico, is estimated at 63 m^3 per second (table 4.4), of which 1.5 m^3/s come from surface systems within the basin, while 42 m^3/s are extracted from the aquifers. The few surviving surface systems are the Magdalena River and

Table 4.4 **Population, urban area, and water use in Mexico City, 1910–1990, and projected values for 2000**

Year	Total population (millions)	Urban area (km²)	Density ('000 pers./km²)	Ground water (m³/s)	Imported water (m³/s)	Total water use (m³/s)	Per capita supply (litres/day)
1910	0.7	40.10	18.0	1.7	0	1.7	210
1940	1.8	117.50	15.0	4.3	0	4.3	206
1950	3.0	215.00	13.9	11.0	0	11.0	317
1960	5.2	383.85	14.1	16.6	3.5	20.1	334
1970	8.7	650.00	13.4	28.7	12.3	41.0	407
1980	13.8	980.00	14.1	36.0	14.0	50.0	313
1990	16.6	1,160.92	14.3	43.5	19.5	63.0	328
1990[a]	15.0[a]	1,160.92	12.9[b]	–	–	–	363[b]
2000[c]	20.0	1,400.00	14.5	44.0	28.2	72.2	320

Sources: INEGI (1991); Instituto de Geografía (1990); GAVM (1995); and our own projections.

a. Estimated by the national census.

b. These values are based on the population estimated by the 1990 census.

c. Projected values.

Table 4.5 **Water supply systems for the Federal District and the State of Mexico, 1988**

Origin	No. of deep pumping wells	Flow (m³/s)
External sources:		
Lerma basin	234	6.0
Cutzamala basin	(surface)	9.0
Internal sources:		
Federal District		
North	62	2.1
South	143	6.4
Centre	96	3.0
East	41	1.1
West	18	0.5
Other wells	209	9.2
Río Magdalena and other surface sources	(surface)	0.8
Private wells	538	1.2
Treated water	–	1.3
State of Mexico[a]	n.a.	18.4
Total	1,341	59.0

Sources: Federal District – DGCOH (1989) and DDF (1997); State of Mexico – SARH (1985b).
n.a. = information not available.
a. Water systems in the State of Mexico, also supplying the urban area, are reported globally.

the Madín Reservoir in the Tlalnepantla River, as well as springs in the Desierto de los Leones and swamp and spring areas adjacent to Xochimilco (table 4.5). The remaining 19.5 m³/s are obtained from sources external to the basin: 6.0 m³/s come from ground water in the Lerma basin and 13.5 m³/s from surface water in the Cutzamala basin (CEAS 1993; DDF 1989, 1991, 1992a; GAVM 1995; Mazari et al. 1992; Murillo 1990). Thus, of the total amount of water used in Mexico City, about 70 per cent is obtained from within the basin and 30 per cent from external watersheds (fig. 4.5).

Water exploitation at these rates has an impact on the three basins (Mazari-Hiriart and Bellón 1993). The aquifers that underlie the city, mainly in the northern and southern parts of the old lacustrine plain, had artesian pressure (i.e. tended to generate free-flowing springs) in the nineteenth century. The positive pressure of the underground aquifers of the Basin of Mexico started to decrease in many areas during the 1920s and is now found in only a few zones such as Chalco

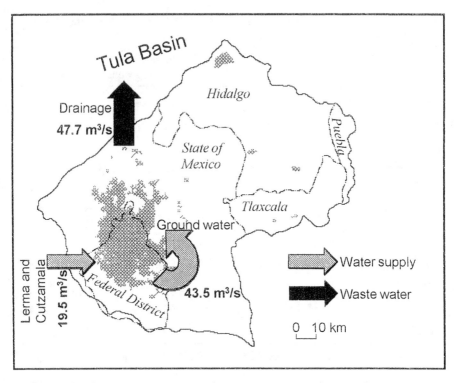

Fig. 4.5 **The flow of water in and out of Mexico City (Source: DGCOH 1991)**

(Mazari and Alberro 1990; Ortega-Guerrero, Cherry, and Rudolph 1993). The majority of the wells are located in or near geological transition zones in areas where the aquifers are semi-confined. The wells are usually 100–200 m deep, although some are as shallow as 70 m or as deep as 300 m. Currently recorded wells number about 1,000 in Mexico City (DDF 1991; Mazari et al. 1992; Mazari-Hiriart and Mackay 1993) and about 3,600 in the whole Basin of Mexico. The hydrological regime in the basin has been significantly affected by the exploitation of ground water. Pumping has reversed the underground hydraulic gradients, and the subsurface water flow in the upper parts of the basin is now directed towards the most heavily pumped zones (Durazo and Farvolden 1989; Marsal and Mazari 1969; Mazari and Alberro 1990; Ortega and Farvolden 1989).

Moreover, the importation of water from external basins has had a considerable impact on the Lerma and Cutzamala hydrological systems, where water is also scarce. The Lerma basin feeds the Chapala Lake in Jalisco, the largest freshwater body in the nation. Chapala's

Table 4.6 **Distribution and consumption of water in the Federal District**

Use	Number of users	Flow[a] m³/s	%
Domestic	1,900,000 households	22	59
Industrial	30,000 industries	5	14
Services	60,000 institutions	4	11
Commercial	120,000 shops	1	2
Losses	–	5	14

Source: Guerrero, Moreno, and Garduño (1982).
a. Water systems in the State of Mexico, also supplying the urban area, are not reported.

water levels have been dropping since the 1970s, with a cumulative decrease of approximately 5 m, partly attributable to the export of water to Mexico City. Surface water in the upper Cutzamala basin was formerly used for generating hydroelectricity, but has lost some of its generating potential as a result of the transference of water into the Basin of Mexico.

The average daily supply of water in Mexico City is around 300 litres/person, which is more than in many European cities (Álvarez 1985; Ramírez 1990a). Yet a considerable part of the city suffers from chronic water shortages, especially during the dry season. The distribution of water usage in the Federal District shows that approximately 59 per cent is for domestic use, 14 per cent for industry, 11 per cent for services, and 2 per cent for commercial use (table 4.6). In the municipalities of the State of Mexico, 80 per cent is used domestically, whereas 15 per cent and 5 per cent are for industrial and commercial use, respectively (DDF 1989).

The close relationship between population growth in Mexico City and water demand dates back to the beginning of the twentieth century (fig. 4.6). According to Ramírez (1990a), the natural capacity of the basin is sufficient to supply water for no more than 8.5 million inhabitants, a situation that was surpassed around 1964. Projected water demand for the year 2000, based on a population estimate of 20–21 million in Mexico City, is over 80 m³/s, which will have to be obtained either from the basin's aquifers or from external sources.

The mean annual input of rainwater into the basin is 744.2 million m³ (23.6 m³/s), some 50 per cent of which infiltrates the subsoil and recharges the aquifers. Some water also makes its way into the aquifers from leaks in the distribution system (Lerner 1986). Leakage may be as much as 25 per cent of the distributional flow in the city (of

83

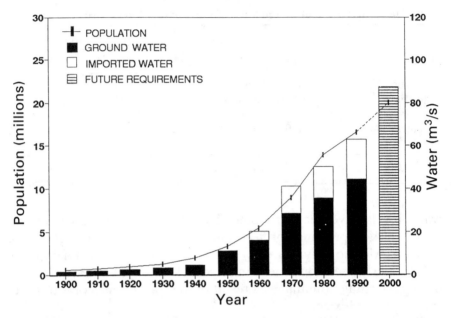

Fig. 4.6 **Population growth and water demand in Mexico City during the twentieth century (Source: modified from Mazari-Hiriart and Mackay 1993)**

the order of 16 m^3/s). Thus the total recharge of the basin's aquifers is some 27 m^3/s. Total extraction from the whole basin's aquifers may be as high as 55.5 m^3/s, considering local use for municipal and agricultural activities outside Mexico City (DDF 1991; GAVM 1995). Thus, although recharge replaces roughly 50 per cent of the extraction volume, there is a deficit of more than 800 million m^3 per year. Plans exist to reduce groundwater extraction from the aquifers of the Basin of Mexico, but policies related to water management are not very clear as regards the replacement of or alternatives to current water sources.

The environmental effects of water management

The modification of the drainage system in the basin since colonial times and especially during the twentieth century, as well as excessive groundwater extraction since the 1930s, have significantly influenced the behaviour of the lacustrine clays and the hydraulic equilibrium conditions of the lower strata of the basin sediments. The main effect of these changes is subsidence, which is also related to deterioration of water quality.

Subsidence

The subsoil where Mexico City has developed and grown over several centuries has been studied extensively with regard to its physical properties and soil mechanics (Alberro and Hernández 1990; DDF 1988a; Hiriart and Marsal 1969; Marsal and Mazari 1969, 1987, 1990; Mazari and Alberro 1990; Reséndiz and Zonana 1969). Studies focusing on the hydrogeological aspects of these lacustrine formations started in the late 1980s (CAVM 1988; DDF 1987b; Durazo and Farvolden 1989; Herrera and Cortés 1989; Mazari-Hiriart 1992; Mazari-Hiriart and Mackay 1993; Ortega and Farvolden 1989; Pitre and Rudolph 1991; Rudolph, Cherry, and Farvolden 1991).

One of the most evident problems of the overuse of ground water is subsidence, that is, the sinking of the ground surface generated by the depletion of the underground aquifers. For a detailed description of this phenomenon, see Marsal and Mazari (1969, 1987, 1990), Mazari and Alberro (1990), and Mazari et al. (1992). Reconstruction of Mexico City's subsidence has been possible by using historical data on levellings conducted since the beginning of the twentieth century, initially in connection with the construction of the water distribution and drainage systems. The topographical measurements show that subsidence peaked in central Mexico City during the 1937–1980 period (figs. 4.7 and 4.8). As early as 1944, the Mexican hydrologist Nabor Carrillo inferred that the main cause of subsidence was the consolidation of the deep underground layers as a result of a drop in the hydraulic pressure of the aquifers, mainly due to pumping within the urban area (see Carrillo 1969). This hypothesis has been confirmed by soil mechanics studies (Carrillo 1969; Marsal and Mazari 1969, 1990).

Since the beginning of the twentieth century, the base level of the city has sunk continuously, as much as 10 m in some parts. The evolution and magnitude of subsidence has been parallel to the volumes of underground water extraction. From the beginning of the century until 1938, the rate of subsidence was 3.3 cm per year; but in the early 1940s it increased to 16.0 cm/yr. The greatest subsidence was recorded between 1948 and 1956, during which period the city sank at a rate of 29.0 cm/yr. This problem forced the closure of extraction wells in the central part of the city in 1954 and their relocation to the north and south of the basin. Although this slowed down the rate of subsidence, it did not stop it completely (Mazari and Alberro 1990; Mazari et al. 1992). From the early 1970s, the rate of sinking in the central part of the city stabilized at 6 cm/yr. On the outskirts of the

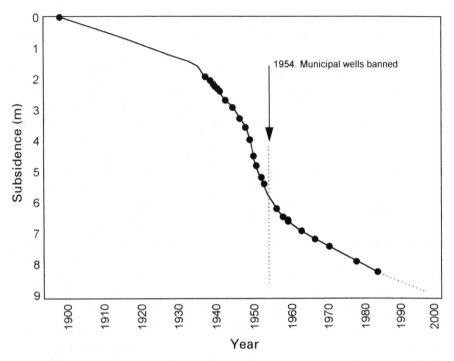

Fig. 4.7 **Subsidence vs. time in central Mexico City (Alameda Central) during the twentieth century (Source: Marsal and Mazari 1990; Mazari, Marsal, and Alberro 1984)**

city, however, the problem has become acute. The rate of subsidence is now 30 cm/yr in Ciudad Nezahualcóyotl, 20 cm/yr in the airport area, and 20–40 cm/yr in Chalco–Xochimilco. These areas are strongly affected by the relatively recent but intense pumping activity (Marsal and Mazari 1990).

Water quality
One of the most critical environmental problems generated by the urban expansion is the threat to water quality. At risk from multiple and diverse sources of contamination as well as overexploitation of the groundwater systems, water quality is a controversial and poorly understood problem that is increasingly affecting Mexico City. For decades, attention has highlighted the bacteriological aspects of water quality. Infectious and parasitic diseases, which can be partially attributed to the poor quality of drinking water, continue to rank among the five most common causes of death in the country, especially for infants (CAE 1990; Martínez-Palomo and Sepúlveda 1990).

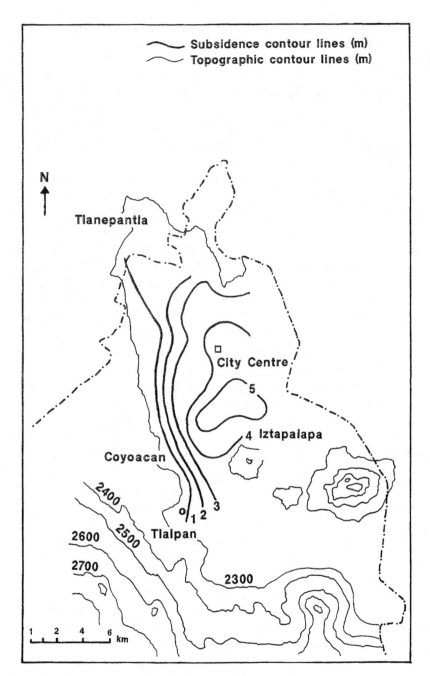

Fig. 4.8 **Subsidence contour lines in Mexico City, 1952–1980 (Note: In spite of the banning of municipal wells, subsidence was still high in the centre of the city. Source: Guerrero, Moreno, and Garduño 1982)**

As a result of overexploitation of the aquifer and the impact of subsidence on the clay aquitard, ions are being released by the clays, affecting water quality. Reported salinity in the aquifer system is 200–400 ppm, except in the central zone of Lake Texcoco, around Cerro de la Estrella, and in the Sierra de Santa Catarina, where concentrations can be as high as 20,000 ppm (DDF 1985; Lesser, Sánchez, and González 1986). Contaminated aquifer areas already exist in some parts of the city, such as Agrícola Oriental and the Sierra de Santa Catarina as well as the central part of Lake Texcoco. Chloride ions have increased in wells of the central part of the urban area (coinciding with leaks in the water distribution system), probably owing to chlorination of the water supply. Wells located in the Sierra de Santa Catarina area and the city centre show an increase in iron and manganese, probably as a result of bacterial production. A considerable increase in nitrates, which are sensitive indicators of pollution from domestic waste, has been detected in the wells running parallel to the Sierra de las Cruces, i.e. in the lacustrine clays of the basin (Lesser, Sánchez, and González 1986), and also in the water sources at the base of the surrounding mountain ranges where the main recharge areas of the basin are located; i.e. in the transition between the lacustrine sediments and the surrounding mountains (Ryan 1989). Ammonium and faecal coliforms, two indicators of contamination by domestic waste, have also been found in ground water from the southern part of the urban area (Ryan 1989).

Problem areas where one or more water-quality parameters have been detected in concentrations that exceed the Mexican drinking-water regulations (DDF 1993) have been recorded mainly in municipalities in the east and south of the urban area, such as Azcapotzalco, Tlalpan, Xochimilco, Sierra de Santa Catarina, Agrícola Oriental, Cerro del Peñón, Cerro de la Estrella, Iztapalapa, Tláhuac, Nezahualcóyotl, San Lorenzo Tezonco, and Santa Cruz Meyehualco (DDF 1993; Lesser, Sánchez, and González 1986; NRC 1995: 107; CNI 1995).

Inorganic compounds that degrade water quality in the basin have been studied and are listed in great detail in the drinking-water regulations. However, Mexico, like many other Latin American countries, is still behind the times in the analysis and regulation of organic chemicals in water. Organic contaminants, mainly synthetic products used by industry, represent a mounting problem since these residues are dumped directly into the drainage system.

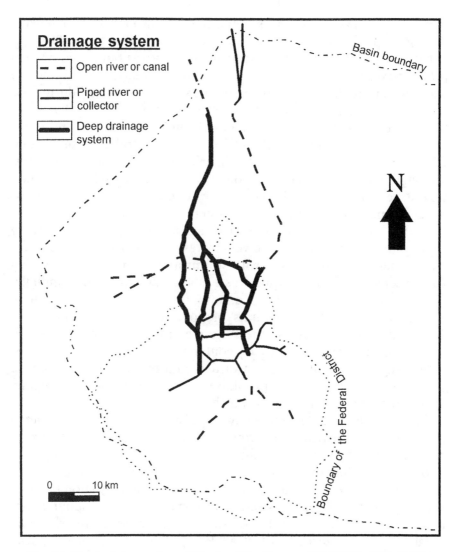

Fig. 4.9 **The drainage system of Mexico City (Source: DDF 1975, 1982, 1988b)**

The drainage system

The contemporary wastewater system of Mexico City includes several unlined sewer canals, sewers, rivers, reservoirs, lagoons, pumping stations, and a deep drainage system (DDF 1975, 1988b; Guerrero, Moreno, and Garduño 1982; see fig. 4.9). About 75 per cent of the population has access to this system; the rest dispose of their sewage through septic tanks and absorption wells (Mejía Maravilla 1987).

During the 1970s, the deep drainage system was built to allow disposal of excess water during the rainy season. Today, both runoff and waste water are disposed of through this system, especially during the rainy season. The system is composed of large (3–5 m diameter) tunnels constructed at depths ranging from 30 m to 50 m, and operating by gravity (DDF 1975, 1988b). In the central area of Mexico City, this system is constructed primarily inside the lacustrine clays, although parts required excavation into the aquifer itself. As the system leaves the basin to the north, the tunnels cross from the lacustrine sediments into the transition zone.

During its passage through the drainage system, the domestic waste water that is collected in the sewers mixes with industrial waste water and, during the rainy season, with stormwater runoff. Approximately 90 per cent of industrial liquid waste, some 1.5 million tons annually (DDF 1992b), passes, untreated, into the city's sewerage system. Given the considerable amounts of domestic and industrial waste flowing through the system, the sewers and unlined canals may well release significant quantities of contaminants into the subsurface, with a high potential for downward migration. The deep drainage system is thought to be leak-proof, but it occasionally requires repairs during the dry season, suggesting that short-term leaks may not be completely ruled out. To our knowledge, no monitoring is conducted in the Basin of Mexico to determine if the deep drainage system may have released significant amounts of contaminants into the aquifer or into the transition zone. Field investigations conducted in the lacustrine clays to assess specific organic contamination migration beneath some of the canals demonstrate that some organic compounds are indeed migrating downwards toward the aquifer (Mazari-Hiriart and Mackay 1993; Mazari-Hiriart et al. 1996). This leakage is of special concern in the northern part of the basin where the canals traverse more permeable regions.

Waste water flows northward into a few reservoirs and finally into the Tula system, in the State of Hidalgo, where some of it is used untreated for irrigation. Waste water is also used to generate electricity at the Zimapán Dam in the Tula River, which has an installed capacity of 280 megawatts (Palacio et al. 1994). Ultimately, the waste water makes its way to the Gulf of Mexico through the Tula–Moctezuma–Pánuco river system.

Even though water treatment and re-use have not been the main strategy for water management in Mexico City, governmental efforts to improve wastewater discharges to water bodies have existed since 1956 when the first wastewater treatment plant was installed in Chapultepec. The two most common treatment systems, both aerobic, are stabilization ponds and activated sludge (IIUNAM 1993). The 1993 installation cost for a wastewater treatment plant based on the activated sludge system, with a capacity of a 1 m^3/s, was US$20–30 million. The cost of treated water in 1994, including operating costs and recovery of investment, was about US$0.20/$m^3$.

A total of 26 wastewater treatment plants in Mexico City process only a portion of the waste water generated in Mexico City. These plants generally operate at less than 50 per cent efficiency and treat approximately 4.3 m^3/s, which represents only about 7 per cent of total waste water (table 4.7). Treated water is used locally as recharge for artificial lakes in Chapultepec, Aragón, and Cuemanco, to recharge the canals in the Xochimilco area, and for the irrigation of green areas within the city (DDF 1992a). About 2.4 m^3/s of treated water are re-used by industry (CEAS 1993).

If the 26 wastewater treatment plants in Mexico City operated at 100 per cent efficiency, the installed capacity could generate approximately 8.6 m^3/s (NRC 1995; CNI 1995), at an annual cost of US$55 million. Until recently, the government subsidized wastewater treatment. At present, new legislation is being implemented that transfers rights and obligations to the users of national hydrological resources, which makes the private sector responsible for discharging waste water within the quality levels established in the legislation on water-quality standards (CNA 1994; DOF 1993, 1995).

Waste

Liquid waste

Untreated waste water is partially eliminated from the basin by means of the deep drainage system and the older surface drainage systems of open channels. The drainage water is used mostly in the State of Hidalgo to irrigate over 85,000 ha for agricultural purposes (Strauss 1988; Cifuentes et al. 1991). The untreated waste water used for irrigation is a significant source of soil and plant contamination. For example, the mean concentration of surfactants in the water used for irrigation is about 13 mg/litre (Mazari-Hiriart 1992). A field irrigated with about 2,000 mm per ha per year (i.e. 20,000 $m^3.ha^{-1}.yr^{-1}$,

Table 4.7 **Wastewater treatment plants in the Metropolitan Area of Mexico City**

Plant	Installed capacity (litres/s)	Working capacity (litres/s)	Type of treatment
Federal District			
Chapultepec	160	106	Secondary
Ciudad Deportiva	230	80	Secondary
Coyoacán	400	336	Secondary
San Juan de Aragón	500	364	Secondary
Tlatelolco	22	14	Secondary
Cerro de la Estrella	3,000	1,509	Secondary
Iztacalco	13	10	Tertiary
Bosques de las Lomas	55	27	Secondary
Acueducto de Guadalupe	80	57	Secondary
Colegio Militar	20	18	Secondary
El Rosario	25	22	Tertiary
Reclusorio Sur	30	13	Secondary
San Luis Tlaxialtemalco	75	55	Tertiary
State of Mexico			
Pintores	5	5	Secondary
Naucalli	40	30	Secondary
San Juan Ixhuatepec	150	30	Secondary
Nezahualcóyotl	200	n.a.	Secondary
U. de Chapingo	40	40	n.a.
Lago de Texcoco (2 plants)	1,500	1,000	Second./Tert.
Termoeléctrica Valle México	450	250	Secondary
P. San Cristóbal	400	250	Secondary
Lechería	30	10	Secondary
Ford	30	30	Secondary
Club Golf Chiluca	20	20	n.a.
Revillagigedo Chiluca	20	20	n.a.
La Estadía Chiluca	20	20	n.a.
Total	7,515	4,316	

Sources: CEAS (1993); DDF (1974, 1992a); Murillo (1990); NRC (1995).
n.a. = information not available.

a conservative volume of irrigation in the area) will receive around 260 kg of surfactants per hectare each year. Heavy metals as a group (lead, cadmium, copper, zinc, and chromium) have shown concentrations as high as 0.78 mg/litre in the waste water used for irrigation (SARH 1985a; Siebe and Fischer 1991). This means that as much as 16 kg of heavy metals may be incorporated every year into a hectare of irrigated agricultural land. A similar situation occurs with boron, which has shown mean concentrations of 1.1 mg/litre in the Gran Canal (DDF 1979), representing about 22 kg of boron incorporated into each hectare of agricultural fields every year.

One of the main causes of water contamination is the practice of dumping industrial waste into the sewage system. A waste-processing plant is urgently needed in the basin, where the only means of disposing of chemical and toxic waste is through the city sewers or by transporting it to distant landfills. The National Commission for Water (*Comisión Nacional del Agua* or CNA) is in the final planning stage for the construction of a large wastewater treatment plant in the Texcoco area, which will be able to treat about 40 m^3/s.

Irrigation with waste water in Hidalgo has also generated a severe problem of microbiological contamination in crop fields. Using most-probable-numbers (MPN) procedures, total coliform counts have been reported in the ranges of 6×10^6 to 2×10^8 MPN/100 ml in the Gran Canal waters, which are used directly for irrigation at Chiconautla. Very high densities of colibacteria have also been reported in vegetables grown at these sites (see DOF 1996a). Median values of faecal coliform counts are 43 MPN/10 g within plant tissues and 96 MPN/10 g in plant surfaces. Some samples, however, have shown faecal coliform counts as high as 3,000 MPN/10 g (Strauss 1986). Additionally, viable amoebic cysts have been found in the canal waters and in irrigation ditches (Rivera et al. 1980). On the basis of epidemiological studies carried out in the Tula Irrigation District in Hidalgo, Cifuentes and colleagues (1991) have concluded that the re-use of waste water in agriculture significantly increases the risk of infection by *Ascaris lumbricoides*, as well as protozoal infections produced by *Entamoeba histolytica*, and promotes diarrhoeal diseases in farm workers and their families.

Solid waste

Solid waste management has been related to the urbanization process followed by Mexico City, being associated with population size, soil use, income level, and consumption patterns (SMA 1978c; Cruz 1995). In pre-Hispanic times (before 1521) 1,000 people were in charge of waste collection in the streets. Waste was partly deposited in dump sites located in marshy areas and partly incinerated to produce light for the city. Some of the organic waste was used as fertilizer. From 1826 to 1883, 14 places were designated specifically as dump sites and some of the solid waste was used for filling in and levelling streets. At the end of this period, waste incineration was favoured as a method that warded off epidemics (AMCRESPAC 1993).

The first governmental rules for clean-up and drainage in Mexico City were published in 1826 and 1836, respectively. Clean-up service regulations for the Federal District were published in July 1941, and abrogated only by new regulations in 1989 (AMCRESPAC 1993). In the 1950s, the solid waste generated in Mexico City amounted to 370 g per capita per day. Given a population of about 3 million inhabitants, it is estimated that 1,220 tons of solid waste per day were generated by the city at that time (SEDESOL 1993). By the end of the 1950s that figure had risen to 2,000 tons per day (AMCRESPAC 1993).

Restrepo, Bernache, and Rathje (1991; see also Castañeda and Jiménez 1986) conducted a detailed analysis of solid waste management in Mexico City for the decade of the 1980s. Based on their data, solid waste can be classified in three hierarchical categories: domestic waste of residential origin; municipal waste (domestic waste plus commercial, office, and institutional waste); and urban waste (municipal waste plus industrial refuse). Solid waste per capita per day in Mexico City in the 1980s amounted to 2.045 kg.

Estimates of total solid waste generation during the 1980s vary from 9,300 tons/day (AMCRESPAC 1993) to 14,000 tons/day (Riva Palacio 1986). As far as domestic waste is concerned, Restrepo et al. reported 5,502 tons/day in 1980 in Mexico City. By 1990, the volume had increased to 6,056 tons/day. The annual quantity grew from 2.0 to 2.2 million tons over the same period. Municipal waste, not including industrial waste, amounted to 11,000 tons/day in 1980, rising to 12,110 tons/day in 1990. During the 1990s, the Federal District alone generated 11,000 tons/day of municipal waste, while Mexico City as a whole was generating approximately 19,000 tons/day by 1993 (SEDESOL 1993).

Mexico City, compared with other places in the country, is the area with the highest concentration of hazardous residues as a result of industrial activities. Industrial residues produced in the whole of Mexico amounted to 164 million tons per year, of which 14,500 tons/day consist of potentially dangerous residues. Mexico City alone produced approximately 5,800 tons/day of industrial waste in 1990 (Ponciano et al. 1996; see also table 4.8), which has to be added to the volume of municipal waste.

The production of waste is growing at an estimated yearly rate of 3 per cent (Deffis Caso 1989). Estimates for the year 2000 show that the

Table 4.8 **Concentration of industries and production of industrial waste in the different municipalities within Mexico City**

Municipality	No. of industries	Industrial waste production (tons/day)
Alvaro Obregón	1,322	473
Azcapotzalco	2,324	917
Benito Juárez	2,879	497
Coyoacán	1,055	617
Cuajimalpa	190	67
Cuauhtémoc	5,948	557
Gustavo A. Madero	3,946	430
Iztacalco	1,897	410
Iztapalapa	3,751	590
Magdalena Contreras	202	7
Miguel Hidalgo	2,521	730
Milpa Alta	128	1
Tláhuac	468	47
Tlalpan	762	143
Venustiano Carranza	2,447	220
Xochimilco	22	87
Total	29,862	5,791

Source: Dirección General de Servicios Urbanos, Dirección de Desechos Sólidos, DDF, unpublished data, 1990.

production of solid wastes will be well above 25,000 tons/day, 48 per cent generated by the Federal District and 52 per cent by the State of Mexico (SEDESOL 1993).

Originally, solid waste disposal sites were located outside the urban area, but as a result of uncontrolled urban expansion they are currently surrounded by urban zones. Until the 1980s most of the solid waste disposal in Mexico City was done in open yards, which represented a serious health hazard. During that decade an effort was made to close all open yards and substitute them with sanitary landfills. Santa Cruz Meyehualco, in operation for 40 years, was closed in 1982, San Lorenzo Tezonco was closed in 1985, and the Santa Fe dump site, which had been in operation for 35 years, was closed in 1987. Several smaller dump sites within the urban area and surroundings were also closed (Restrepo, Bernache, and Rathje 1991; DDF 1988c). Some of the closed sites were transformed into recreational areas: Alameda Poniente, a large commercial development, was constructed on the filled area of the Santa Fe dump site; Parque Cuitláhuac was created on the former dump site of Santa Cruz

Meyehualco, and Alameda Oriente on the former dump site of Bordo Xochiaca (DDF 1988c). Santa Catarina stopped operating as an open-yard dump site in the 1980s, and 30 ha were redesigned to operate as a landfill storing 2,700 tons of waste per day.

In 1985, Bordo Poniente (a landfill with an area of 150 ha and a storage capacity of 2,700 tons/day) started operation in the Texcoco area, followed in 1987 by Prados de la Montaña on the western side of the city (30 ha and 2,100 tons/day). Both landfills were planned to operate for 15 years, and, together with Santa Catarina, they currently receive 7,500 tons/day of the municipal waste generated by the Federal District (DDF 1988c; Castillo et al. 1995), which represents 65 per cent of the waste generated in the city. No systematized information exists on solid waste generation and disposal in the State of Mexico, which has 12–15 registered dump sites.

These landfills were designed as final disposal sites for municipal waste, and thus are not lined or outfitted specifically for the containment of hazardous waste (Mazari-Hiriart and Mackay 1993). Nevertheless, owing to the lack of industrial waste disposal sites, all of the landfills have been receiving mixed domestic and industrial waste for years.

It has been suggested that, as in the past, the huge amounts of solid waste generated daily by the city should be processed to separate and recycle what is possible; the remaining garbage could be used through a combustion process or anaerobic digestion in special landfills to collect the biogas produced (Mulás 1995). As well as the dramatic increase in the generation of solid waste since the 1950s, there has been a change in composition. Between 1950 and 1990, the non-biodegradable content of solid waste increased from about 5 per cent to 40 per cent (Cruz 1995; SEDESOL 1993).

The proportion of organic garbage in the domestic waste of Mexico differs markedly from the waste production patterns in developed countries. For example, the United States generates domestic waste with a low proportion (less than one-third in weight) of organic residues, whereas Mexico City's domestic waste contains on average some 53 per cent of organic residues (table 4.9). It is especially rich in vegetable and fruit refuse, which has a high potential value as compost (Restrepo and Phillips 1985). Municipal waste, too, has a high organic matter content (about 47 per cent), and also some 34 per cent of potentially recyclable material. Domestic waste constitutes the main portion, contributing 53 per cent of the total volume, whereas commerce and services account for 37 per cent (Cruz 1995). Accord-

Table 4.9 **Mean composition and production of domestic waste per inhabitant in Mexico City (1987 values) and in the United States**

Component material	United States		Mexico City	
	g/day	%	g/day	%
Metals	69.2	6.7	9.7	2.4
Newspaper/magazines	111.8	10.8	15.3	3.8
Packing paper	98.2	9.4	20.5	5.1
Other paper	96.2	9.3	41.8	10.4
Plastic	60.9	5.9	28.9	7.2
Glass	108.7	10.5	28.9	7.2
Kitchen organics	142.7	13.7	181.7	45.2
Garden organics	179.6	17.3	33.0	8.2
Other	172.7	16.6	41.8	10.4
Total	1,040.0	100.0	401.6	100.0

Source: Restrepo, Bernache, and Rathje (1991).

ing to Restrepo, Bernache, and Rathje (1991), residential domestic waste can be divided into three main categories: organic kitchen waste, paper, and other recyclable products, which together account for about 72–81 per cent of total municipal waste.

A technological response in Mexico City to waste management started in the 1940s, when three waste management plants went into operation: Tetepilco, Azcapotzalco, and Aeropuerto. In the early 1970s the first storage facility and transfer station was constructed in the Federal District, and in 1974 a solid waste facility started operating in San Juan de Aragón (AMCRESPAC 1993). Two plants for the selection and recycling of solid waste, Bordo Poniente and San Juan de Aragón, were in operation in 1994 (DDF 1994). The San Juan de Aragón plant has never functioned at its full capacity. Designed to process 500 tons per day, the plant actually processes around 16 per cent of its installed capacity (Reséndiz Meza 1989).

Informal methods of waste recycling are much more important than official waste-processing plants. Restrepo, Bernache, and Rathje (1991) have calculated that some 300 tons of waste (or about 3 per cent of the city's domestic refuse) are recovered daily through the domestic sale of used paper and glass, and that around 1,500 tons are recovered by the operators of the waste-collection trucks, who classify and select usable waste during transportation and transfer. Finally, some 7,000 families subsist on the recovery of saleable waste directly from the dump sites (Reyes 1984). Known locally as *pepenadores*

Table 4.10 **Atmospheric emissions estimated for the Metropolitan Area of Mexico City, 1994**

Pollutant[a]	Sources			Total
	Industry	Services	Vehicles	
Absolute emissions (tons/yr)				
TSP	6,358	1,077	18,842	26,277
SO$_x$	26,051	7,217	12,200	45,468
CO	8,696	948	2,348,497	2,358,141
NO$_x$	31,520	5,339	91,787	128,646
HC	33,099	398,433	555,319	986,851
Relative emissions (% of total pollutant)				
TSP	24.2	4.1	71.7	100
SO$_x$	57.3	15.9	26.8	100
CO	0.4	0.0	99.6	100
NO$_x$	24.5	4.2	71.3	100
HC	3.4	40.4	56.3	100

Source: SEMARNAP (1996d).
a. TSP: total suspended particles; SO$_x$: sulphur oxides; CO: carbon monoxide; NO$_x$: nitrogen oxides; HC: hydrocarbons.

(scroungers), this group of people collects and recycles between 15 per cent and 35 per cent of municipal waste.

Air quality

Another serious problem associated with the uncontrolled growth of the city, and perhaps the most obvious one, is the high levels of atmospheric pollution that have persisted in Mexico City since 1970 (SAHOP 1978; SMA 1978a, 1978b). This problem is particularly critical during the cold season (December–February), during which the low temperatures stabilize the atmosphere above the basin and the air pollutants accumulate in the stationary mass of air that hovers, entrapped, above the city (SEDUE 1986; Velasco Levy 1983). Early studies of the lead (Pb) and bromine (Br) content in the air in Mexico City showed that, quantitatively, most of the air pollution originated from automobile exhaust (Barfoot et al. 1984; Sigler Andrade, Fuentes Gea, and Vargas Aburto 1982). According to Bravo's (1987) detailed report, vehicles produce most of the carbon monoxide and hydrocarbon residues in the basin, but fixed sources are responsible for a large proportion of the suspended particles and most of the sulphur oxides (table 4.10). During the 1980s, the number of cars in

Table 4.11 **Number of vehicles in Mexico City, 1978–2000**

Year	Vehicles ('000)	Population (million)	Urban area (km^2)
1978	1,600	12.8	949.9
1980	2,054	13.8	980.0
1983	2,205	14.6	1,031.1
1986	2,839	15.5	1,084.8
1990	3,070	16.6	1,160.9
2000[a]	3,900	20.0	1,400.0

Sources: Legorreta (1988 and 1995) for the numbers of vehicles, and DDF (1986) for population and urban area.
a. Projected values.

the city increased at an annual rate of more than 4 per cent (there were some 2 million cars in 1979 and more than 3 million in 1994; see table 4.11). The total amount of suspended particles during the dry season increased at approximately 6 per cent per year between the late 1970s and early 1980s (calculated from Fuentes Gea and Hernández 1984). Thus, in the early 1980s the deterioration in the air quality in the Basin of Mexico during the dry season was higher than the rates of population growth and urban expansion. The problem became so alarming that in the early 1990s the newly created National Commission on Human Rights assigned a working group the task of preparing a detailed report (Restrepo 1992), which is still one of the most comprehensive analyses of the problem. This unexpected initiative pushed the problem of air pollution into a new framework that regarded the right of the people to a healthy environment as a basic human right. The late 1980s and early 1990s produced a series of new measures to curb air pollution, chiefly through the use of unleaded gasoline and the installation of catalytic converters in all new cars. Although these innovations appear to have managed to stop the growth of air pollution levels, they have yet to succeed in bringing these levels down.

Until 1986, lead was probably the most harmful pollutant in the atmosphere of the basin (Salazar, Bravo, and Falcón 1981; table 4.12). Prior to that date, only leaded gasoline was sold in Mexico City and the concentration of lead in the air increased steadily with the number of cars, in some areas reaching values as high as 5 $\mu g/m^3$ during the 1970s and 1980s (Halffter and Ezcurra 1983; the Mexican standard for atmospheric lead is 1.5 $\mu g/m^3$). High lead concentrations were particularly hazardous in the areas of greatest traffic in the

Table 4.12 **Average concentration of lead in the atmosphere of Mexico City in 1970, compared with some cities in the United States**

City	$\mu g/m^3$
Mexico City	5.1
Cincinnati	1.4
Philadelphia	1.6
Los Angeles	2.5
New York	2.5

Source: Bravo (1987).

north of the city, where in the 1980s the maximum allowable standard was violated more than 55 per cent of the time (fig. 4.10). Among its many deleterious effects, a high concentration of lead in blood retards intellectual development in children (Albert and Badillo 1991; WHO and UNEP 1992) and, in general, causes alterations in neural development. The problem became so critical that, in September 1986, the state-owned oil company (PEMEX) replaced regular gasoline with low-lead fuel in which synthetic oxidizing additives partly replaced the action of leaded compounds (table 4.13). Additionally, in 1991 unleaded gasoline started to be sold in Mexico, and all new cars were required to be fitted with a catalytic converter and to use unleaded fuel. Figure 4.11 shows the increase in the consumption of unleaded gasoline after that date. The lead in the city's environment did indeed decrease dramatically as a result of these two efforts (fig. 4.12). It is estimated that atmospheric emissions of lead decreased from about 2,000 tons/year in 1986 to around 150 tons/year in 1994. As a result, a sustained decrease in the proportion of schoolchildren with high levels of lead in the blood has been observed: between 1990 and 1992, the proportion of schoolchildren with low-risk lead levels (0–10 μg of lead per 100 ml of blood) increased from 16 per cent to 45 per cent (Restrepo 1995; fig. 4.13).

However, the beneficial decrease in lead emissions produced by the change in gasoline also gave rise to unexpected and harmful side-effects. Although the atmospheric concentration of lead indeed fell, ozone concentrations above the city rose quickly as a result of a reaction between ultraviolet solar radiation, atmospheric oxygen, and gasoline residues (Bravo et al. 1992; fig. 4.14). The interaction of pollutant oxides of nitrogen (NO_x) and non-methane hydrocarbons (NMHCs) with solar radiation occurs via a complex set of chemical reactions (see Blake and Rowland 1995; Dickerson et al. 1997). The

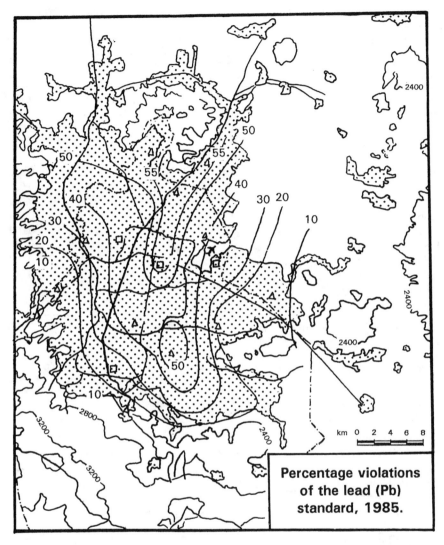

Fig. 4.10 **Percentage of days that the standard for atmospheric lead (1.5 $\mu g/m^3$) was exceeded in 1985 (Source: Jaúregui 1990)**

final result can be summarized in the following simplified equation, which takes place in the presence of nitrogen oxides (NO_x):

$$NMCH + 4O_2 + 2\,hv \rightarrow 2O_3 + CARB,$$

where *hv* represents a photon, or quantum of light, and CARB represents carbonyl compounds (i.e. the result of the photochemical

Table 4.13 **Concentration of lead tetra-ethyl in Mexican gasolines, 1978–1991 (ml/litre)**

Year	Type of gasoline	
	Regular	Extra
1978	0.77	0.77
1979	0.77	0.018
1980	0.77	0.018
1981	0.66	0.018
1982	0.48	0.018
1983	0.44	0.018
1984	0.22	0.018
1985	0.22	0.011
1986	0.14	0.011
1987	0.14	0.011
1988	0.14	0.011
1989	0.14	0.011
1990[a]	0.14	0.011
1991	0.14[b]	–
1991	0.00[c]	–

Source: Bravo, Sosa, and Torres (1991).
a. Last year that Extra gasoline was sold.
b. For pre-1991 vehicles.
c. For 1991 vehicles with a catalytic converter.

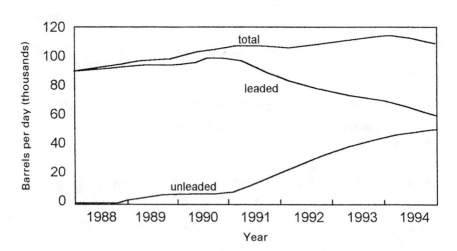

Fig. 4.11 **Average consumption of gasoline in Mexico City, 1988–1994 (Source: SEMARNAP 1996d)**

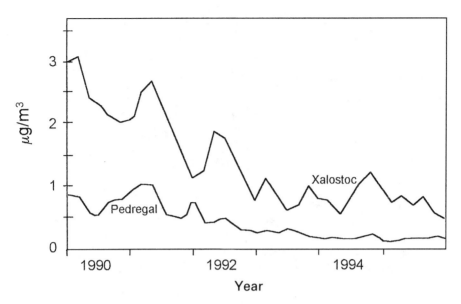

Fig. 4.12 **Mean levels of lead in the atmosphere of Mexico City for Xalostoc (an industrial area with high levels) and El Pedregal (a residential zone with low levels), 1990–1995 (Source: SEMARNAP 1996d)**

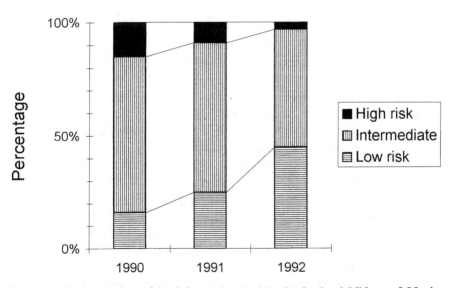

Fig. 4.13 **The evolution of lead levels in the blood of schoolchildren of Mexico City (Note: low risk = lead concentrations of 0–10 μg/100 ml blood, intermediate = concentrations of 11–20 μg/100 ml blood, and high risk = concentrations of 21–30 μg/100 ml blood. Source: modified from Restrepo 1995)**

103

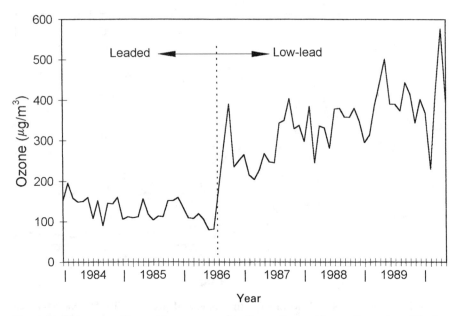

Fig. 4.14 **Mean monthly maximum concentrations of ozone in south-western Mexico City, 1984–1990 (Note: the broken line indicates the date when the concentration of lead tetra-ethyl was lowered in regular gasoline. Source: modified from Calderón-Garcidueñas et al. 1992a and Bravo 1987)**

oxidation of the NMHCs, such as aldehydes or ketones), which can further break down to produce additional ozone (O_3). The rate of production of smog depends on the concentrations of these pollutants (NO_x, produced by most combustion processes, and NMHCs, produced by the emission of unburnt or partially burnt hydrocarbons) and on the intensity of solar near-UV (300–400 nm) radiation, which produces the photons necessary to trigger the reaction. Because the combustion of unleaded gasoline is less complete than that of leaded fuel, the elimination of lead tetra-ethyl from gasolines in the Basin of Mexico resulted in a significant increase in the amount of hydrocarbons emitted with the exhaust gases of motor vehicles (Bravo et al. 1992; SEDESOL 1994d; Riveros 1995; Riveros et al. 1995).

The present ozone concentration in Mexico City during hours of high solar radiation (11.00 to 16.00 h) is, on average, around 0.15 ppm (300 $\mu g/m^3$; see RAMA 1996a), 10 times the normal atmospheric concentration, well above the one-hour maximum limit in the United States and Japan (Aznavourian 1984), and high enough to damage most of the urban vegetation (Skärby and Sellden 1984). Because of

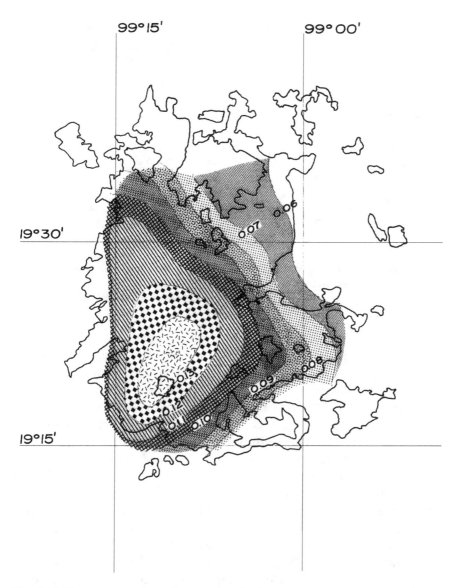

Fig. 4.15 **The concentration of ozone (ppm) above Mexico City (Source: Jáuregui 1990)**

the time-lag involved in the formation of ozone, the highest ozone concentrations occur near midday, on sunny days, and mostly towards the south-west of the city in the direction of the prevailing winds (fig. 4.15). During the winter of 1991–92, the ozone levels in this area exceeded the maximum allowable standard (0.11 ppm or 216 $\mu g/m^3$)

105

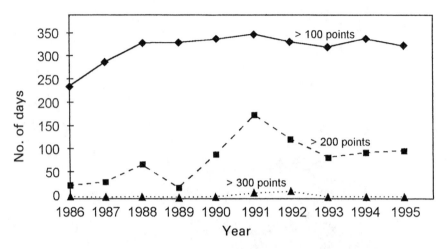

Fig. 4.16 **Number of days on which air-quality indices exceeded level 100 (unhealthy), level 200 (dangerous), and level 300 (alert), 1986–1995 (Note: see chap. 5 for a discussion of the air pollution index for Mexico City. Source: SEMARNAP 1996d)**

almost every day and generated continuous health complaints from the population. During some days, ozone reached concentrations as high as 0.6 ppm (1,200 μg/m^3), a level that, by any standard, is considered highly harmful for humans (WHO and UNEP 1992) and plants. In terms of Mexico's air-quality indices (see chap. 5), air pollution has reached "dangerous" levels on about 30 per cent of days since 1991 (fig. 4.16). The main pollutant has been ozone.

In 1991, catalytic converters became mandatory in new cars sold in Mexico. It was hoped that this would lower the emissions of the reactive organic compounds that are the by-product of the combustion of unleaded gasoline and act as ozone precursors. The concentration of ozone, however, has stubbornly remained at high levels. It is not yet known if the lack of response to the new automobile standards is due to the slow upgrading of vehicles on the road, or to the poor maintenance of the converters themselves, or to other sources, such as unburnt leakages of liquefied petroleum gas (LPG) from domestic and industrial stationary tanks, incomplete combustion of LPG in badly regulated burners, or vaporized emissions from uncapped or leaky fuel tanks, which may also contribute significantly to the generation of ozone-precursor hydrocarbons (Blake and Rowland 1995; Riveros 1995; Riveros et al. 1995). The high annual growth rate of the number of vehicles has possibly also played its part in countering the effectiveness of the new measure.

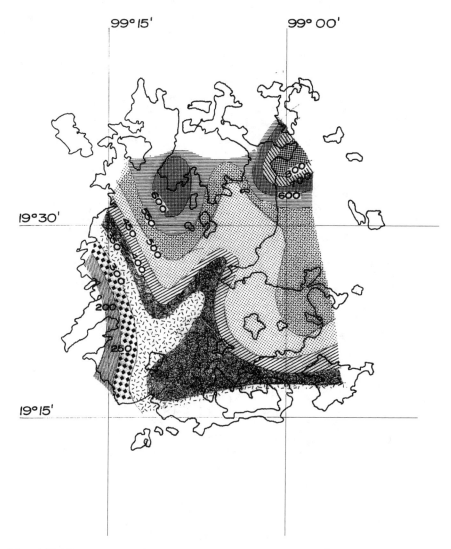

Fig. 4.17 **The concentration of suspended particles (μg/m^3) above Mexico City (Source: Jáuregui 1990)**

Other pollutants too have considerable impact on the atmosphere of Mexico, but their spatial distribution differs from that of ozone. Particulate pollution is highest towards the north-east of the city, where the urban area borders the dusty bowl of the now dry Lake Texcoco, and in the north, in the industrial quarters of Azcapotzalco and neighbouring municipalities (fig. 4.16). Sulphur dioxide is highest in the north, where most of the industries are located (fig. 4.17). In

107

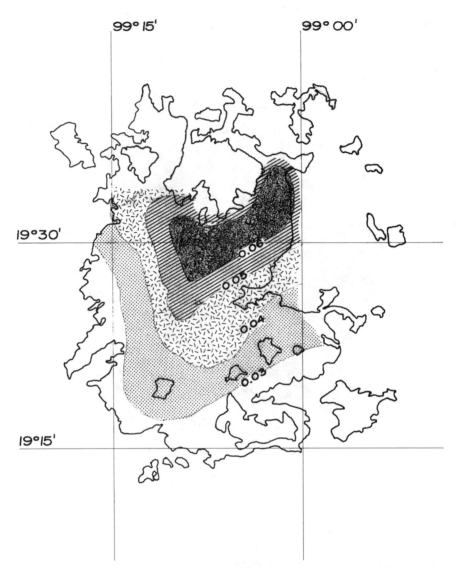

Fig. 4.18 **The mean concentration of sulphur dioxide (ppm) above Mexico City (Source: Jáuregui 1990)**

some parts of the city, particularly towards the east-central area, the concentration of total suspended particles exceeds both Mexican and international air-quality standards more than 50 per cent of the time (Fuentes Gea and Hernández 1984).

Table 4.14 **Maximum allowable standards for the six main air pollutants in Mexico City**

Pollutant	Symbol	Mean value[a]	Period of averaging
Breathable suspended particles	PM-10	150 $\mu g/m^3$	24 hours
Carbon monoxide	CO	12 mg/m^3 (11 ppm)	8 hours
Ozone	O_3	216 $\mu g/m^3$ (0.11 ppm)	1 hour
Nitrogen dioxide	NO_2	395 $\mu g/m^3$ (0.21 ppm)	1 hour
Sulphur dioxide	SO_2	365 $\mu g/m^3$ (0.13 ppm)	24 hours
Lead	Pb	1.5 $\mu g/m^3$	3 months

Sources: RAMA (1996a) and SEDUE (1985).
a. These values correspond to a level of 100 on the Metropolitan Index of Air Quality (IMECA) – see table 5.5.

The breathable fraction of suspended particles, or PM-10 (i.e. particulate matter with diameter of 0.3–10.0 µm), is particularly important, because these particles, which form 40–60 per cent of the total suspended particles, are small enough to lodge permanently in human lungs and represent a serious health hazard (WHO and UNEP 1992). On average, the mean peak concentration of PM-10 in the air of Mexico City is around 250 $\mu g/m^3$, almost twice the Mexican maximum allowable standard of 150 $\mu g/m^3$ (table 4.14). This average, however, masks the extremely biased spatial distribution of this pollutant: the southern parts of Mexico City in general have low concentrations of PM-10, whereas in the industrial north-eastern districts (Xalostoc) the situation is critical, with 168 days per year (46 per cent of the year) above the maximum allowable standard (RAMA 1996a).

Carbon monoxide (CO) is higher in the central part of the city, where vehicular traffic is more intense (fig. 4.19). A study by Fernández-Bremauntz (1993) has shown that the concentration of CO in public transport in central Mexico City ranges between 34 and 132 mg/m^3, a value dangerously above the maximum allowable standard (12 mg/m^3 or 11 ppm; table 4.14) and sufficiently high to cause significant physiological effects on humans in less than one hour (Santos-Burgoa and Rojas-Bracho 1992; WHO and UNEP 1992).

Because wind speeds are extremely low in the elevated and topo-

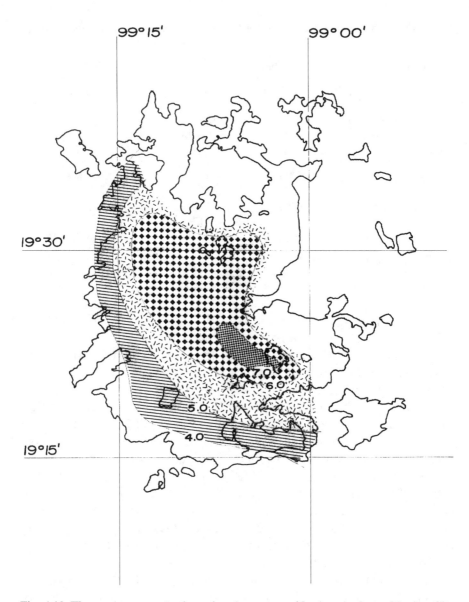

Fig. 4.19 **The mean concentration of carbon monoxide (ppm) above Mexico City (Source: Jáuregui 1990)**

graphically closed Basin of Mexico, horizontal air movements are not a major cause of dispersion of air pollutants. On the contrary, the main cause of atmospheric dispersion is the turbulent ascent of hot air at midday during warm, sunny days (Velasco Levy 1983). For this

110

reason, the colder months of the year (December to March) are a particularly hazardous time in terms of air pollution, because thermal inversions occur frequently during these periods (RAMA 1996a). When a thermal inversion occurs, the lower layers of the atmosphere, which are in contact with the ground, cool more rapidly than the upper layers and a stationary, thermodynamically stable mass of cold air settles above the city (Ezcurra 1991a).

5

The driving forces of environmental change

The rapid rise and the enormous power of the Aztec state were based on the political control of much of Meso-America and on the subordination of hundreds of different groups that paid tribute to the emperor. Aztec wealth depended to some extent on the concentration of high-quality goods (e.g. metals, obsidian, tropical fruits, high-protein food) and labour collected as tribute from conquered groups. The Basin of Mexico, which initially allowed the rise of the Aztec culture through the appropriation and use of the highly productive *chinampa* technology, became a partly subsidized ecosystem receiving inputs of matter and energy from other areas.

This tradition, maintained under Spanish rule, has now reached overwhelming proportions. Few ecosystems in the world are so altered and so far from self-sufficiency as the Basin of Mexico is at present (Ezcurra and Sarukhán 1990; Mazari-Hiriart and Mackay 1993). With much of the forests cut, most of the *chinampa* lands turned into urban developments, and practically all of the lakes dried up, the supply of raw materials and energy generated within the basin does not suffice for even a small fraction of the almost 20 million residents. Thus, the Basin of Mexico imports vast amounts of food, energy, wood, water, building materials, and many other products from other ecosystems

112

Table 5.1 **Energy consumption in the Mexican Republic and in the Basin of Mexico, 1970–1975**

| Source of energy | Consumption (m^3 of oil, or equivalent) | | | |
| | 1970 | | 1975 | |
	Mexico	Basin of Mexico[a]	Mexico	Basin of Mexico[a]
Oil	34,060,003	9,215,600 (27.1%)	48,081,005	13,202,132 (27.5%)
Electricity	2,320,482	753,874 (32.5%)	3,708,698	1,065,554 (28.7%)
Coal	1,470,000	–	2,616,000	–
Total	37,850,485	9,969,474 (26.3%)	54,405,703	14,267,686 (26.2%)

Source: Ibarra et al. (1986).
a. The numbers in parentheses indicate the proportion used by the Basin of Mexico with respect to the whole country.

that, in effect, subsidize the water and energy flows of the basin. With 20 per cent of the population of the country, the basin consumes around 27 per cent of the country's oil and nearly 29 per cent of its electricity (table 5.1). Mexico City is at the hub of an immense system of concentration of power and labour, and also of appropriation of natural resources. The social domination of some groups by others is expressed in geographic and environmental terms, as a system of appropriation of natural resources from other regions and other social groups.

Although mortality has been reduced significantly during recent decades, there has been a marked shift in its principal causes (table 5.2). Whereas in the first half of the twentieth century infectious diseases were the most common cause of death, now diseases associated with modern industrial life and with contamination (heart disease, cancer, and accidents) have moved into the top five, together with pneumonia and gastro-enteritis, two infectious diseases associated with the degradation of air and water.

The ultimate driving force of environmental change is an immense system of subsidies, both in terms of natural resources (ecological subsidies) and in terms of financial resources (economic subsidies). We can, however, recognize four main mechanisms, or proximate causes, driving accelerated environmental change in the Basin of Mexico: (a) population change, (b) governmental policy, (c) distribution of wealth and resources, and (d) concentration of technological capacity. We shall discuss them separately in the following sections.

Table 5.2 **Changes in the 10 highest causes of mortality in Mexico between 1955–57 and 1980**

1955–57			1980		
Cause of death	Mortality rate (per 10,000)	%	Cause of death	Mortality rate (per 10,000)	%
1. Gastro-enteritis	227.5	17.5	1. Heart diseases	74.9	11.7
2. Influenza and pneumonia	202.0	15.5	2. Accidents	71.1	11.1
3. Early childhood diseases	135.3	10.4	3. Influenza and pneumonia	56.9	8.9
4. Heart diseases	91.4	7.0	4. Enteritis and diarrhoeic diseases	55.1	8.6
5. Malaria	66.4	5.1	5. Malignant tumours (cancer)	39.2	6.1
6. Accidents	48.1	3.7	6. Perinatal afflictions	34.3	5.4
7. Homicides	38.0	2.9	7. Cerebro-vascular diseases	22.6	3.5
8. Malignant tumours (cancer)	37.8	2.9	8. Cirrhosis and other chronic diseases	22.1	3.5
9. Bronchitis	32.7	2.5	9. Diabetes mellitus	21.7	3.4
10. Tuberculosis	31.2	2.4	10. Nephritis and nephrosis	10.5	1.6
Other causes	390.0	30.0	Other causes	231.6	36.2
Total	1,300.4	100.0	Total	640.0	100.0

Source: Santos-Burgoa and Rojas-Bracho (1992); DGE (1989).

114

Table 5.3 **Population in Mexico City, 1519–1990 (million)**

Year[a]	Federal District	State of Mexico	Total
1519 (Conquest)	0.3	–	0.3
1620 (Colony)	0.03	–	0.03
1810 (Independence)	0.1	–	0.1
1910 (Revolution)	0.7	–	0.7
1940 (Cardenist Period)	1.8	–	1.8
1950	3.0	–	3.0
1960	4.8	0.4	5.2
1970	6.8	1.9	8.7
1980	8.8	5.0	13.8
1990[b]	9.3	7.3	16.6
1990[c]	8.2	6.5	15.0

Source: DDF (1987a), and projections by the authors.
a. Pre-1950 dates have been chosen as approximate indicators, and correspond with the important historical dates indicated in parentheses.
b. Values projected by the authors.
c. Values of the 1990 population census.

Population change

The real size of the present population of Mexico City is not known for sure. Officially, the 1990 census reported a figure of 15 million for the whole megalopolis (table 5.3). This figure, however, seems unrealistic when compared with the growth of the urbanized area during the 1980–1990 decade and with historical trends in population growth rates. On the one hand, the present size of the urbanized area, as estimated by remote sensing techniques, multiplied by the historical population density (14,500 persons per km^2), suggests a total population of about 16.6 million in 1990 and 18.5 million in 1995. On the other hand, a projection of the 1980 population values at a conservatively low growth rate of 1.5 per cent (the growth rate between 1940 and 1980 always exceeded 2 per cent) gives a total population of 16 million for 1990 and 17.3 million for 1995. This is in agreement with Corona (1991), who concluded that the national census underestimated the total population of the country by some 2–6 million people. Finally, the current total use of water in the city (63 m^3/s) and the historic per capita use (300 litres/day) also suggest a total population of around 18.1 million for 1995. Thus, we may assume that the 1995 population of the larger Mexico City was some 18 million people.

Between 1950 and 1980, the average annual growth rate of the population of Mexico City was 4.8 per cent. The population, however, has grown more quickly in the industrial zone of the State of Mexico, north of the Federal District, where the average rate of increase between 1950 and 1980 was 13.6 per cent, compared with 3.3 per cent in the Federal District. As chapter 3 of this book indicates, much of the high growth rate of the city has been due to the continuous arrival of migrants from economically depressed rural areas (Goldani 1977; Stern 1977a, 1977b; Unikel 1974). In the 1950–1980 period, 5.43 million immigrants arrived in Mexico city. This influx was responsible for 38 per cent of the growth of the city (Partida 1987). Between 1970 and 1980 alone, 3.25 million immigrants arrived in Mexico City (Calderón and Hernández 1987). If this effect is taken into account, the intrinsic annual growth rate of the city for that period can be calculated as approximately 1.8 per cent, considerably lower than the national average, which was around 3.0 per cent for the same period. It is immigration, more than reproductive growth, that has maintained the high rate of increase of the population of Mexico City (Goldani 1977). Between 1970 and 1980 around 650 babies were born every day, while some 1,100 new immigrants arrived daily to stay in the Basin of Mexico. Many of the new-born babies, of course, were born to recently arrived immigrants, a phenomenon that further increased the growth rate of the population by elevating the natural birth rates. Assuming that the figure of about 18 million inhabitants in Mexico City for 1995 is correct, then the growth rate for the 1980–1995 period was around 1.8 per cent, considerably lower than the rates for the previous decades. The population is still growing, but it is also quite clearly going through a demographic transition, and the growth rates seem to be slowing (fig. 5.1).

The net population densities (fig. 5.2) of Mexico City have stabilized since 1930 at around 14,500 persons/km^2. In the 1920–1930 decade, a dramatic decrease in population densities coupled with the introduction of inexpensive and efficient public transportation (trams and buses) into Mexico City changed the urban trace from a concentrated city that hinged around its central area into a more dispersed metropolitan area with a lower population density and a growing number of alternative commercial centres. In spite of this decrease, the population densities of Mexico City are still high in comparison with other cities in the world: slightly higher than Tokyo or Caracas; twice as high as New York, São Paulo, and Buenos Aires, three times as high as Paris, and four times as high as London. Only some Asian cities, such as Bombay, Calcutta, and Hong Kong, show population densities higher than Mexico City's (Ward 1991).

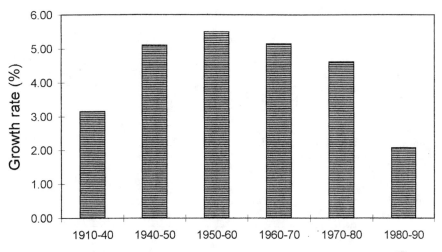

Fig. 5.1 **Population growth rates in Mexico City, 1910–1990 (Source: DDF 1987a)**

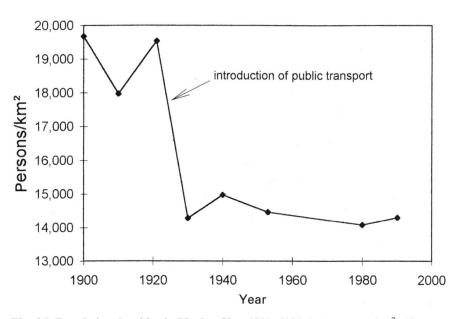

Fig. 5.2 **Population densities in Mexico City, 1900–1990 (persons per km^2) (Source: DDF 1986)**

Severe environmental problems notwithstanding, the Mexican model of development has given priority to improving the quality of life in the large cities, where social demand is more concentrated, at the expense of the rural areas, which have become comparatively

117

Table 5.4 **Evolution of the quality-of-life indicators for the Basin of Mexico, 1950–1980**

Indicator	Basin of Mexico				Mexican Republic 1980
	1950	1960	1970	1980	
Life expectancy at 1 year of age (years)	55.0	60.8	63.2	65.2	64.4
Infant mortality (%)	12.0	7.9	7.4	4.3	7.1
Adult literacy (%)	83.8	88.4	92.6	95.6	83.0
Houses with running water (%)	n.a.	35.0	53.0	67.0	n.a.
Houses with drainage (%)	n.a.	33.0	63.0	81.3	n.a.
Houses owned by their residents (%)	n.a.	34.0	50.0	52.7	n.a.

Source: Ibarra et al. (1986).
n.a. = information not available.

poorer. From 1950 to 1980 the basin experienced marked improvements in demographic and domestic indicators of quality of life (table 5.4), but the changes at the national level have been less dramatic (Ezcurra 1990a). This difference in trends is, of course, much more pronounced if the Basin of Mexico is compared with the depressed rural areas from which most of the immigrants come. Such public services as education, drinking water, and drainage are rare in the poorer areas of central and southern Mexico, which provide (at a cheap price) many of the products that are consumed in the basin, and also generate most of the new immigrants that move into the area. In the Mixtec region, for example, the proportion of houses with drinking water is less than 4 per cent, and most of the towns do not have drainage. Similar contrasts hold for educational levels.

In short, the population growth rate emerges as the main driving variable of environmental change. Between 1940 and 1980, with a growth rate of approximately 4–5 per cent, the population doubled every 15 years, and with it the demand for water, electricity, transportation, housing, and other services. The number of cars has grown at an even higher rate than the population, doubling every decade. These rates *per se* have exacted a huge environmental toll, as more people necessarily use more resources and generate more waste and more pollution.

Governmental policies

Governmental policies have acted as a driving force of environmental change in several ways. In zealously promoting the concentration of employment and economic activity in the basin, they have provided infrastructure and services in Mexico City much more abundantly than in the rest of the nation. Governmental policies have promoted urban expansion, subsidized resources that sustain employment, provided cheap subsidized transport within the city, and fostered the concentration of education and health services in the Basin of Mexico.

Like Tenochtitlan, Mexico City since colonial times has enjoyed the status of the heart of Mexico. The colonial government established a currency mint-house (La Casa de Moneda) in Mexico City to control commercial transactions. Besides, Mexico City was the seat of the political and administrative powers, and much of the infrastructure constructed at that time was oriented to facilitating communication with the rest of the country. These factors influenced the concentration process that continued during the Independence period and throughout the nineteenth century, when the Federal District was created.

Completion of the railway and electrical systems between 1870 and 1910 and then, from 1930 onwards, the construction of wide city streets for automobiles and buses, the development of a water supply network, and the expansion of the electricity network represented very important infrastructural advantages for the establishment of industries. By the 1940s, investment in the Federal District represented approximately 40 per cent of the federal government's total investment in the country. In 1958, federal investment per capita in the Federal District was five times higher than in Guadalajara or Monterrey (Bataillon and Rivière d'Arc 1973).

Particularly since 1940, governmental policy appeared to be oriented to creating a wide industrial base in the country through specific programmes and legislation that had a great impact in the capital city. Mexico City's metropolitan growth, initiated in the 1950s when the urban area started to spread over the territory of the State of Mexico, is attributable to intentional measures taken by the local government. In 1950, the government of the Federal District prohibited the construction of residential developments within its territory, a decision that stimulated urban expansion into the contiguous municipalities of the State of Mexico. (This prohibition was abolished in 1970.)

119

Several important construction projects accelerated this urban expansion. The construction of the Mexico–Querétaro highway in 1957 and the extension of the peripheral freeway (*Periférico*) in 1968 provided the city with rapid communication between the Federal District and the municipalities of the State of Mexico in the north. The consequent demand for land for industries and housing triggered a real development boom that completely transformed the north of the city. In their attempts to attract capital and investment, the local municipal governments of the State of Mexico made great efforts to erect housing developments and to regularize illegal settlements and thus contributed significantly to accelerating the expansion of the urban area over good agricultural land. Naturally, private developers also acted in the same way. As an example of this rapid process, Schteingart (1989) indicates that, between 1958 and 1963, 87 new residential developments for the middle and working classes were constructed in 15 metropolitan municipalities of the State of Mexico, particularly in Tlalnepantla, Naucalpan, Ecatepec, and Atizapán. The 1970 lifting of the ban on new developments in the Federal District spawned an even greater acceleration in the approval of residential developments in the State of Mexico. The years 1970–1975 saw about 29,000 housing programmes approved for residential developments in the Federal District and 166,100 in the State of Mexico.

One important form of government intervention that has promoted the occupation of land in the Basin of Mexico has been the regularization of *ejido* land (state-owned land given to peasant communities for agricultural use) and land owned by communes of native peoples. Such land is legally reserved for agricultural production but frequently invaded by low-income groups for unauthorized housing developments. A pragmatic policy has prompted the authorities to recognize these illegal settlements and to provide the squatters (known in the local Mexican jargon as *paracaidistas*, i.e. "paratroopers") with basic services. This practice, in turn, has encouraged a vicious circle of land invasion, eventual governmental recognition of the new settlers, and a prosperous black market in communal land. Indeed, land invasion is often promoted by the same *ejido* authorities (*comisariados*), which see in the creation of urban developments an opportunity to reap greater economic benefit than they might obtain from land cultivation. And governmental authorities, which have only limited capacity to make cheap land available to the working population that migrates into Mexico City, have tolerated the whole process, thus exacerbating the problem.

Several governmental bodies were set up to deal with this problem. The Commission for the Regularization of Land Tenure (Comisión para la Regularización de la Tenencia de la Tierra, or CORETT) was created at federal level and worked very actively in Mexico City. At state level, the Commission for Land Regularization (Comisión para la Regularización de la Superficie Territorial del Estado de México, or CRESEM) was created in the State of Mexico. In essence, the programmes for regularization of land tenure and land use have been important catalysts of the urbanization process. This situation has also forced the government to supply infrastructure and public services to populations unable to enter the private land market.

The government has also played a role by relocating populations affected by extraordinary events, such as the 1985 earthquake. Following that event, the government relocated many former inhabitants of central areas to peripheral zones, mainly in the metropolitan municipalities of the State of Mexico to the north of the city, where the local governments supplied them with new dwellings. The resettled population complained about the general condition of their houses, the lack of basic services such as water and electricity, and inadequacies in social infrastructure, particularly in relation to schools and transport (Icazuriaga 1992).

Above all, governmental policy promoted industrial development in Mexico City, thus providing employment and attracting population. The Law on New and Essential Industries, passed in 1951, granted fiscal exemptions to firms establishing in the national territory. The most favoured region was Mexico City, which housed a great number of industries, either as individual companies or as part of "industrial parks" in the metropolitan municipalities. The exemption from taxes in the Federal District was abolished in 1954, but this did not happen in the State of Mexico, which recorded a notable increase in the number of industries. This lack of coordination of governmental industrial policies continued in subsequent years. While the Federal District was considered to be an area of industrial saturation, the State of Mexico avidly courted the establishment of industries. By 1970, the State of Mexico was receiving 20 per cent of all credit granted at the national level by the Fund to Guarantee and Promote Small and Intermediate Industry (Icazuriaga 1992). Obviously, this situation accelerated the growth of the city towards the north.

Finally, it is worth noting that urban planning failed to control the expansion of the city. In addition to the provision of infrastructure and roads, other actions worked to consolidate the metropolitan area. For instance, the planning and establishment of a model municipality in the form of a self-contained "new town," Cuautitlan–Izcalli, complete with all the essential services, in which the population could live, work, and have access to services without long journeys, fell short of the original aims. The location, which was very vulnerable to the direct influence of Mexico City, simply became part of the metropolitan area. Such developments, particularly given the absence of a metropolitan body to coordinate urban planning in the whole city, led to contradictory measures and to conflict between the two entities involved, namely the Federal District and the State of Mexico.

Ever since large-scale industrialization began in the basin early in the twentieth century, governmental policies have lagged behind environmental problems, which were not until recently even on the list of governmental priorities. Following an ancient, pre-Hispanic tradition, the government has treated the basin as the focus for decision-making, wealth, and resources, frequently at the expense of the development and environmental quality of other regions. In more recent times, the government seems to have grown wary of the large urban concentration, but it does not seem to be willing to risk taking the unpopular measures required to control demographic concentration and environmental deterioration.

Traditionally, the official response to environmental deterioration in the Basin of Mexico has been to export the problem away from the region or to concentrate the problem in poor and degraded districts, rather than to solve it in an environmentally sound manner. Solid waste, for example, was disposed of in open dump-yards surrounded by poor neighbourhoods until 1986, when the government realized that the yards were leaching toxic lixiviates into the soil and contaminating the air. Because the yards had become a matter of concern for the whole basin and not just for the immediate neighbourhood, the government took steps to confine the dumping of waste to trenches designed specifically for that purpose.

A system of ecological subsidies sees to it that many of the problems generated by the growth or by the sheer size of Mexico City are, in effect, exported to neighbouring areas. The chronic shortage of water in the basin, for example, has been in great part transferred to the Lerma and Cutzamala basins, from where water is imported at a rate of 19.5 m^3/s (Bazdresch 1986). Meanwhile, contaminated waste water drains into the Tula basin, in the State of Hidalgo, where, until recently, it was used for the irrigation of vegetables and other crops.

This practice contributed to the spread of parasitic diseases such as amoebiasis and cysticercosis, and also contaminated agricultural soils with as much as 260 kg of detergents or 22 kg of boron per hectare per year (Ibarra et al. 1986). Although irrigation with waste water has now been banned in the region, alternatives are still not accessible to most farmers, who often have to resort to using the polluted waters illegally to save their crops.

Mexican public policy towards the health hazards involved in environmental pollution has been to play down the real magnitude of the risks involved. For example, the Metropolitan Index of Air Quality (Índice Metropolitano de Calidad del Aire, or IMECA) has been largely copied from the National Ambient Air Quality Standard (NAAQS; see EPA 1994b) of the United States, which in turn was derived from the index of Ott and Thom (see Thom and Ott 1975). However, IMECA downplays the risks attendant on different levels of atmospheric pollution. That is, for a similar concentration of air pollutants, the Mexican standard informs the population of much milder risks than are really involved (table 5.5; Ezcurra 1991b). Similarly, during the winter season, when atmospheric thermal inversions occur and air quality is unacceptably poor almost every day (Ezcurra 1991a), the health authorities routinely inform the public to guard against influenza and other respiratory diseases, ignoring completely the effects of air pollution. This tends to give people the impression that their respiratory ills are normal seasonal ailments, unrelated to environmental degradation.

The distribution of wealth and resources

Apart from the ecological interpretation of the natural resource subsidies channelled into the basin, the urban growth of Mexico City has also involved the concentration of wealth and an economic subsidy implicitly granted by the rest of the nation to the residents of the capital city. The cost of public transportation in Mexico City (buses, trolleys, and the metro train) in the 1980s and 1990s fluctuated between US$0.07 and US$0.15 per trip, a fixed tariff that is independent of the distance travelled. The metro train, which transports 4.6 million passengers per day (DDF 1997), thus generates revenue of some US$500,000 per day, but the real cost of operating the system was of the order of US$1.5 million per day in the 1980s (Bazdresch 1986) and around US$2 million in the 1990s. The shortfall is ultimately met by all taxpayers, many of whom do not benefit from the service in any

123

Table 5.5 **Comparison of the Mexican air quality index (IMECA) against Ott and Thom's index and the National Ambient Air Quality Standard (NAAQS) of the United States, for similar pollution levels**

Index[a]	IMECA description	Ott and Thom	NAAQS
0–50	Favourable environment for all sorts of physical activities.	Good	Below NAAQS
51–100	Favourable environment for all sorts of physical activities.	Satisfactory	Below NAAQS
101–200	Slight reaction in predisposed persons.	Unhealthy	Above NAAQS
201–300	Reaction and relative intolerance towards physical exercise in persons with breathing or cardiovascular problems. Slight reaction in the population in general.	Dangerous	Alert
301–400	Diverse symptoms and intolerance towards physical exercise in healthy people.	Dangerous	Warning
401–500	Diverse symptoms and intolerance towards physical exercise in healthy people.	Dangerous	Emergency
501+	(Not described)	Significant harm	Significant harm

a. A description of IMECA-100 thresholds is given in table 4.14.

way. Similarly, the real costs of water distribution in Mexico City are some US$0.20–0.30/m^3, largely as a result of the high costs of pumping water into the Basin of Mexico from the Lerma basin (Bazdresch 1986; see also table 6.2). Consequently, the government spends some US$450 million per year to supply water to the Basin of Mexico. The revenue obtained from the service, however, is of the order of US$42 million, less than 10 per cent of the total cost. Other services, such as electricity, gas, garbage collection, and road maintenance are subsidized nation-wide and not just in the Basin of Mexico. However, because the city receives these services in a higher proportion than the rest of the nation, it receives a higher share of the subsidy, as in the case of energy discussed at the beginning of the chapter. This is, again, particularly true for rural areas that export their produce to the city but do not benefit from the cheap urban services.

The marked improvements in demographic and urban indicators of quality of life since 1950 in the Basin of Mexico have exceeded those for the country as a whole and especially those of impoverished rural areas. These improvements have not been equally distributed in social and spatial terms, however, and pronounced inequalities prevail in this particular region. Increasing social and economic polarization could become a major driving force of environmental degradation and damage to the human population. Affluence usually translates into high per capita consumption, with obvious impacts on the environment of the basin: for example, a high per capita use of cars exacerbates air pollution problems. Poverty, the opposite of affluence, is the major driving force of migration into Mexico City, and breeds inappropriate provision of public services, poor-quality housing, and an increasing number of low-income and underemployed groups.

Recent economic crises have affected the standard of living of numerous social sectors. According to the 1990 census data, 20 per cent of the employed population in the Federal District earned less than 1 minimum wage (m.w.), and an additional 41 per cent earned 1–2 m.w. This means that about 60 per cent of the total employed population in the DF was in an unsatisfactory economic situation (González Salazar 1993). At the beginning of 1995 (shortly after the financial crisis in December 1994) survey data reported that 11 per cent of the employed population in Mexico City earned less than 1 m.w. (around US$5 per day), and 52 per cent received 1–2 m.w. In short, some 63 per cent of the working population was below the poverty level. Poorly qualified occupations in the commerce and service sectors were particularly affected. In contrast, in the same year, 3 per cent of the employed population earned more than 10 m.w. (table 5.6). These figures underscore the unequal distribution of wealth and the widespread presence of poverty in Mexico City.

If we look at income levels and their distribution in Mexico City, it is notable that municipalities in the east have the highest proportions of the economically active population that earn less than 1 m.w. In municipalities such as Chalco, Chimalhuacan, La Paz, or Ixtapaluca this proportion is usually more than 50 per cent. In the central and western administrative units, such as Benito Juárez, Miguel Hidalgo, or Tlalpan, the poorer social groups represent less than 30 per cent, whereas the middle and upper classes account for more than 10 or 15 per cent. The high proportion of low-income population in peripheral municipalities, mostly those to the east, can be explained by three factors: first, some peripheral municipalities still include a significant number of people engaged in agricultural occupations, although these productive activities tend to decrease with urban expansion; second, peripheral populations include a sizeable proportion of unskilled

Table 5.6 **Employed population in Mexico City by income levels, 1995**

Income level[a]	Employed population	
	No.	%
Less than 1 m.w.	654,111	10.99
1–2 m.w.	2,419,810	40.66
2–3 m.w.	1,145,110	19.24
3–5 m.w.	566,368	9.52
5–10 m.w.	410,194	6.89
More than 10 m.w.	194,289	3.26
No income	277,400	4.66
Not specified	284,184	4.78
Total employed population	5,951,466	100.00

Source: INEGI (1995).
a. Defined in minimum wages (m.w.).

migrants who have recently been incorporated into the urban economy; and, third, poor émigrés are abandoning the central areas of Mexico City in search of cheaper land or dwellings in the periphery (Aguilar and Godínez 1989).

In the 1970–1990 period, the highly qualified labour force, formed by professional and technical workers and executive personnel (managers and top-level administrators), recorded a yearly growth rate of around 4–5 per cent. This was among the highest growth rates in labour demand for the period and gave these two high-level categories the greatest relative participation in the occupational structure (table 5.7). They experienced a total gain of some 600,000 jobs in the period, mainly in the manufacturing and service sectors. A high growth rate was also observed in the category of commerce personnel, which showed a net increment of 456,000 jobs and an annual growth rate of almost 5 per cent. Service workers and drivers, with some 350,000 new jobs, had a slower growth rate (2.4 per cent), while the ranks of blue-collar workers increased at a rate of 2.1 per cent, to 454,000 employees. As a result of the speedy urbanization process, the number of agricultural workers decreased rapidly by 3.6 per cent. In short, at the same time that unemployment and poverty seem to be increasing in Mexico City, a high proportion of the demand for jobs is occurring in the highly skilled technical occupations. Thus, it is possible to argue that the 1980s and 1990s witnessed a trend towards social polarization in the urban labour market of Mexico City.

Table 5.7 **Change in the occupational structure in Mexico City, 1970–1990**

Occupational structure	1970	1990	Increase	% growth rate
Metropolitan Area of Mexico City	2,756,696	4,901,361	2,144,665	2.88
Professionals and technicians	273,846	701,007	427,161	4.70
Executive personnel	138,115	307,583	169,468	4.00
Administrative personnel	426,624	781,734	355,110	3.03
Commercial workers	299,815	756,523	456,708	4.63
Service workers	573,599	920,446	346,847	2.36
Agricultural workers	90,790	43,879	−46,911	−3.64
Blue-collar workers	861,720	1,315,931	454,211	2.12
Not specified	92,187	74,258	−17,929	−1.08

Source: DGE (1990).

In support of this hypothesis, it is worth emphasizing that the downward trend in demand for medium-skilled labour is forcing its historical middle-class clients either to climb into technical, highly skilled occupations or to settle for employment in less skilled occupations. This intermediate group, represented by administrative personnel and skilled manual workers, once accounted for the highest proportion in the occupational structure, but present trends reveal a loss of its former relative importance. Although these categories registered a net gain in jobs in the 1970–1990 period, their relative participation in the labour market either remained stable or declined. These changes are associated with the loss of dynamism of the manufacturing sector and the shrinking of the public sector – a major employer of administrative personnel – owing to privatization processes in the state-owned industries.

Furthermore, urban poverty in the basin is accentuated by high levels of underemployment and unemployment. In 1974 it was estimated that 5.7 per cent of the economically active population were unemployed while 35.3 per cent were classified as underemployed. Thus, a total of 41 per cent of the city's population lacked a secure income (Cornelius 1975; Ward 1981). According to more recent data, the percentage of unemployed increased to 7 per cent in 1995, mostly as a result of the economic crisis of 1994. This event has also maintained underemployment at very high levels and has pushed some 25 per cent of the economically active population into the informal economy or into marginal occupations (Banco Nacional de México 1996).

127

As a result of the dynamics of changing employment demand, the urban economy has experienced a rapid increase in informal economic activities. In 1989, the National Chamber of Commerce (Cámara Nacional de Comercio, or CANACO) estimated that more than 112,000 informal businesses existed on the streets of Mexico City. Most of these were selling products or services on the city's sidewalks (Bustamante 1993).

One unionized group of these informal traders has established mobile stalls in areas where there are high concentrations of consumers, such as the historical centre of Mexico City. Most of their merchandise has entered the country illegally and thus evades fiscal control. These activities, which have resulted from the recent changes in the labour market and the contraction in demand for intermediate-skilled jobs, have proliferated throughout the metropolitan area but are especially concentrated in the central part of Mexico City, such as the *delegaciones* Cuauhtemoc, Venustiano Carranza, and Miguel Hidalgo.

Another group of informal businesses is represented by the legal and officially recognized mobile markets (*mercados sobre ruedas*) that move location within the urban area every day. They offer not only basic goods such as food and clothing (their traditional supply) but also electronic equipment and other (often illegally) imported goods in growing quantities. In 1991, there were some 70 registered locations for these markets in the metropolitan area, accounting for about 1,734 stalls and 4,335 workers.

A third group of informal merchants is represented by food-stands selling *tacos* and traditional foods. They have proliferated mainly around the subway stations, operating under unsanitary conditions and posing an additional public risk because of their use of gas bottles for cooking. In 1990, there were an estimated 19,000 stalls in the Federal District alone (Bustamante 1993). In general, the state authorities have had to tolerate the proliferation of informal traders and the increase in marginal commercial activities owing to the recurrent economic crises that the country has experienced since the early 1980s, the lack of job opportunities, and the low purchasing power of the majority of the population.

The dearth of economic opportunities shows up in other socio-economic aspects, such as housing conditions. Although demographic growth has declined in the basin, census data report a large expansion in popular self-constructed housing units in the 1980–1990 period. This process took place chiefly in the peripheral areas of the east and south-east of the basin, in the municipalities of Iztapalapa (70,000 additional dwellings), Chalco (41,000), Chimalhuacán (33,000), Nezahualcóyotl (24,000), and La Paz (8,000). The increase in low-income settlements is attributable to the illegal occupation of land by poorer groups. This land lacked public infrastructure. The rapid growth of these marginal settlements and the eventual political need to supply them with public services caused a worsening in the overall supply of public services for the rest of Mexico City during the 1980s. For example, between 1980 and 1990, the provision of drinking water within dwellings diminished for the entire metropolitan area, from 67.2 to 64.3 per cent of actual demand (Coulomb 1992). This decrease was even more dramatic in the metropolitan municipalities of the State of Mexico, which showed a drop from 62 to 54 per cent.

It is predictable that, in spite of falling growth rates in the Basin of Mexico, the short-term pressures to occupy peripheral land without services will be maintained and will act as a major driving force of urban expansion and conurbationization. The growing polarization of incomes makes these marginal lands likely alternatives for the poorest of the poor, even though the periphery is increasingly further away from prospective work places and promises inadequate social services, poor environmental quality, and high transport costs.

Technological capacity

Because the basin concentrates the largest part of the nation's industry and hence the largest amount of technological know-how, it has been relatively easy to take a complacent view regarding environmental deterioration and to rely on technological means to restore damaged environments. Environmental problems have not been regarded as such, in part because of this "technological-fix" mentality that seeks solutions through technological change, largely on the supply side. After all, did not economic and technological growth between 1950 and 1980, on average, lead to increases in the material standard of living for the people of the Basin of Mexico during a time of major environment change?

In the case of water use, for example, the relentless depletion of the basin's aquifer was not judged a serious problem because it was thought that water could be brought from other basins with the proper technology. This line of reasoning prompted the development in the early 1970s of a plan to pump water from a series of neighbouring watersheds in the states of Morelos, Tlaxcala, and Puebla

(Guerrero, Moreno, and Garduño 1982). This extreme faith in the greater technological capacity of the Basin of Mexico compared with the rest of the nation has postponed the solution of environmental degradation, on the presumptuous view that economic development takes priority and that, when the time comes to solve environmental problems, the technological tools will be readily at hand.

Some statistical data indicate the concentration of technological capacity in the basin. Looking at the 500 largest enterprises in the country according to their total sales, in 1993 Mexico City accounted for 56 per cent (280 firms) of the total; of these, 70 per cent were in the manufacturing sector, 16 per cent in the commercial sector, and 13 per cent in the service sector. In the group of the 20 largest enterprises in the country (table 5.8), 15 are located in Mexico City itself. These firms are linked either to industrial or to service activities. Most importantly, some of these economic groups represent, or have been until recently, a real economic monopoly in their own spheres, for example PEMEX (Petróleos Mexicanos, the state-owned oil company), Teléfonos de México (telephone and communications), or Televisa (television and communications). Most of these firms represent powerful interests linked to a complex network of economic relations and a highly developed technological capacity.

Although the past decade has seen a strong deconcentration of manufacturing activities away from the Basin of Mexico, the services sector has continued to grow at a rapid rate in Mexico City (table 5.9). During the 1980s, a loss of dynamism in manufacturing figured in a loss of about 94,000 jobs and 4,430 establishments, which led to negative growth in this sector. During the first half of the 1990s, however, industrial activities showed signs of recovery, with 12,000 new jobs and 13,000 new establishments.

The crucial point of this industrial concentration is that it is the industrial subsectors with more advanced technology and a higher capacity for innovation that have the highest representation in the basin. Analysing the share of all industrial subsectors in the basin in relation to the country as a whole (table 5.10), it is evident that particular subsectors – printing and publishing; chemical substances and oil products (including petrochemical processes and the manufacturing of plastic products); basic metallic industries; and metallic products (including the automobile industry) – are strongly concentrated in the basin. Although the relative concentrations of these industrial subsectors declined between 1980 and 1994 owing to the deconcen-

Table 5.8 **Geographical distribution of the 20 largest enterprises in Mexico, 1994**

Rank	Company	Location	Sector	Sales (US$m.)	No. of workers
1	Petróleos Mexicanos	México, D.F.	Oil and gas	95,159,781	n.a.
2	Teléfonos de México	México, D.F.	Communications	29,213,112	63,254
3	CIFRA	México, D.F.	Supermarkets	15,637,293	46,898
4	VITRO	Garza García. N.L.	Glass and other products	14,190,324	36,694
5	Chrysler de México	México, D.F.	Automobile	13,525,647	10,445
6	General Motors de Mexico	México, D.F.	Automobile	12,750,629	76,426
7	Grupo CARSO	México, D.F.	Various[a]	11,353,396	41,525
8	CEMEX	Monterrey, N.L.	Cement	10,644,632	20,997
9	Valores Industriales	Monterrey, N.L.	Beverages	9,392,695	35,097
10	ALFA	Garza García. N.L.	Various[b]	9,352,822	23,412
11	Fomento Económico Mexicano	Monterrey, N.L.	Beverages	9,256,493	34,551
12	Controladora Comercial Mexicana	México, D.F.	Supermarkets	9,060,252	28,431
13	Gigante	México, D.F.	Supermarkets	9,046,276	32,515
14	Empresas ICA Soc Controladora	México, D.F.	Construction	7,937,639	25,267
15	Grupo Televisa	México, D.F.	Communications	6,441,994	20,965
16	Grupo Modelo	México, D.F.	Beverages	6,353,843	37,559
17	Grupo Industrial BIMBO	México, D.F.	Food	6,073,810	39,425
18	DESC	México, D.F.	Various[c]	5,535,695	19,288
19	Cía. Nestlé	México, D.F.	Food	4,813,000	5,801
20	IBM de México	México, D.F.	Computing	4,768,310	1,674

Sources: Anon. (1995a, 1995b).

a. Secondary and tertiary sectors, e.g. tobacco and financial services.

b. The production of steel and activity in the petrochemical and food industries.

c. Secondary and tertiary sectors, e.g. the chemical industry and administrative services.

n.a. = not available.

131

Table 5.9 **The number of establishments and jobs in Mexico City's Metropolitan Area, by sector, 1980–1994**

	Establishments				Employed workers				Growth rates, 1980–94 (%/yr)	
	1980	1986	1989	1994	1980	1986	1989	1994	Establishments	Workers
Total	274,522	290,661	320,766	470,328	1,739,066	1,820,033	1,902,787	2,417,283	3.85	2.35
Manufacturing	35,676	33,352	31,246	44,252	893,369	844,983	799,427	812,033	1.54	−0.68
Commerce	159,759	166,943	187,849	267,023	444,517	514,744	578,392	754,181	3.67	3.78
Services	79,087	90,366	101,671	159,053	401,180	460,306	524,968	851,069	4.99	5.37

Source: Calculated from INEGI (1994b).

Table 5.10 **Industrial establishments and employed workers in Mexico City's Metropolitan Area, by subsector, 1980–1994**

Industrial subsector	Establishments				Workers			
	1980		1994		1980		1994	
	No.	As % of national total	No.	As % of national total	No.	As % of national total	No.	As % of national total
Total	35,367	28.0	44,031	16.6	875,641	41.0	832,117	25.6
Food products, beverages, and tobacco	10,392	20.8	14,351	15.7	114,259	26.2	135,500	19.4
Textiles, garments, and leather	5,745	31.8	5,868	13.3	142,707	40.2	131,957	24.1
Wood industry	3,709	27.0	3,482	11.0	37,021	41.1	30,386	18.1
Paper, printing, and publishing	3,350	51.2	5,499	36.5	70,751	60.2	91,135	46.2
Chemical substances, oil and coal products	2,124	51.0	2,698	38.0	136,356	52.8	160,443	42.2
Non-metallic products	1,051	12.6	1,478	6.1	26,126	22.6	30,875	16.8
Basic metallic industries	198	50.1	84	26.2	25,877	26.6	12,706	21.5
Metallic products, machinery and equipment, and precision instruments	7,912	34.4	9,674	20.9	298,872	47.5	222,510	23.1
Other manufacturing industries	886	46.9	698	14.9	23,672	27.6	16,605	37.8

Sources: 1980 data – Garza and Rivera (1994: 14); 1994 data – INEGI (1994b).

tration of industrial activities, the total number of establishments in the Basin of Mexico increased for most of these subsectors.

One associated feature of economic restructuring in Mexico City is the growth of advanced services that support the so-called producer services: financing, real estate, professional services, insurance, marketing, publicity, design, and research. These productive activities take advantage of new developments in telecommunications and air transportation and enlist technology transfer to support the industrial process and to make the capital city more competitive in terms of technological capacity. These types of services grew by 52 per cent in the 1980–1989 period, with an annual growth rate of 5 per cent, which was the highest increase for all types of services in the same period. Moreover, this group of producer support services shows productivity levels above the national averages (Aguilar 1993; Garza and Rivera 1994).

In another vein, technological capacity has acted as a direct agent of environmental change by enhancing people's access to and use of the natural resources of the basin. More and more people are acquiring an increasing ability to consume resources, be it through the use of electrical and water systems, or through the use of personal automobiles. Simply stated, the concentration of technology in the basin increases resource use and environmental damage, especially compared with the country as a whole. It is important to note that technological capacity also implies technological innovation, specialization, and diversification of economic activity, which all enhance the overall level of technology available to users.

Economic development and environmental degradation

For nearly 2,000 years the Basin of Mexico has been one of the most densely populated areas of the world. Since those ancient times, the inhabitants of the basin have used their political power to obtain advantages over other areas of the nation. The economic development of Mexico City after the Mexican Revolution (i.e. since 1930) has been promoted by governmental policies, local private enterprises, and foreign capital. The main objective has been massive industrial development, frequently at the expense of social equality. The direct driving force of urban growth has been the use of public resources allocated to the industrial and financial sectors. As a result of the rapid but highly unbalanced growth, the basin now confronts an unsustainable pattern of urbanization and land use, as well as an uneven and socially conflictual distribution of population and wealth.

Despite the existence of a wealthy social sector that includes government officers, private executives, public bureaucracy, and a large middle class with a high capacity to consume, most of the city consists of poor districts inhabited by workers and underemployed people. These social groups are formed mostly by recent immigrants into the basin, who left rural Mexico in search of some of the services and goods that the basin seems to promise.

The concentration of wealth and the rapid development of the basin have had no impact on environmental protection. Decision makers have prioritized economic growth at all costs, in general taking a complacent view with regard to environmental deterioration. The assumption is that the technological development associated with rapid economic growth will eventually be able to restore degraded ecosystems and repair environmental damage.

6

The vulnerability of the basin

One cannot be optimistic about Mexico City's future prospects. It would appear by any interpretation that Mexico City is rapidly reaching its ecological limits, given its technology. The greatest challenge at present is to promote action before matters get out of control. In this chapter we will analyse these issues in detail.

Vegetation and open space

The projection of present trends shows that, after the year 2000, Mexico City will have changed from the patchy mixture of urban and rural environments that was typical of the first half of the twentieth century to an overcrowded urban environment with little vegetation and open space for its inhabitants (table 6.1). The city will spread over 1,400 km^2 with a population of around 20 million, spilling in parts over the boundaries of the basin into the adjacent cities of Toluca, Querétaro, Cuernavaca, or Puebla to form an immense conurbation. Most (92 per cent) of the megalopolis will be houses and roads, whereas only 6 per cent of it will be occupied by parks, private gardens, and public spaces. Taking into account the whole conurbation that forms the megacity, some 25 million people will live in the basin, enjoying only 5 m^2 of green area per person. In some parts of

Table 6.1 **Green areas per person in the Metropolitan Area of Mexico City, 1950, 1980, and 1990, and projected values for the year 2000**

	1950	1980	1990	2000
Population (million)	3.0	13.8	16.6	20.0
Total urban area (km^2)	215	980	1,161	1,400
Total urban green areas (m^2/person)	29.0	9.9	7.6	5.6
Parks, gardens, and other recreational areas (m^2/person)	9.0	5.9	5.6	5.0

Mexico City the situation will be substantially worse; many inhabitants of the future city will have less than 1 m^2 of open public spaces for recreational use, as is already the case in Azcapotzalco.

It is interesting to note, for comparison purposes, that different international standards define some 9 m^2 per person as the minimum amount of open space (in the form of public parks and recreational areas) necessary to maintain an adequate quality of life in urban areas (see Guevara and Moreno 1987; Halffter and Ezcurra 1983).

Green areas in the basin include different types of zones. Guevara and Moreno (1987) recognized five categories: (a) nature reserves and protected natural areas, (b) agro-pastoral fields, (c) urban parks and gardens, (d) highway, sidewalk, and boulevard garden-beds, and (e) open plots. Each of these categories has its own problems of management and vulnerability.

Nature reserves and protected natural areas

Most of the basin's 20 national parks and protected areas were established between 1936 and 1939 during the Presidency of Lázaro Cárdenas. Only one national park, Desierto de los Leones, had been established before this period (1917). Additionally, in 1983 a protected area was created in a small part of El Pedregal de San Angel, to protect the remnants of the vegetation and fauna that are endemic to the *pedregales* (lava flows) of the southern part of the basin. Other recently protected zones include part of the central region of the El Ajusco range, in Lomas del Seminario, where both irregular settlements and an upper-class settlement had started to develop illegally. It is in these humid southern ranges that most of the water recharge into the basin's aquifers occurs, largely regulated by the existing remnants of the original vegetation. People were transferred from this zone, now decreed as a reserve (Parque Ecológico de la Ciudad

137

de México) with a centre for research and educational activities. Other zones, such as El Cerro de Guadalupe, had also been colonized by squatters and are now being re-established as protected zones. The future of these reserves is not assured, for population pressure on these areas is strong, and both economic and political interests could at some point acquiesce to their occupation by squatters. In the design of programmes intended to rescue reserves invaded by urban settlements, the social factor merits consideration. People who are forced to leave these zones need an alternative place to settle, without reproducing the damaging patterns, and to increase their quality of life.

Most of the reserves in the basin no longer represent natural or protected areas. In fact, most of the *c.*80,500 formally protected hectares are so deteriorated they can hardly be considered green areas any more. Some of them have lost all their vegetation and have been incorporated into the urbanized area.

The deterioration of the national parks of the Basin of Mexico started almost immediately after their creation. For example, during 1946–1952, one of Mexico's largest paper factories was officially allowed to log the forests in the protected parts of El Ajusco. Desierto de los Leones, Cumbres del Ajusco, Dinamos de Contreras, and Miguel Hidalgo are among the few zones that can still be considered as effective protected zones, although they face the problem of increasing human use for recreation, with growing erosion on their trail-paths, and the additional problem of tree dieback owing to high levels of atmospheric pollution. The new reserves of El Pedregal and Lomas del Seminario have also managed to avoid being invaded or overly degraded by human use, although from a conservationist point of view their size is smaller than it should be for a protected zone.

Agro-pastoral zones

As a result of the growing occupation of agricultural land by urban expansion, the proportion of the basin's area used for agriculture and for raising cattle is constantly decreasing. Though these land uses are rapidly disappearing, some zones in the basin can still qualify as agricultural areas. Such is the case of the relatively small towns near Popocatépetl and Iztacchíhuatl, which still produce corn on a relatively large scale. Many of the inhabitants of these towns do not work in agriculture, however, but travel into the city to work. Despite the selling of most *haciendas* for urban development during the first decades of the twentieth century, traditional agriculture still occurs in some areas of the Basin of Mexico, especially in the south-east and the north. In a few places, small crops are raised in *solares*, the orchards or small plots that surround the houses.

The most common and important species is corn, the staple cereal of Mexico, of which different traditional varieties are still harvested in the basin. Other crops harvested around Mexico City include beans, different types of chilli, and squash. Oats, tomatoes, beans, potatoes, agaves, and nopales (*Opuntia* cacti) are still harvested in the agricultural plots of the satellite towns of Mexico City, such as Milpa Alta, which have not yet been engulfed by the rapid urban growth. In some of these places it is still possible to see the traditional use and harvest of native semi-domesticated fruit trees such as *Crataegus mexicana* (*tejocote*), *Prunus capulli* (*capulín*), and nut trees (*Juglans* sp.; see García-Mora 1978, 1979; and Pisanty 1979). In many cases, individual trees of these species are all that is left from former forests. Some towns in the southern and south-eastern parts of the basin, such as Tepetlixpa, Atlautla, Nepantla, and Ecatzingo, are important fruit producers, taking advantage of the conditions that prevail in this part of the basin where temperate and subtropical climates meet. Apricots, pears, apples, peaches, plums, avocados, *guanabanas*, and *chirimoyas* (*Annona* spp.) are common products of this agricultural region.

Some agricultural weeds, known locally as *quelites*, are still consumed as greens, following the traditional usage of Aztec agriculture (see also chap. 2 for a description of the historical uses of agricultural weeds as food supplements). *Gaura coccinea, Reseda luteola, Argemona ochreoleuca, Lopezia racemosa, Bidens pilosa, Galinzoga parviflora, Amaranthus hibridus, Chenopodium album, Portulaca oleraceae*, and *Marrubium vulgare* are among the most common ruderals of corn fields (Rzedowski 1975; Villegas 1976). Many of these species are edible, and others are used in traditional medicine. Most of them are used as fodder for domestic animals.

However, the agricultural or semi-agricultural use of land is restricted to regions outside the urban area. As the result of an average annual decrease of 7.4 per cent in their extent (Ezcurra and Mazari-Hiriart 1996), agro-pastoral fields have almost completely disappeared from the urban area. The contrast between the massive urban development and the small towns that still prevail in the basin is surprising, as is the quick incorporation of the latter. One of the main casualties of this rapid change is the knowledge of traditional

Mexican agriculture, which is disappearing as fast as the agricultural fields.

Urban parks and gardens

Recreational areas of different sizes, shapes, and characteristics make up this category of green areas. Parks once abounded in all districts of Mexico City, but growing automobile use has centred the attention of urban projects on the creation of wider streets, parking lots, malls, and large buildings, leaving little vegetated land for essential but less profitable uses. Mexico City exhibits an irregular distribution of green areas, and some districts, such as industrial ones, lack any open space. At present, the city provides around 5 m^2 of green recreational areas per inhabitant (including both public parks and private gardens; see table 6.1). However, if private gardens are removed from the calculations, Mexico City offers on average less than 3 m^2 of public green areas per inhabitant, and as little as 0.4 m^2 in many areas.

Some protected areas serve as recreational zones. Unfortunately, the immense number of park visitors that Mexico City can generate makes the management of these zones particularly difficult. Probably the most illustrative place in this sense is Chapultepec, whose vegetation we described in chapter 4. The Chapultepec park, one of the most popular places for walks since pre-Hispanic times, now includes three sections. The first corresponds to what is left of the original forest. Many of the native *ahuehuetes* (swamp cypresses) are ailing and diseased, mostly as a result of the drying-up of the water table, but also as a result of atmospheric pollution and of insect pests that attack the debilitated plants. The tramping of the millions of people who annually visit the park has compacted the soil of the forest. The water springs that once existed on the lower parts of the slopes have decreased, and the water table has dropped, severely affecting the forest. The introduction of many alien tree species, especially *Eucalyptus*, which has proved to be a highly competitive weed, displaced some of the native plants in the Chapultepec forests. By 1980 the forest contained approximately 80,000 trees, a substantial portion of which were exotic species: 50,000 of the introduced alien *Ligustrum lucidum* (*trueno*), nearly 2,000 of *Taxodium mucronatum* (the native *ahuehuetes*), and 28,000 of various species, including exotics such as *Eucalyptus* spp., *Gingko biloba*, *Sequoia sempervirens*, and *Araucaria* spp. The tree population is no longer dominated by tall trees such as the *ahuehuetes*; instead, nearly half of the forest is composed of low trees such as *Ligustrum lucidum* (S. Castillo, personal communication). The second section of Chapultepec park is a recreation and educational zone, which includes Mexico City's zoo, an amusement park, and several museums, alternating with patches of trees dominated by *Eucalyptus*. The third section occupies the upper slopes and piedmonts of the Sierra de Las Cruces, and some of the original fir forests (*Abies religiosa*) are still to be found in its ravines. The rest of this section has been almost completely invaded by planted eucalyptus forests.

Parks harbour different species of trees, but less and less care has gone into using parks as places to preserve the original and extremely valuable biological diversity of the basin. Old, traditional parks, such as La Alameda, Parque México, Parque España, and Parque de los Venados, are more diverse in their plant species composition than the more recent ones, which contain mainly *Eucalyptus*. Recent research (S. Castillo, personal communication) found 42 tree species in Parque México, 35 in Parque Ignacio Chávez, and 34 in Parque España. All three parks had existed for more than 50 years and belonged to a traditional district of the old city in the *delegación* Cuauhtémoc. In contrast, the newer parks are extremely species poor; for example, Jardín los Angeles, a park of recent creation, contained only five tree species. *Ligustrum lucidum*, *Fraxinus uhdei*, and *Eucalyptus* spp. were the most common species in a sample of 20 new parks. Among the larger and traditional urban parks, the most important (because of their size and their tree diversity) are Chapultepec and Bosques de Aragón, parts of which are still covered with the original native vegetation. Notably, the latter has an area covered by a native oak forest, which makes it particularly important in terms of the preservation of biological richness, while the former has part of the swamp cypress forest that once covered it (Guevara and Moreno 1987).

Highway, sidewalk, and boulevard garden-beds

Although small and inaccessible for human recreation, the vegetated areas in the centre of large avenues and boulevards, together with the lawns at the sides of the large highways that traverse Mexico City, may represent an important proportion of the city's green areas, especially in the central, north-central, and eastern sections of the city. Many of the central courses (*camellones*) of the old boulevards, which ornamented the urban landscape with flowers and foliage, were eliminated in the late 1960s when streets were widened to speed

141

up the urban traffic. The *camellones* that survived the widening of the streets often have large old ash trees (*Fraxinus uhdei*) and various palm species, especially *Phoenix canariensis* and *Washingtonia robusta*. These individuals have been slowly disappearing, victims of air pollution and pests. Because of the growing scarcity of open and vegetated areas in Mexico City, some of the roadside lawns and *camellones* are used as playgrounds, although in most cases they are in the middle of broad avenues with heavy traffic.

Open areas

This last category is represented by a heterogeneous mixture of empty plots, graveyards, and abandoned fields. The fate of most of these is invasion by the African grass *Pennisetum clandestinum*, which tends to cover the ground almost completely, preventing the recovery of the original vegetation. Open areas do not contribute significantly to the "greening" of the environment in Mexico City. They do not represent an efficient alternative for the protection of plant species, nor are they a source of the environmental benefits that forests and parks usually provide, but they can play an important role in the recreational activities of the population.

Even where the natural vegetation is at least partially represented, most of the green areas in the Basin of Mexico are treated as recreational zones, with no ecological or conservationist purpose. Their management, design, and spatial distribution have been strongly dependent on recreational considerations. Green areas contain many non-indigenous species. This is the case with many of the most common tree species such as *Eucalyptus* sp., an Australian genus, *Schinus molle*, a South American tree, *Jacaranda mimosaefolia*, from Brazil, or *Ligustrum lucidum*, from Asia. The original species of the basin are only rarely used for planting, because the alien species frequently have higher growth rates, fewer predators, or both. These are important considerations, but this practice is accelerating the depletion of the original richness of environments and species in the basin and the progressive loss of animal species of the region because herbivores can no longer find the native plants on which they feed.

It is evident that the protection of the few remaining natural areas and the restoration of as much as possible of those that have been affected by urban development should be a priority in any programme aimed at rescuing the Basin of Mexico from the ecological crisis it faces. Vegetated areas are important not only to the quality of life of the city dwellers but also to the hydrological cycle of the basin.

Water quantity and quality

During the twentieth century, the Basin of Mexico has evolved from a high level of self-sufficiency in water resources to dependence on imports from other regions (fig. 6.1). Although Mexico City derives more than 70 per cent of its water supply from the aquifer system that underlies the metropolitan area, recent pressures on the aquifer account for a mean draw-down of 1 metre/year in specific areas (the south and north-west of Mexico City and north of Zumpango) and a degradation of water quality. The continued overexploitation of this system is inevitable at present, even though serious problems related to subsidence and to water quality have been noted for decades and seem to be increasing (see chap. 4).

The first important problem associated with water is the availability and re-use of the resource. Assuming a daily quota of 300 litres per person, a recharge rate of around 27 m^3/s can supply water for 7–8 million people. In theory, this is a reasonable carrying capacity for the population of the basin. It is estimated that, by the year 2000, some 75 m^3/s of water will be needed to supply the needs of the more than 20 million inhabitants of Mexico City. In the short term, this will demand either a higher rate of pumping from the basin's aquifer, further increasing the problem of subsidence, or that some 40 m^3/s of water be pumped from outside the basin, at a prohibitive economic and social cost. In the longer term, it will necessarily mean obtaining extra water (with the attendant implications for storage and distribution) from the catchment of rainwater during the wet season and the efficient treatment and re-use of waste water.

The extension of the city to its future area of 1,400 km^2 will also mean the deforestation of a significant part of the surrounding areas which now act as hydrological regulators for the already severely disrupted water cycle of the basin. In this way, the growth of the city will negatively affect its capacity to capture water, contributing even further to the shortage of water.

Subsidence of the central metropolitan area continues and there is some evidence that it is increasing again, as a result of heavy pumping in the eastern Texcoco area. Subsidence velocities on the outskirts (Chalco–Xochimilco) are similar to or worse than those observed in the central part of the city several decades ago (Marsal and Mazari

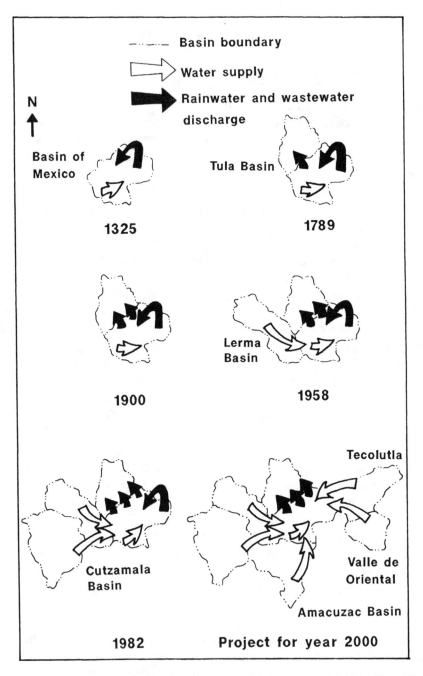

Fig. 6.1 **Evolution of the hydraulic system supplying water to Mexico City, 1325–1982, and projected developments for the year 2000 (Source: Guerrero, Moreno, and Garduño 1982)**

144

1990). Comparative data have been presented by Mazari and Alberro (1990) for several specific sites in the metropolitan area. Among other problems, the subsidence of the ground surface at the bottom of the Basin of Mexico has changed the topographical gradient on which the flow of the surface drainage depends (fig. 6.2). Thus, the basin depends increasingly on pumping waste water out of the basin through the deep drainage system, with concomitant costs in energy.

Several potential outside sources to supply water to Mexico City have been identified. These include increasing the amount of water extracted from the Cutzamala system from 13.5 to 17 m^3/s (CEAS 1993). The National Water Commission has also been considering the Temascaltepec, Amacuzac, Tecolutla, Tula, Oriental, and Libres rivers (fig. 6.1). Exportable flow estimates from these systems are 5, 11, 15, 2.5, and 7 m^3/s, respectively (CEAS 1993), giving a total of increment of 40.5 m^3/s. According to estimates of water demand, all of this would be needed to meet Mexico City's projected demand for the year 2000. However, because of the immense costs involved in the construction and operation of pumping systems, this project has not been realized.

These plans imply an enormous environmental impact on the basins from where the water is to be pumped. The projects would entail the modification and limitation of activities for the inhabitants of neighbouring basins and involve a very high social cost, because they would reduce the amount of water available for electricity generation and for irrigation.

Pumping from external sources into the Basin of Mexico, which is at a mean altitude of 2,240 m, is inefficient and very expensive in terms of energy costs. Although there are no official figures on this matter, an estimation can be easily calculated based on the fact that elevating 1 m^3 of water an altitude of 10 metres demands a fixed energy input of 98 kilojoules, plus the additional energy demanded by the mechanical inefficiency of the system. The pumping system from the Cutzamala basin, for example, has to elevate the water flow some 1,100 m, which requires a constant energy input of 190 MW (SARH 1985b; see also table 6.2). Thus, it can be calculated that, in order to move the 43.5 m^3/s that are obtained from within the basin, and the 19.5 m^3/s that come from external watersheds, plus the waste water in the deep drainage system, an average energy consumption is needed of around 370 MW (i.e. the system uses 3–4 million MW hours per year; Castillo 1991). For comparison, this energy input is 53 per cent of the energy produced at peak operation (750 MW) by the thermo-

145

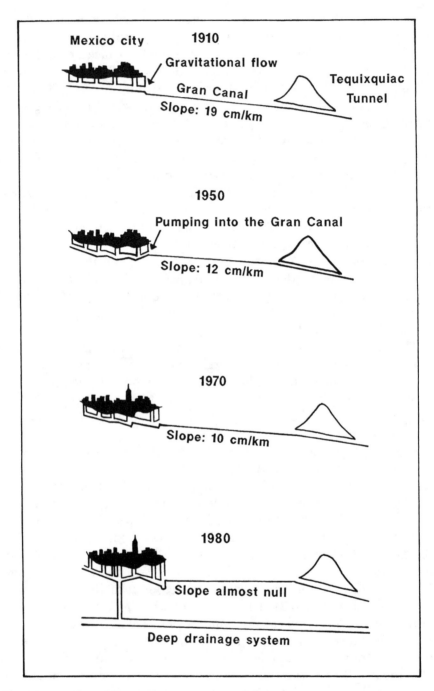

Fig. 6.2 **The effect of subsidence of the ground surface on the drainage system of the Basin of Mexico, 1910–1980 (Source: Guerrero, Moreno, and Garduño 1982)**

Table 6.2 **Estimated energy cost of moving water into and out of the Basin of Mexico**

Type of pumping	Required power (MW)
Pumping from the Cutzamala and Lerma basins (18 m^3/s; 1,000 m elevation)	250
Pumping from the wells of the Basin of Mexico (depth 40–100 m; 50 m^3/s)	65
Deep drainage system (100 m^3/s)	25
Moving water in the network	30
Total energy cost	370
Economic cost of energy expenditure per day	US$890,000
Economic cost per m^3	US$0.20

electric generating plant of the Valley of Mexico, which supplies energy to the city, 33 per cent of the energy produced at peak operation by Chicoasén, one of the largest (1,200 MW) hydroelectric reservoirs in Mexico, and approximately 31 per cent of the energy that the two nuclear generators at Laguna Verde are producing (1,280 MW).

The energy costs involved in pumping water into, within, and out of the Basin of Mexico, which amount to almost US$900,000 per day, appear at present to be one of the most important factors limiting the growth of Mexico City. It has been proposed that urban-industrial corridors should be developed in places with water availability, easy drainage, communication, and transportation services. Some of the proposed corridors are: Amozoc–Tehuacán in the State of Puebla, Cuautla–Tequesquitengo in Morelos, San Juan–Acaponeta in Nayarit, and lower Papaloapan in Oaxaca and Veracruz (Ramírez 1990b). Apart from the economic costs of developing such areas, there is a lack of political will to decentralize the capital city in this way.

The quality of the water supply is also endangered. The main water-quality problems detected in Mexico City are (a) bacterial contamination (including potentially pathogenic micro-organisms such as bacteria and parasites), (b) chemical pollution (including toxic salts, heavy metals, and organic compounds), and (c) contamination of vegetable crops through irrigation with waste water. No comprehensive analysis exists of the potential routes through which contaminants may invade groundwater resources. However, the growing number of reports of groundwater contamination, and the fact that the ground water that is used by the population of the basin is separated by a subsiding clay aquitard from the highly con-

147

taminated surface waters, suggest that the water supply of Mexico City could be one of the most vulnerable of its environmental aspects. It is likely that, in coming decades, groundwater contamination will become a growing problem in Mexico City.

Mazari-Hiriart and Mackay (1993) have described the potential for groundwater contamination in the Mexico City area. They observe that the most important route for contaminants to reach the aquifers may be through sedimentary material in the transition zone. Other areas of potential vulnerability, such as fractured zones of lacustrine clay, have shown higher permeabilities than generally assumed. The authors highlight the vulnerability of the aquifer system by identifying potential contaminant sources in the metropolitan area, such as petroleum refining, transport and storage, gasoline stations, commercial and industrial sources, and the wastewater disposal system.

Studies are under way to determine if there is any significant migration of contaminants from some of the wastewater canals into the lacustrine zone, but few efforts have addressed the transition zone, where most of the recharge to the aquifers occurs. This activity would appear to be of relatively high priority considering the proximity of supply wells in that area, as well as the increase in extraction. The potential for subsurface contamination from unlined sewage canals also exists in the lacustrine area, which has significant downward hydraulic gradients that are likely to increase with time (Pitre 1994). In fact, relatively recent research appears to confirm the infiltration of contaminated water at the confluence of the Gran Canal and the Río de los Remedios (Mazari-Hiriart 1992; Mazari-Hiriart et al. 1996; Pitre 1994). Organic contaminants (halogenated solvents and surfactants) have been detected at low concentrations at depths consistent with migration dominated by fracture flow; indeed fractures have been observed in cores at this site down to 15 m deep (Pitre 1994).

Regarding the drainage system, little information on the extent of leakage is available. Sewer pipes are unlikely to be in good condition, owing to improper installation or more likely to deterioration or disruption by building activities, subsidence, and earthquakes. As the city grows without control into the transition and mountainous areas, leakage from some of the newer portions of the system could be significant, given essentially unimpeded access to the aquifer.

Noticeable degradation in water quality shows up in several specific areas in the south and east of the lacustrine zone. In the south, the *chinampa* agriculture that still exists is fast disappearing owing to the falling water table and the recharge of the canals of Xochimilco

148

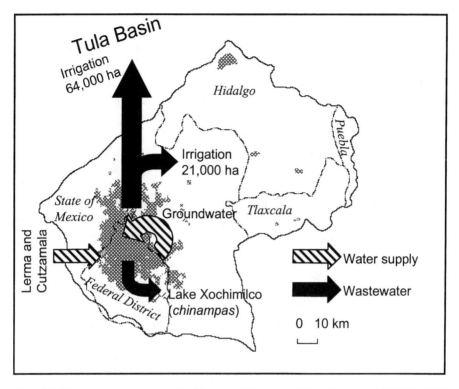

Fig. 6.3 **Wastewater flows in the Basin of Mexico, 1982 (Source: SAHOP 1977; Guerrero, Moreno, and Garduño 1982)**

with partially treated waste water (fig. 6.3). Although sewage receives secondary treatment in the Cerro de la Estrella plant, the nutrients in the waste water have eutrophied and polluted the canals.

Waste

The management of solid and liquid waste presents a serious and unsolved environmental problem for the whole of Mexico, despite governmental efforts to improve transport, processing, and final disposal. According to official statistics (see chap. 4 of this book), some 65 per cent (7,500 tons/day) of the municipal waste of the Federal District is disposed off adequately, but the final destination of the remaining 35 per cent is unaccounted for and hence unclear. The situation is worse in the State of Mexico, where no official landfills exist, and clandestine dump sites have proliferated. Most experts believe that solid waste disposal will remain a problem until a better disposal

149

service is implemented, until stricter regulations are applied (Aguilar Sahagún 1984), and, above all, until waste-processing plants are built to cope with the large output of garbage produced by the city (Monroy Hermosillo 1987; Trejo Vázquez 1987).

The problem regarding waste disposal gets more complicated when considering existing facilities for the adequate disposal of industrial hazardous waste. There are seven hazardous waste landfills for the whole country, four of which are private sites; only three are public sites, and they are all located far from Mexico City in Nuevo León, San Luis Potosí and Sonora (Ponciano et al. 1996). Considering that Mexico City has the highest industrial concentration of the nation (about 48 per cent of all industries) and accordingly produces a high volume of hazardous waste, its management of solid waste will continue to be problematic.

Current disposal sites for both hazardous and non-hazardous liquid and solid wastes pose the threat of contaminating soils, especially in areas of permeability, as well as ground water, owing to leaching. Considering that ground water is the source of 70 per cent of the city's drinking water, adequate waste management is crucial to reducing the vulnerability of the basin at large and of Mexico City in particular.

Air quality

The levels of air pollution in Mexico City represent a serious danger to human health. Calderón-Garcidueñas et al. (1992a, 1992b) evaluated the histopathological changes of the nasal mucosa in inhabitants of south-west Mexico City, the area of the basin where ozone concentrations are highest. In a careful experimental design, they compared the nasal mucosa from three groups of health workers and navy employees: (a) long-term residents of the Port of Veracruz (a low-ozone environment), (b) persons resident for fewer than 31 days in Mexico City, and coming from non-polluted locations, and (c) subjects who had lived in the south-west of Mexico City for more than two months (the mean residence time of this group was about 10 years).

Basal cell hyperplasia was present in 98 per cent of all patients from group (c) (long-term residents of Mexico City), whereas the long-term residents of Veracruz presented this syndrome in only 5 per cent of cases. Additionally, the hyperplasia in the Veracruz group formed only small patches, occupying less than 25 per cent of the biopsy surface, whereas in Mexico City residents it covered more than 50 per cent of the sampled tissue in almost 50 per cent of the patients evaluated. Although none of the Veracruz patients showed additional effects, the residents of Mexico City showed varying degrees of squamous cell metaplasia (55 per cent of patients), keratinization (23 per cent), epithelial dysplasias (81 per cent), vascular submucosal proliferation (100 per cent), and submucosal chronic inflammation (98 per cent). Group (b) (the short-term residents of Mexico City) showed intermediate values of incidence. Although the authors suggest that high levels of ozone are possibly the main cause of these histopathological changes, they do not discard the hypothesis that other potential environmental carcinogens are likely to be involved in the extremely high level of tissue anomalies present in the respiratory tracts of the inhabitants of Mexico City.

Margulis (1992) used standard dose–response curves to quantify the health effects of pollutants in Mexico City. He then calculated the economic costs of pollution by integrating the average individual cost associated with the levels of each pollutant (in terms of the cost of treatment, lost wages, or death) for the whole population of the city (which he estimated as *c*.17 million in 1992). He estimated a total annual cost related to particulate matter pollution of US$850 million, a cost of US$102 million for ozone, and a cost of US$125 million for atmospheric lead. (As explained previously, the impact of lead seems to have decreased since 1992, but it is also likely that the health effects of ozone have increased.) In short, the aggregated "hidden" cost of atmospheric pollution, as estimated by the known effects of pollution on human health, is around US$1.1 billion per year.

Atmospheric pollution also has a considerable influence on the quality of rainwater. For the 1983–1986 period, reports indicate a significant decrease in the pH of incoming rainwater in Mexico City, owing to the increasing concentration of sulphur and nitrogen oxides in the air (Páramo et al. 1987; also Bravo 1987). In the urban parts of the basin, the average pH of rainwater is around 5.5, and a few rain events have been recorded with pH values as low as 3.0.

The direct effect of pollution may have major consequences upon the conservation of the few green areas that are still used and enjoyed by the urban inhabitants. Little is known about the effects of pollutants such as ozone and lead, among many others, on plants in the high-altitude environment of the Basin of Mexico. Observations by plant physiologists, however, allow us to presume that pollutants are already a major problem both in the city and in the surrounding

151

areas, because phytotoxic gases are easily windborne. In Mexico City and its environs, at least three gases (ozone, sulphur dioxide, and peroxyacetyl nitrate) reach concentrations that are well above the known toxic threshold for plants (Bauer 1981). Thus, the effects of air pollution are not restricted to the urban areas; they also have considerable impact on the natural ecosystems surrounding the basin. Krupa and Bauer (1976) reported over 20 years ago the noxious effect of windborne ozone on the forests of El Ajusco. They reported chlorotic bands in the needles of *Pinus hartweggii* and in *Pinus leiophylla*, the former being more susceptible than the latter. It is presumed that these bands precede the death of the needle. Even though at the date their study was published the levels of ozone attributable to human activities were way below the current levels, 5–10 per cent of the sampled trees registered significant damage as a result of air pollution.

Later studies (Hernández Tejeda, Bauer, and Krupa 1985; Hernández Tejeda and Bauer 1986, among others) have detected specific effects of pollution on the growth and photosynthetic rates of trees. Hernández Tejeda, Bauer, and Ortega Delgado (1985; see also Bauer 1981; Bauer and Krupa 1990; and Bauer, Hernández Tejeda, and Manning 1985), for example, found that the ozone produced above the city and carried by the dominant winds to the Sierra del Ajusco, south-west of the basin, significantly reduced the chlorophyll content and the growth of *Pinus hartweggii*, the dominant pine species in the high mountains (*c.*3,500 m) around the basin.

Different effects have been observed in trees such as ash (*Fraxinus* spp.), sycamore (*Platanus* spp.), and *Eucalyptus globulus*, which show different types of damage (e.g. different levels of foliar injury, early senescence and loss of leaves at the end of summer and the beginning of autumn, and chlorotic patches along leaves) caused by ozone and other atmospheric oxidants (Bauer and Krupa 1990). Native species, such as *Pinus hartweggii* and *Pinus leiophylla*, which cover and protect the south-western slopes of the basin, show chlorotic banding and mottling in their needles, as well as premature needle loss and branch mortality, caused by oxidant agents (Bauer and Krupa 1990). The increased mortality of the temperate forests surrounding the basin, reported by Bauer and collaborators in different studies, is particularly worrying in environmental terms and indicates significant endangerment in the basin. The immediate cause of the forest decline is attack by scolytid bark-beetles (*Dendroctonus* spp.) on the conifers, but many foresters associate the new and increased aggressiveness of

Table 6.3 **Emission standards for automobiles in Mexico and in the United States (g/km.vehicle)**

	1975		1985		1994	
	Mexico	USA	Mexico	USA	Mexico	USA
Hydrocarbons	2.50	0.90	2.60	0.25	0.25	0.15
Carbon monoxide	29.20	9.40	24.20	2.09	2.11	2.09
Nitrogen oxides	(no standard)	1.93	2.20	0.61	0.62	0.25

Sources: Bravo (1987), SEDESOL (1994c), and EPA (1994a) for the 1985 and 1994 data in the United States.

Table 6.4 **Lead content of regular gasoline in England and Germany, compared with Mexico (ml of lead tetra-ethyl per litre of gasoline)**

Country	1980	1987	1991
England	0.28	zero	zero
Germany	0.15	zero	zero
Mexico	0.77	0.14	0.14 (leaded)
			zero (unleaded)

Sources: Bravo (1987) and SEDESOL (1994c).

this pest (which in the past never proved capable of producing widespread tree mortality) with the stressful environmental conditions generated by high ozone levels in the air, possibly coupled with the effect of acid deposition.

The economic cost of the effects of pollution on the tree vegetation surrounding the basin has not been calculated, but is most likely also very high. Apart from the aesthetic importance of these forests and their direct impacts on erosion control and on the conservation of biological diversity, possibly their most important service is the regulation of the water cycle and the recharge of the aquifers. Because the water balance of underground water is so strongly disrupted in the basin, no one has calculated in detail the future costs of the non-renewable exploitation of the aquifers or the future value of the recharge that is being lost through deforestation. This deficit, however, strongly questions the mid-term sustainability of the Basin of Mexico, and may be as limiting for the future development of the basin as the air pollution problem.

There is still room, however, for measures to control atmospheric pollution in the Basin of Mexico. For decades, the Mexican standard for maximum allowable exhaust emissions in new vehicles was two to three times more permissive than that of, for example, the United States, although the gap has been closing (tables 6.3 and 6.4). Even at present (1997), the vehicles assembled in Mexico for the export market have tougher emission-control standards than those assembled for the domestic market. Environmental regulations controlling emissions in Mexico have lagged, on average, some 10 years behind the same measures in the developed world. Catalytic converters, which need unleaded gasoline, were required in new cars from 1991, but older models still run without them. In 1995, some 68 per cent of all cars were still pre-1991 models (SEMARNAP 1996d). As the mean life of a car in Mexico City is around 10 years, the measure has not yet succeeded in curbing pollution levels, although it does seem to have stabilized current levels and stopped further increases.

More widespread use of public transportation, coupled with restrictions on the use of private vehicles, would certainly ease the air pollution problem. Buses, metro trains, trolleys, and taxis are responsible for only 23–30 per cent of all vehicular emissions, yet they transport 81 per cent of all passengers (Bravo 1986). The average emission of pollutants per passenger using private vehicles is 10 times higher than that of passengers using public transportation. Thus, implementation of these simple measures (emission control plus encouragement of public transport) would produce a significant improvement in the quality of the air in the basin in a relatively short time.

7

The response to the environmental problem

The construction of an environmental conscience

The Mexican highlands, and especially the Basin of Mexico, are among those regions of the world that have suffered the greatest environmental alterations in history. When the Europeans arrived in Mexico in 1519, they found the region already greatly transformed by waterworks constructed for the *chinampa* agriculture, by deforestation in the north of the basin, and by faunal extinction (Ezcurra 1992). The rate of environmental change, however, has increased continuously since then, and, with the mounting ecological deterioration, awareness of the problem by different social groups has increased accordingly.

The development of the Spanish Colony in Mexico hinged on an intentional transformation of the environment to adapt it to the introduced European crops and animals and to new means of transportation. Roads replaced canals and *chinampa* agriculture gave way in many areas to Castillian-style dryland farming. Forests were cut to induce the growth of grasslands and to supply wood for construction. In the mid-eighteenth century, Antonio de Alzate, one of the first Mexican scientists, expressed some concern about the potential effects of draining and drying the highland lakes and of displacing the native wetlands for dry ecosystems. Towards the end of the century, Alexander von Humboldt, in his *Political Essay on the Kingdom of the New Spain* (written in about 1795 and published in 1811) also expressed serious concern about the future effects of the rapid deforestation that was taking place on the slopes of the Mexican highlands. In the early twentieth century, Miguel Ángel de Quevedo campaigned for the planting of trees in the Basin of Mexico and predicted that large-scale environmental degradation would ensue if deforestation continued at its current rapid rate.

In spite of these early dire forecasts, general consciousness of the problem of environmental degradation failed to spread until the late 1970s, at first mostly in response to the problems of urban pollution in Mexico City. The economic development of Mexico during the 1936–1976 period, spanning the presidencies of Lázaro Cárdenas to López-Portillo, basically relied on the non-sustainable use of natural resources and reflected little awareness of the negative environmental consequences that would follow.

By the mid-1970s, many Mexicans recognized the need to confront the accumulating environmental problems. The conclusions of the United Nations Environmental Conference in Stockholm in 1972, and the continuing attention attracted by books such as Rachel Carson's (1962) *Silent Spring*, synergized with the growing perception that air quality in the industrialized cities was rapidly deteriorating, that industrial pollution was increasing, and that the new agricultural technologies carried a hidden cost in the exhaustion of water resources and the dissemination of biocidal residues. Both governmental authorities and different sectors of the Mexican society started to react.

Trends in governmental institutions

The evolution of environmental policies

Since 1970, Mexican environmental policy has passed through two main phases: the first, 1970–1982, involved the presidential terms of Luis Echeverría and José López-Portillo; the second, 1983–1992, involved the mandates of Miguel de la Madrid and Carlos Salinas de Gortari.

During the first phase, air pollution in Mexico City provided early evidence of non-sustainable use of the environment and prompted thinking about controlling emissions and planning environmental use in the large cities (Mexico, Monterrey, and Guadalajara). Some early governmental measures were taken at the beginning of the 1970s. President Luis Echeverría proposed a Law on Environmental Protection (DOF 1971), and his successor, José López-Portillo, created the Subsecretariat of Environmental Improvement (Subsecretaría de Mejoramiento del Ambiente, or SMA), in the Ministry of Health (Secretaría de Salud, or SSA). The emergence of this interest in the early 1970s is linked to the debate that was stimulated by the Stockholm Conference of 1972.

During the second phase, environmental policy acquired a higher political status through the creation of governmental agencies exclusively devoted to the environment and through an increase in specific environmental regulations and programmes. At the beginning of his mandate, in 1982, President Miguel de la Madrid created a new ministry of state called Secretaría de Desarrollo Urbano y Ecología (SEDUE; Ministry of Urban Development and Ecology). During his election campaign, he had repeatedly declared the urgent need for a national ecological awareness to put a stop to the "historical immorality" of the destruction of nature. In this new ministry, ecological issues carried the same administrative weight as those of urban development, but many aspects of environmental problems were still dealt with by other ministries such as fisheries, forestry, agriculture, and water resources. One of the first actions of SEDUE was to draft a new Environmental Protection Law, which was published in January 1984 (DOF 1984; SEDUE 1987).

In 1985, the National Commission on Ecology (Comisión Nacional de Ecología, or CONADE) was established with the objective of defining priorities in environmental matters and coordinating the different public institutions dealing with environmental actions. This Commission worked effectively until 1988, and was responsible for the first State of the Environment Report published for Mexico (CONADE 1992). One result of these changes in national policies was an administrative change in the government of the Department of the Federal District (DDF), which incorporated a Commission on Ecology in 1984; a year later, a General Directorate of Urban Planning and Ecological Protection was established to make decisions dealing directly with the urban environment of Mexico City.

Up to the mid-1980s, however, actions to prevent pollution were limited, mainly owing to the deep economic crisis confronting the country since 1982, a situation aggravated by the 1985 earthquake in Mexico City. In this context, the environmental problem lost priority in relation to financial constraints and basic living conditions.

157

From 1986 onwards, social pressure mounted owing to the lack of effective action to prevent environmental deterioration and the ever-increasing levels of air pollution in the city, particularly during winter. As a result, in 1986 the government of the Federal District formulated new programmes and enacted specific regulations that defined more stringent pollution control measures.

At the beginning of 1986, SEDUE announced a set of 21 anti-pollution measures applicable to Mexico City. Among these, the following were the most important:

1. the conversion of 2,000 state-owned public service buses to run on new, low-emission engines;
2. the extension of non-polluting urban electric transport to include 4.7 km of new lines for underground trains and 116 km of new lines for tramways, trolleys, and light trains;
3. the creation of sanitary landfills in which to dump solid wastes and the covering-up of the old open-space dumps;
4. the institution of a programme for the gradual substitution of oil by natural gas as fuel in the thermoelectric generators in the basin;
5. the supply of low-lead gasoline to the Metropolitan Area of Mexico City;
6. the establishment of a programme gradually to incorporate anti-pollution devices in new automobiles.

For the first time these measures tried to quantify actions and to give specific time-periods to accomplish them.

Together with these measures, which were mainly oriented to controlling air pollution, the Urban Development Plan for the Federal District, approved in 1987, established an ecological reserve of 85,554 ha to the south of the basin and in the neighbouring state of Morelos, in the Ajusco and the Chichinautzin ranges, where urban expansion was to be restricted, agricultural activities stimulated, and forest areas preserved and expanded. The main rationale behind this action was to preserve the southern forests of the basin, which are the most important water catchment areas for the city.

In 1989, under the newly assumed mandate of Carlos Salinas de Gortari, the definition of an official environmental policy proceeded and clearly became a political priority. At the national level, a new Law on Ecological Equilibrium and Environmental Protection (DOF 1988) had been passed a few months before the end of the de la Madrid administration, and the 1990–1994 National Development Plan included a National Programme for Environmental Protection. The National Institute of Statistics, Geography and Information

(Instituto Nacional de Estadística, Geografía e Informática, or INEGI) started to record the loss of natural resources in its national accounting report (INEGI 1994a).

As part of a more direct political response to the serious air pollution problem, in 1990 the federal government, together with the governments of the State of Mexico and the Federal District, announced a joint Programme against Atmospheric Pollution in the Metropolitan Area of Mexico City. This programme included four main policy decisions: (1) to rationalize the urban transport system; (2) to improve the quality of fuels used in the basin; (3) to install systems to control polluting emissions from vehicles, industries, and service facilities; (4) to regenerate natural areas subject to high ecological disturbance. To a great extent, this new programme was a continuation of SEDUE's "21 measures" from the previous administration – the strategies were clearly more oriented towards the control of critical air pollution levels. The main actions taken in this new programme included the following measures:

1. the control of emissions of atmospheric pollutants in service facilities such as public baths, dry cleaning shops, and laundries, which frequently did not comply with technical standards because of their old equipment and a notorious lack of maintenance;
2. regular and systematic inspection of industries in the basin in order to verify the correct functioning of their pollution-monitoring and emission-control equipment, which became mandatory for all industries;
3. mandatory checking, for both official and private vehicles, of exhaust emissions every six months;
4. banning the use of each car for one day a week, according to the numbers on the licence plate, with the objective of decreasing the circulation of vehicles by approximately 500,000 cars on average during working days;
5. a decrease in the levels of lead in gasoline, and the introduction of unleaded gasoline from 1991 onwards as the use of catalytic converters became mandatory in all new petrol-driven vehicles;
6. increased substitution of oil by natural gas in the two thermo-electric generating plants in the Basin of Mexico.

A paradigm shift in the wake of the Earth Summit

The year 1992 was extremely important for environmental institutions in Mexico. As a consequence of the growing number of industrial accidents in many parts of the nation (Martínez de Muñoz et al. 1992), which had in turn generated a series of recommendations from the National Commission on Human Rights, in March 1992 the federal environmental administration was separated into two more autonomous new offices: a National Institute of Ecology (Instituto Nacional de Ecología, or INE), which was basically in charge of drawing up environmental regulations and of administering the protection of the environment and natural resources; and an Environmental Protection Attorney General (Procuraduría Federal de Protección al Ambiente, or PROFEPA), a new office in charge of law enforcement in environmental matters and largely responsible for satisfying the popular demands that generated the recommendations of the Commission on Human Rights. Additionally, the former SEDUE was reorganized into a new Ministry of Social Development (Secretaría de Desarrollo Social, or SEDESOL). This administrative shift shows the development of a new paradigm in the federal administration, which had previously regarded the environment as basically a part of the complex set of urban problems.

The Mexican government participated actively in the preparatory meetings preceding the United Nations Conference on Environment and Development (UNCED) in 1992. Following the paradigm of sustainable development that UNCED attempted to implement on a global scale, the federal administration began to regard environmental affairs more as problems of socio-economic development (SEMARNAP 1996e, 1996f), closely linked to problems of poverty and social progress. Also prompted by UNCED, the federal government took an active interest in the protection of the natural heritage of Mexico. In early 1992 it created the National Commission for the Knowledge and Use of Biological Diversity (Comisión Nacional para el Conocimiento y el Uso de la Biodiversidad, or CONABIO), an organization devoted to surveying the biological richness of Mexican ecosystems.

New economic and political tools for ever-growing environmental problems

Also in 1992, modification of Article 27 of the Mexican constitution (*Constitución Política de los Estados Unidos Mexicanos*, 1992) ended the process of agrarian reform and land allotment, thus opening the possibility of ending the communal ownership of land under the *ejido* system for those *ejidos* and indigenous communities wishing to do so.

The overexploitation of natural resources in excessively subdivided communal lands was one of the arguments put forward for this constitutional amendment. Although the new version of Article 27 states that one of its objectives is to preserve the environmental equilibrium, some Mexican conservationist groups have voiced concern about the future impact that this constitutional change may have on the pressures to privatize and sell potentially valuable land, such as the forest ecosystems surrounding the Basin of Mexico or the remaining *chinampa* fields in Xochimilco.

SEDESOL proposed, among other things, to decentralize decision-making on environmental matters. The executive powers of the National Institute of Ecology were down-scaled, and its role as a regulatory institution assumed precedence. Many powers that were previously held by the federal government in Mexico City were passed to the delegates of SEDESOL in the states, or to the state and municipal governments themselves (INAP 1991). During the term of Salinas de Gortari many state governments produced their own environmental laws and regulations, and some began to administer programmes formerly operated by the federal administration. As an example, during this period and as a result of the growing concern about the deteriorating air quality of the Mexico City, the Department of the Federal District (DDF 1995; RAMA 1996a, 1996b) created the Metropolitan Commission for the Prevention and Control of Environmental Pollution in the Valley of Mexico (Comisión para la Prevención y el Control de la Contaminación Ambiental en la Zona Metropolitana del Valle de México, or CPCCA), with the participation of the government of the State of Mexico and the federal authorities (DOF 1992). As one of its first actions, the Metropolitan Commission produced a strategic plan for the prevention of industrial catastrophes in the Basin of Mexico and an action strategy to minimize risks in the event of a large-scale industrial accident in Mexico City (CPCCA 1992). Water management in the basin is also undertaken through a complex set of state and federal governmental organizations, including the Department of the Federal District and the Commission for Water and Sanitation of the State of Mexico, at the state level, and the National Water Commission (Comisión Nacional del Agua, or CNA) and the Ministry of Health (SSA), at the federal level.

The new emphasis on regulatory action by the National Institute of Ecology led to the publication of 58 Normas Oficiales Mexicanas (Official Standards) dealing with different aspects of the environment, including standards on wastewater quality, atmospheric emissions, air pollutants, toxic waste, and natural resources, including a list of endangered species (SEDESOL 1994c). The publication of these standards allowed the regulation of industrial emissions in the Basin of Mexico. The new standards also provided a formal regulatory framework for environmental impact studies and ecological planning. In addition, these new regulations brought new analytical techniques (such as risk assessment and cost–benefit analysis) in decision-making and priority-setting into the governmental discourse.

Environmental sustainability as a major political concern

During the 1994 elections the environment occupied an important niche in the party platforms. The Partido Verde Ecologista (Ecologist Green Party) came fifth in the elections, after the three large parties (Partido Revolucionario Institucional, Partido de Acción Nacional, and Partido de la Revolución Democrática) and the medium-sized Labour Party (Partido del Trabajo). In December 1994, shortly after assuming office, the Zedillo administration created a new ministry (DOF 1994b) to encompass all federal environmental functions, including those dealing with "brown ecology" (environmental pollution) and "green ecology" (natural resources management). The Ministry of Environment, Natural Resources, and Fisheries (Secretaría de Medio Ambiente, Recursos Naturales y Pesca, or SEMARNAP) consolidated functions previously dispersed among different federal agencies: the protection and management of natural resources such as water, forests, and fisheries; waste management and pollution control; the management of national parks and other protected natural areas; and the enforcement of environmental law.

The creation of this strong ministry highlights the ever-increasing importance that the federal authorities now accord to the environmental problems of Mexico. It also underscores an effort to institutionalize sustainable development initiatives by integrating governmental activities that may affect the environment and that were previously separated, such as forestry, fisheries, and conservation, or energy use, transportation, and urban design.

In July 1996, the Internal Rules (Reglamento Interno) of SEMARNAP were published (DOF 1996c). They cover three sub-secretariats (Planning, Natural Resources, and Fisheries) and five deconcentrated, or autonomous, institutions (*órganos desconcentrados*): the National Water Commission (CNA), the Mexican Institute of Water Technology (Instituto Mexicano de Ciencia y Tecnología del Agua, or IMTA), the National Institute of Ecology (INE), the Environmental Protection Attorney General (PROFEPA), and the National Institute of Fisheries (Instituto Nacional de la Pesca, or INP). Furthermore, this new organizational structure separates the management of natural protected areas from the management of wildlife, raising the former into an autonomous Coordination Unit. SEMARNAP has faced its great responsibilities and the financial difficulties imposed by current policies of governmental reductions by seeking for programmes of decentralization even stronger than those implemented by SEDESOL, on the one hand, and by trying to develop alliances with non-governmental organizations (NGOs) and the private sector to manage specific aspects of the environmental policies, on the other. An ambitious programme of decentralization with the states and federal delegations is being discussed (SEMARNAP 1996a, 1996c).

As a result of the growing autonomy, a new environmental law has been passed for the Federal District (DOF 1996b), and Environmental Commissions are now working both in Congress and in the Senate. More specifically, SEMARNAP has elaborated a programme to decentralize the administration of the national parks, and to cooperate with NGOs and research institutions in the management of biosphere reserves (SEMARNAP 1996b, 1996c). For this purpose, SEMARNAP has created an independent Advisory Council on Protected Areas, and is working with NGO representatives to convert a Global Environmental Facility donation to Mexico of US$25 million into a private trust fund. Additionally, in cooperation with the SSA, the DDF, and the government of the neighbouring State of Mexico, SEMARNAP has developed a new and comprehensive programme to improve air quality in Mexico City (SEMARNAP 1996d).

Current perspectives on governmental policies

The implementation of governmental policies and the establishment of end-of-pipe standards may have curbed the increase in atmospheric pollution, but high levels have persisted and new dimensions of the problem have appeared. Indeed, some pollutants (for example, ozone) frequently exceed what are considered acceptable limits, and globally the air quality index (IMECA) surpasses 200 points for most of the year, indicating that at least one pollutant is well above the healthy limit. These levels of pollution represent a serious danger to

Table 7.1 **Investment in the seven largest projects of the Programme against Atmospheric Pollution in Mexico City, October 1990 – December 1995**

Project	Institution in charge	Investment US$m.	%
1. Production of gasoline that meets international standards of quality	PEMEX	811	34.8
2. Closure of the "18 de Marzo" refinery in Mexico City	PEMEX	500	21.4
3. Supply of unleaded gasoline (*Magna Sin*) for vehicles with catalytic converters	PEMEX	345	14.8
4. Replacement of public transport vehicles (*Ruta 100*) with 3,500 vehicles with low pollution emissions	DDF	137	5.9
5. Introduction of catalytic converters for taxis and public transport (vans and micro-buses)	State of Mexico, DDF	121	5.2
6. Supply of low-lead oxygenated gasoline for pre-1991 vehicles	PEMEX	119	5.1
7. Production of diesel with a low sulphur content	PEMEX	118	5.1
Subtotal (7 projects)		2,151	92.2
Total (41 projects)		2,333	100.0

Source: SEMARNAP (1996d).

human health and to natural ecosystems, and they call for new measures.

Policy measures have influenced, and to some extent controlled, the upward trend of specific pollutants such as lead, carbon monoxide, and sulphur dioxide. The 1990 Programme against Atmospheric Pollution concentrated its efforts on the improvement of gasolines (table 7.1). Of the total investment in this programme between 1990 and 1995, the seven largest projects (17 per cent of the total number of projects) accounted for 92 per cent. This confirms a bias in favour of improving air quality by means of producing better fuels and controlling emissions. Mexican gasolines now comply with international standards in terms of chemical composition, and are considered to be as good as those in developed countries. Until the end of 1996, Mexico produced two types of gasoline: an unleaded gasoline (*Magna Sin*); and one with a 92 per cent lead reduction (*Nova*). In 1997, low-lead gasoline was removed from the market, leaving only unleaded gasolines for sale. Diesel oil was improved by decreasing its sulphur content by 95 per cent, while burner oil was substituted by natural gas and, to a lesser extent, by industrial gas with a lower sulphur content (DDF 1997).

The 1990 programme also included the *"Hoy no circula"* ("Don't drive today") measure, which required automobile owners to forgo using their cars one day each week. The *"Hoy no circula"* measure was originally established in December 1989, and at first received wide public support: official statistics showed that gasoline consumption in the Basin of Mexico fell by around 12 per cent (Menéndez Garza 1993). Every workday, between 5 a.m. and 10 p.m., certain cars were banished from the city's streets, on the basis of the last digit of their licence plate. But people displayed little willingness to shift to the use of public transport, already generally perceived as providing an inadequate service. By buying additional cars, drivers could acquire plates that allowed them to drive every day. Thus, the programme, coupled with the financial and economic bonanza of the presidency of Carlos Salinas de Gortari (1988–1994), generated a dramatic increase in the demand for cars (fig. 7.1). Whereas average car sales per year between 1982 and 1988 were around 100,000 vehicles, between 1989 and 1994 they climbed to around 200,000 vehicles.

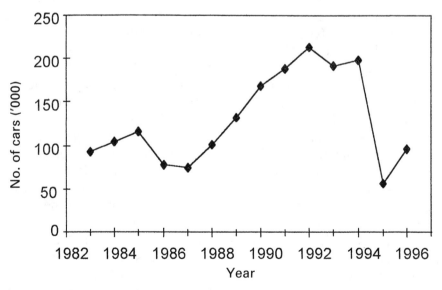

Fig. 7.1 **Estimated sales of passenger cars in the Basin of Mexico, 1983–1995 (Source: Legorreta 1995)**

Accordingly, the number of cars on the roads rose from 2 million in 1980 to more than 3 million in 1990, and an estimated 3.5 million in 1995 (INEGI 1997; AAMA 1996; see also table 4.11). By 1994, the daily consumption of gasoline in Mexico City was some 2 million litres above the 1989 level (a 25–30 per cent increase). Thus, the final result of the programme was completely opposite to its initial objectives, because it contributed to the dramatic increase in the number of cars in Mexico City.

In 1995, as a result, on the one hand, of the obvious failure of the programme and, on the other, of the establishment of more stringent emission standards for new cars, the environmental authorities decided that new cars with catalytic converters and fuel injection could be used every day without restriction if they were able to pass a new, more stringent, exhaust emissions test. As old models are removed from circulation, the "*Hoy no circula*" measure will gradually disappear. Indeed, this relaxation of the restriction, combined with the economic crisis of December 1994, led to a collapse in car sales in 1995 and 1996 (fig. 7.1).

The government of President Ernesto Zedillo, who took office at the end of 1994, had to design a programme to handle the new dimensions of environmental degradation in the basin. All the new strategies and measures were included in the "Programme to Improve Air Quality in the Valley of Mexico, 1995–2000" (DDF 1997), whose objectives are to decrease by the year 2000 the emission of hydrocarbons by 50 per cent, of nitrogen oxides by 40 per cent, and of suspended particles by 45 per cent, and to decrease the mean values of the air quality index (IMECA) throughout the year. To achieve these objectives, the programme intends to work largely on the inventory of emissions of the Basin of Mexico, in order to (a) reduce emissions from industries and services, (b) reduce vehicular emissions, (c) make urban transport more efficient by regulating the total number of kilometres travelled by motor vehicles, and (d) control soil erosion and promote programmes of ecological restoration.

This new programme and its revised structure of aims and strategies (table 7.2) demand some comments. First, the new measures place great importance on the incorporation of n_ ˖ technologies into productive activities and vehicles, which will entail modernization of industrial processes and new emission standards. Such a measure has long been neglected because technological innovation requires, among other things, significant investment. Attention is now given to credits, economic incentives, and international financing. Secondly, a

166

Table 7.2 **Objectives, aims, and strategies of the Programme to Improve Air Quality in the Valley of Mexico, 1995–2000**

Type of strategy	Main objectives of the programme			
	Clean industry	Clean vehicles	Efficient transport and new urban order	Ecological restoration
Technological development	Improvement and incorporation of new technologies			
Energy use	Improvement and substitution of energy sources			
Policy tools	Integration of metropolitan policies on urban development, transportation, and environment			
	Inspection and control of industries and vehicles		Wide supply of reliable and safe public transport	
Economic tools	Economic incentives			
Social participation	Development of environmental information and education programmes; promotion of public participation			

Source: SEMARNAP (1996d).

specific emphasis on the coordination of metropolitan policies linked to public transport and the environment reflects a concern to avoid the kinds of contradictory measures sometimes taken in past by the Federal District and the State of Mexico. The new approach tries to promote better land-use planning that incorporates a reference to the carrying capacity of ecosystems and their compatibility with productive activities. It demonstrates a wider coverage of issues, such as the consolidation of urban neighbourhoods and the restoration of ecological zones, which is indirectly related to air quality. To support its actions and their potential impacts, the programme champions environmental education and social participation. The strategy also considers the creation of a feedback mechanism to enable society to correct and improve the whole programme. The setting up of new evaluation and information mechanisms will enlist the participation of relevant institutions such as universities, social and private sector organizations, and the legislative bodies of the Federal District and the State of Mexico. Finally, an executive body will be in charge of the coordination and operation of the programme, integrated by the members of the Metropolitan Commission for the Prevention and Control of Environmental Pollution in the Valley of Mexico.

Many factors have contributed in the past to the slow response of official environmental policy to the obvious environmental criticality of the basin. First, there has been a marked delay in the application of the technical standards that regulate atmospheric emissions. Although the atmospheric problem was clear to many experts by the mid-1970s, strict government control started only when air pollution was overwhelming in its magnitude. There is, of course, a time-lag in the effect of policy measures. For example, the mean life of a car in Mexico City is approximately 10 years. Thus it is obvious that the effect of catalytic converters, for example, will be slow to be noticed.

Secondly, the political will to apply continuous and strict anti-pollution measures has been weak in relation to the economic interests of the main polluting industries. Cases in point include the automobile industry, which for years avoided the incorporation of anti-pollution devices in new models, and Mexico City's industrial sector, which long evaded the installation of emission controls. Industries have enjoyed favourable treatment from governmental policy makers who did not wish to scare the large companies away by burdening their production costs with emission control measures. Not until the 1990–1991 winter did many industries begin to suffer formal closure and high penalty charges as a result of not complying with environmental legislation.

Lastly, the real dangers imposed by air pollution were consistently minimized by government agencies (see the discussion about the air quality index in chap. 5). Not only were the real consequences of air pollution played down, but the indices measuring air quality were averaged over time and over different stations, in such a way that local peaks in the concentration of pollutants became hidden. This self-deluding attitude was shared by most public officers, many of whom honestly believed that the problem was not so serious as some scientists and civil organizations contended.

Thus, the perception of the environmental problem by government decision makers translated into a focus mainly on the control of air pollution and only secondarily on the regeneration of heavily disturbed or eroded natural areas. Two aspects that are rarely mentioned in the official environmental discourse as driving forces of environmental degradation are poverty and social inequality. The public administration has responded with strict measures against what it perceives as potential sources of political trouble, but the lack of a long-term perspective may lead to ephemeral solutions. For example, the decrees that made car exhaust checks mandatory and forced citizens to stop using their cars one day in the week were aimed at reducing emissions by 10–20 per cent. Yet, with the number of cars growing at a rate of more than 4 per cent a year, the measures will be effective only in the short term; the problem will persist and even escalate for several years.

Trends in non-governmental institutions

The starting point: A concern for resource degradation

Concern about the environmental degradation of the Basin of Mexico dates back to the early days of the colonial city. In the early 1600s, Enrico Martínez strongly opposed the way the hydrology of the basin was being transformed. After a long period of debate with the colonial government (Palerm 1973), he finally imposed his views, and in 1603 became chief engineer for the first drainage project in Mexico City. Some of his ideas, such as siphoning water out of the basin, led to the desiccation of the basin's lakes. Although his concerns about floods and the use of water were valid, the solution he proposed was harmful in the long term.

Concerns about the effect of deforestation on the basin's water balance and about the draining of the lakes were voiced in the seventeenth century by other naturalists such as Antonio de Alzate and Alexander von Humboldt. These concerns, however, were basically the expression of academic interests; they did not represent a true social response to environmental change. The environment did not appear on the social agenda of the inhabitants of the Basin of Mexico until many years later.

During the nineteenth century, the few explicit environmental worries that arose basically related to the fate of the forests. Upper-class citizens, linked either with the first non-Hispanic governments or with the long dictatorship of Porfirio Díaz, were worried about the depletion of forested land. On the one hand, the need to make "idle lands" economically productive was a priority according to the prevailing paradigms of that time. Although von Humboldt (1811) had given clear warnings about the negative consequences of deforesting the basin's slopes, the ruling classes had little knowledge of the ecological services of forests as efficient regulators of water flows. On the other hand, the non-sustainable exploitation of natural resources was blamed on the indigenous groups who logged the forests for wood and for coal. More attention was devoted in the nineteenth century to the damaging effects of the logging of old-growth forests by impov-

169

erished Indian villagers than to the massive use of wood for mines, railroads, and houses and of coal for the higher classes and for the development of incipient Mexican industry. This view sparked a fever of expropriation of Indian communal lands.

The process reflected a change in the whole concept of nature and of the relation between society and nature. Land appropriation, which eventually led to the Mexican Revolution at the beginning of the twentieth century, at first had the support of many intellectuals, who viewed this new mode of natural resource use as progressive. Two names appear to mark a turning point in environmental consciousness: Miguel Ángel de Quevedo and Enrique Beltrán.

Quevedo was born in Guadalajara in 1862 into a prosperous family. He studied hydraulic engineering in France, where he also developed a deep appreciation of nature. He returned to Mexico and, travelling through the basin on one of his engineering jobs, he became keenly aware of the devastating effects of deforestation, particularly the impressive floods attendant on the removal of old forests. Subsequently, still as a hydraulic engineer, Quevedo started an intense campaign against deforestation. He encountered many opponents, who did not regard the destruction of forests as a serious concern, but he also rallied enthusiastic followers, who in 1901 founded the Junta Central de Bosques and appointed Quevedo as its first president. Though mainly a technological association engaged in lobbying, the Junta was, in a way, the first social environmental movement in the Basin of Mexico and indeed in the country. Shortly after its creation, the Junta was being actively consulted by the government of Mexico City.

Quevedo was active for many years, and he made many contributions. He was an enthusiastic supporter of the creation of national parks, which increased from 2 to 34 in only 10 years (Simonian 1995). Among his best-known actions was the creation of a beautiful tree nursery that is still in operation in the now densely populated district of Coyoacán. By 1914, Los Viveros de Coyoacán were annually producing 2.4 million trees, many of which were later transplanted to different parts of the basin in order to protect soils from erosion and to help prevent floods. Others were planted in parks and streets. These nurseries are still one of the most important sources of young trees and seedlings for reforestation.

Though Quevedo's reforestation efforts were extremely important owing to their immediate effect on natural and transformed landscapes and their impact on the way the management of resources was

170

conceived, some of his actions had unexpected consequences. Particularly counterproductive was the introduction of *Eucalyptus* into the basin. While studying and travelling in Europe, Quevedo had been surprised by the quick growth of these trees and by their lack of pests. He concluded that they were the perfect trees for reforesting the basin, and he viewed the planting of *Eucalyptus* as the best strategy to prevent soil erosion, dust storms, and floods. Unfortunately, the trees became weedy invaders in the mild environment of the Basin of Mexico, and have replaced the original vegetation in many parts, with serious ecological repercussions (see chap. 6).

For a long time Quevedo managed to influence governmental decisions dealing with green areas, reforestation, and the protection of forests. President Porfirio Díaz took Quevedo's opinions seriously, as did Francisco I. Madero, who succeeded Díaz after leading the Mexican Revolution that ousted him from power. In 1914, when Victoriano Huerta became president, however, Quevedo had to leave the country because the new government regarded the Junta Central de Bosques as subversive. Unfortunately, this was not the last time that environmental movements would be identified as subversive. Many of the areas that Quevedo and his followers had reforested were destroyed after he went into exile in France.

After Huerta's defeat, Quevedo returned to Mexico and helped to draft the texts on Mexico's natural resources that were incorporated in the country's 1917 constitution. The following 15 years saw an active but weary Quevedo trying to convince governmental agencies of the importance of protecting wildlife and forests. Most of his efforts during this politically unstable period were unsuccessful but they opened the way for future decisions. In 1934, Lázaro Cárdenas became Mexico's last military president. Though he was a General, Cárdenas led a mostly civilian cabinet. He was very influenced by Quevedo's views and appointed him as the head of the Department of Forestry, Fish, and Game. Quevedo was again leading the way in the protection of forests, this time through the creation of numerous protected areas (basically natural parks) throughout the country.

However, the non-economic services provided by forests – water, clean air, conservation of wildlife, and recreation – received short shrift from powerful emerging financial groups, who wanted to use the forests for wood and paper. Besides, Quevedo was worried about the environmental consequences of the post-Revolution agrarian reform that distributed land to *campesinos* and would, he predicted, transform many well-preserved natural forests into agricultural land.

This concern came across as anti-indigenous and incompatible with the socialist-leaning government of Cárdenas, who finally decided to close the Department of Forestry he had created. Once again a common citizen far removed from governmental activities, Quevedo continued his advocacy on behalf of trees and nature conservation until his death in 1946.

Miguel Ángel de Quevedo stands out as one of the first environmentalists of the twentieth century in Mexico, whose passion for trees earned him the popular label "El Apóstol del Arbol" (The Apostle of Trees). He represented what was to become a typical characteristic of all environmental movements and initiatives in decades to come: environmentalism stereotyped as radical and subversive whenever it challenged powerful economic and governmental interests. Quevedo's perseverance made him, in a way, a pioneer of the Mexican environmental movements of the twentieth century.

Other independent, non-governmental environmental initiatives and efforts slowly developed in the country, particularly in the Basin of Mexico. Actions by professionals and scientists such as Alfonso Herrera, who, like Quevedo, commanded great respect in Mexican society, generated a growing awareness of the importance of conserving forests and wildlife. Indeed, it was one of Herrera's disciples, Enrique Beltrán (1903–1994), who started to talk about conservation in the broader context of preserving natural resources. Beltrán, a biologist, was one of the most important Mexican conservationists of what might be called the foundational period of environmental movements. For some time, he eschewed governmental administration, since he rejected Quevedo's opposition to the indigenous peoples' right to use their forests. He disdained the Department of Forestry, Fish, and Game created by Cárdenas and headed by Quevedo, and he blamed some of Quevedo's ideas for the destruction of the forests of Mexico.

In sharp contrast with Quevedo, Beltrán thought that, to conserve renewable resources, society should not refrain from using them but should instead learn how to use them wisely. Beltrán's ideas are very much along the lines of the sustainability paradigm that permeates most current conservation movements. At the time, though, his views frequently struck observers as contradictory. In order to protect forests, he wanted forests to be used, but in a regulated way. He was against declaring new protected areas because the national parks established by Cárdenas, even a short period after they had been declared, had no operational funding. In a way, Beltrán was fighting against the same barrier that many other conservationists would confront several decades later. His scientific background allowed him to envisage the sustainable management of resources, but reconciling use with protection was not easily imagined and even now it is under discussion. Beltrán was also one of the first conservationists to talk about environmental education. In 1952, he created the Instituto Mexicano de Recursos Naturales Renovables (Mexican Institute for Renewable Resources) with the aim of drawing up an accurate reliable inventory of natural resources in Mexico, making this information freely available, and seeking appropriate ways of using natural resources without destroying them. Like Quevedo, Enrique Beltrán represented a turning point in environmental paradigms and concerns in the nation at large.

Although both men lived in Mexico City and worked on many aspects of the environment of the Basin of Mexico, their interests extended beyond this particular region. In the 1940s, other conservationists started to work actively in other parts of Mexico. The most notable example is Miguel Álvarez del Toro, who founded, in the state of Chiapas, a regional zoo and a research institute that has received international recognition. In 1951, Gonzalo Blanco Macías founded Amigos de la Tierra (Friends of the Earth), a non-governmental organization that promoted the conservation of soil, water, and wildlife. Although based in Mexico City, Amigos de la Tierra worked with *campesinos* and landowners throughout the country, so this movement cannot be identified as an exclusive and direct response to the basin's problems.

Biosphere reserves and biological diversity

Mexican ecological activism hinged largely on the growing urban problems of Mexico City. Beginning in the late 1970s, some groups began to lobby for the protection of the nation's biological diversity and against the growing deforestation. The 1970s witnessed the creation of several institutions, partially funded by government but largely the result of efforts by non-governmental persons or groups.

The Centro de Ecodesarrollo (CECODES; Centre for Eco-development), based in Mexico City, was created in 1972 under the direction of Iván Restepo, who has played an important role in informing citizens about the environmental problems of Mexico through newspaper articles and notes. Basically because of its militant nature, CECODES ceased to receive governmental support and closed in the late 1980s. However, it re-opened in 1992 as a fully independent, non-governmental research institution.

In 1974, Gonzalo Halffter, a very active ecologist, created the Instituto de Ecología (Institute of Ecology), a civil association. Conceived as a research organization, the institute also conducted applied activities such as environmental impact assessments. Under Halffter's direction, the Institute of Ecology started promoting the concept of biosphere reserves in Mexico. Although the idea, which had been developed by a group of ecologists in UNESCO's Man and the Biosphere Programme (MAB), is now fairly well accepted, it was radically new in 1975. Biosphere reserves were to be protected areas where the indigenous populations living inside the area or in the surrounding "buffer zones" were encouraged to use their natural resources in a sustainable manner. This was quite a departure from the "natural park" concept, basically a pristine area free of human influence. The Mexican biosphere reserves were among the first in the world to become operational and part of the MAB network of reserves.

Many of the concepts discussed at UNCED in 1992 were already to be found in MAB's ideas about biosphere reserves almost 20 years earlier: (a) the need to protect biodiversity globally through a network of protected areas, (b) the urgency of preserving cultural diversity together with natural diversity, (c) the involvement of local populations in the protection of biological diversity, and (d) the promotion of the sustainable use of natural resources. The Institute of Ecology also launched a programme and a series of publications that tried to generate awareness about the non-sustainable nature of natural resource use in Mexico City, and drew public attention to the importance of some of the surviving natural ecosystems around the megalopolis. Although the institute is an academic research centre and not, strictly speaking, an NGO, its work opened the way for many experiments developed later by NGOs within the basic paradigm of sustainable resource use.

In 1975, the Instituto de Investigaciones de los Recursos Bióticos (INIREB; Research Institute for Biotic Resources) was founded by Arturo Gómez-Pompa, a biologist deeply concerned by the prevailing strategies for the management of natural resources and the effects of those strategies on environment and society, especially on the impoverished rural population. Although INIREB established its headquarters in Jalapa, Veracruz, and its interests were basically oriented towards the Mexican tropics, another line of research was

174

the *chinampa* system the Aztecs had created in the basin. INIREB invested a lot in research in this area and opened local offices in Mexico City to facilitate investigations into the *chinampa* regions of Xochimilco, Tláhuac, and Misquic. Later, this group tried to promote a system of tropical *chinampas* in Tabasco and Veracruz. INIREB closed in 1988, when its facilities merged with those of the Institute of Ecology.

The emergence of ecological activism

Environmental activism and environmentally oriented NGOs are a relatively new phenomenon in Mexico, but both have grown extremely rapidly in recent years.

Before 1980, small groups of citizens had rallied sporadically and mostly in urban areas to prevent specific actions – such as the widening of streets at the expense of vegetated areas – that could damage the environment. This type of action spawned the likes of the Green Brigades (*Brigadas verdes*), formed in 1977 under the influence of the radical green movements in Europe. The brigades emerged as a social response to a very specific problem: the decision to widen the streets of Mexico City in order to speed up urban traffic occasioned the cutting down of many trees and the paving over of sidewalk lawns. The movement was unsuccessful in stopping these measures, but it enlightened the inhabitants of Mexico City about the growing deterioration of their environment.

Although most of the inhabitants of the basin witnessed the relentless increase in environmental problems over a long period, they possessed little information on the real magnitude of the problem and could contemplate few governmental actions that would convince people that the issues were being taken seriously. On the other hand, not every citizen regarded environmental degradation as an issue of great concern. The few official reports produced at the time only added to the general perception that the number of industries in the city was growing, with some associated and localized effects. For example, no reports on air quality were produced by the Department of the Federal District before the 1980s, and the few official reports produced by the Subsecretariat of Environmental Improvement (SMA 1978a, 1978b) basically linked air pollution to the industrial districts of Mexico City.

A collective social response to the ecological problems of the basin materialized very slowly, partly owing to lack of information about

175

the ecological processes taking place in the basin as a whole and about the possible effects of, for example, the excessive extraction of water or the high levels of air pollution. The media encouraged this general indifference, and school programmes simply did not include environmental issues in their curricula.

Air pollution was the first signal of real problems, and, as noted above, it prompted policy changes in the 1970s and especially in the 1980s. Despite this rise in official concern and the creation of new governmental offices, the basin's environment continued to deteriorate at increasing rates.

This scenario favoured the birth of modern environmental non-governmental associations, such as ProNatura, founded in 1981 by a group of conservationists and entrepreneurs (Andrés Marcelo Sada, Pedro Domecq, Hector Ceballos Lascurain, and Mario Ramos), and Movimiento Ecologista Mexicano (Mexican Ecological Movement, or MEM), founded by Alfonso Ciprés Villarreal. In 1983, the Asociación Ecológica de Coyoacán (Coyoacán Ecological Association) was formed, and in 1984 the Alianza Ecologista Nacional (National Ecological Alliance) was established. In 1985, the poet Homero Arijdis rallied the support of 100 prominent artists and intellectuals and formed the Grupo de los Cien (Group of 100).

Other non-governmental organizations that were set up in this period are Biocenosis, Pro-Mariposa Monarca (later re-named Monarca A.C.), and Amigos de Sian Ka'an. Most of these NGOs either began in, or drew many of their members from, Mexico City. However, their focus was not the basin, or at least not exclusively – with the exception of the Coyoacán Ecological Association. By the 1980s, Coyoacán, originally a small town some distance from Mexico City, had long been engulfed by the metropolis. It had poor districts alternating with trendy upper-class areas, where intellectuals and politicians liked to live. The association, a classic product of an area such as Coyoacán, was worried about the potential loss of "ecological equilibrium." The association defined itself as having no links with political, religious, governmental, or industrial groups. Despite its relatively limited scope of action, it managed to remain active for more than a decade, and enjoyed an influential role among the other environmentalist associations.

By 1984 several groups had come and gone. The survivors united in the Red Alternativa de Ecocomunicación (Alternative Network of Eco-Communications). The constituents of this network organized their work around the development of alternative technologies, eco-

176

logical conservation, anti-nuclear activities, domestic action to avoid pollution, and new philosophies opposed to the ecologically disruptive lifestyle that prevailed in the large Mexican cities. This group represented a starting point for other social experiments addressing the preservation of the environment and its sustainability.

The year of the great earthquake, 1985, marked a turning point in the societal response to environmental problems. Added to the tragedy of the earthquake, air pollution that year reached unprecedented levels, attributed at first to the dust produced by collapsing buildings. When air pollution did not diminish in 1986, after most of the destroyed buildings had been cleared, it became evident that atmospheric pollution was rapidly increasing. Around this time, governmental advertisements filled the media, urging people to lead an environmentally sound life, albeit without specifying what this really meant or explaining how to attain a lifestyle that was less harmful to the environment. Slogans such as "la contaminación somos todos" ("we all pollute") betrayed a lack of knowledge among governmental policy makers about the real complexity of the problem. Thus, the messages exhorted the inhabitants of the basin to keep their cars tuned, to stop littering, and to protect urban trees, but made no mention of industries or automobiles as sources of pollution. The authorities at that time actually seemed to believe that every citizen was individually responsible both for the serious environmental crisis and for its solution. It was soon evident to citizens and government officials alike that, unfortunately, the problem was much more complicated than that, and could not be addressed solely through appeals to individual conscience.

Owing to the severe increase of air pollution levels, schools started changing their time schedules and prohibited students from outdoor activities during the winter, when the risk of a thermal inversion over the basin is highest. People suddenly became aware of the magnitude of the problem and that it was affecting everyone. A persistent demand for information characterized this period, and news services started to give daily reports of air-quality measurements. Nowadays, this information is routinely available from newspapers, television, and radio news services. Individual responses were accompanied by a social awareness; environmental issues became part of everyday conversations and the concepts of pollution and environmental risk became part of common knowledge and language.

The growing expressions of concern about the environment by the citizens of the basin led the different political parties to include environmental issues in their campaigns during the 1988 presidential elections. They were also motivated by the aftermath of the 1985 earthquake and a surge in *organizaciones de barrios* (neighbourhood organizations) that questioned the government's handling of the problems of the megacity.

A taxonomy of NGOs

During the 1980s, non-governmental environmentalism started to organize outside the research centres and academic institutions and became more and more a matter for militant groups and political parties. Many eco-activist organizations appeared, with different aims and with varying ideologies. The 1985 earthquake in Mexico City was a crucial experience, sparking a spontaneous organization of urban society and also inducing a discussion on environmental risks and the limits to growth that confronted modern megalopolises. From then onwards, the number of environmental associations increased dramatically.

Sandoval and Semo (1985) and Quadri (1990) described four basic kinds of ecological groups in Mexico in the mid-1980s:

1. Some NGOs had developed as opponents to governmental policies, particularly those involving the environment, and adopted many aspects of the ideology of the European anti-nuclear groups.
2. Other groups had evolved around a concern about the extinction of species and the destruction of ecosystems and were less concerned about issues of industrial pollution and urban ecology. Some of these groups included industrialists and businessmen and frequently presented a less radical ideology.
3. Other groups were searching for alternative and environmentally sound technologies that could be applied both in cities and in the countryside. These NGOs were often linked with rural or suburban popular organizations.
4. NGOs that wanted to give environmentalism a political connection tried to link their actions with those of political parties, the government, and the media.

By 1986, many environmental NGOs had merged into a coalition known as Pacto de Grupos Ecologistas (Pact of Ecological Groups). This coalition, together with the Mexican Ecological Movement, co-ordinated the actions of many ecological groups between 1986 and 1988. The coalition failed to stick together, however, and the Pact disintegrated in 1989. Since then, apart from the national NGOs that have continued operating in Mexico, local chapters of international NGOs have also established in the country. Some, such as Greenpeace and Oilwatch, are devoted to the surveillance and monitoring of environmental regulations and ecological protection. Others, such as the Worldwide Fund for Nature and Conservation International, are dedicated to the conservation of nature. These organizations are contributing significantly to linking Mexican environmental groups to the global international perspective.

Recent trends in NGO organization

The rather intense activism of the mid-1980s slowly declined after the contentious and fraudulent elections of 1988. During the government of the controversial Carlos Salinas de Gortari, though many groups survived, they tended to remain isolated after the disintegration of the Pact of Ecological Groups. Public disputes between their different members became common and this in turn lessened the interest and the confidence of non-organized citizens.

During this period, environmental issues were discussed by some groups when the ecological issues of the North American Free Trade Agreement (NAFTA) became public, but the lack of a well-organized, united environmental movement was evident, all the more so in comparison with the US groups working around this theme. As a result of intense lobbying by US organizations, the new free trade agreement was accompanied by the North American Agreement for Environmental Cooperation. This created environmental obligations that were trusted by their promoters to avoid the unwanted environmental consequences of free trade.

The reasons for the decline in interest have little to do with improvements in environmental conditions in the basin. The causes of this relative change in attitude are not very clear, but can probably be related to the disenchantment that set in when the real magnitude of the problem became evident, along with the lack of quick, efficient, short-term solutions. The participation of some of the environmental leaders in government posts also had a certain immobilizing effect. The political climate, too, together with the pulses of activity generated by elections, may have been a significant influence.

Although the influence of urban environmental NGOs ceased to grow after 1989 (it nevertheless has not decreased), environmentally motivated groups continue to spring up in rural Mexico. In 1992, the National Institute of Ecology published a "Green Directory" of environmental organizations. The second edition (SEDESOL 1994b) listed around 130 NGOs dealing with environmental issues in the Basin of Mexico. Also in 1992, the National Commission on Human Rights (Comisión Nacional de Derechos Humanos, or CNDH) published its *Recomendación 100*, which recommended that the federal and state authorities take urgent action to solve the critical environmental problems – most of them caused by the oil industry – confronting the *campesinos* in the Tabasco lowlands. In many parts of Mexico, indigenous groups have started to lay claim to the management of their own natural areas. For this purpose, they have made alliances with urban conservationist organizations in the Basin of Mexico and even with international organizations.

The traditional urban environmental groups have extended their interests into the conservation of biological diversity in natural ecosystems. The Coyoacán Ecological Association, for example, now also hosts a group known as Comisión de Selvas Mexicanas (Commission for Mexican Tropical Forests). The Group of 100, although still concerned about the environment in general, is now more concerned about conservation issues such as whales, marine turtles, the international trade in endangered species, monarch butterflies, and the management of biosphere reserves.

The growing interest in environmental issues is also visible in the number of training programmes that Mexican universities and higher education institutions now offer. Whereas in the late 1970s virtually no university courses were directly and objectively aimed at environmental issues, the "Blue Directory" published by INE in 1994 (SEDESOL 1994a) lists more than 150 different courses and training programmes oriented towards environmental problems in the Basin of Mexico.

After the tense 1994 elections, which were held in the aftermath of an immense political crisis generated by three dramatic political assassinations, a currency devaluation crisis struck the Mexican economy. This crisis in turn generated strong restrictions on government expenditure on environmental improvements in general. The political and economic climate changed drastically in a very short period of time. The new Ministry of Environment, Natural Resources, and Fisheries (SEMARNAP), which was formed in 1994, created a Consultative Council on Sustainable Development. This became the arena of harsh confrontations between the government and environmental NGOs. It is difficult to implement the paradigm of sustainable development in the context of rapidly increasing levels of poverty and unemployment and a widening gap between the rich and the poor.

It is extremely hard to predict how the social responses to environmental issues – which are far from being resolved in the Basin of Mexico – will develop in the new situation, dominated as it is by an economic and political crisis and by the new commercial conditions created by NAFTA. All the same, new social and environmental movements can be expected to continue to be organized around the basin's critical environmental situation.

Environmental networks

Mexican governmental organizations have been slow to adopt the new communication technologies. The Internet and electronic network systems have been more a tool of NGOs and academic organizations. In general, a growing number of people are using the Internet for communication, and this is already a well-established trend in the ranks of NGOs and environmental researchers. Mexico has an electronic network of NGOs that operates its own server (*La Neta*) in Mexico City with very low subscriptions. In addition, the National University (UNAM) offers direct dial-up connections to its server at low cost for the public in general, and free for university employees. The SEMARNAP offices are getting wired, and the Internet is becoming more and more a means of communicating between institutions.

The Sustainable Development Network (Red de Desarrollo Sustentable, or RDS) is a project financed by the United Nations Development Programme (UNDP). It operates in the Centre of Studies and Training for Sustainable Development (Centro de Estudios y Capacitación para el Desarrollo Sustentable, or CECADESU), an offshoot of SEMARNAP that is located in Mexico City. The main objective of the RDS is to facilitate communication between governmental and non-governmental organizations, and to build bridges of understanding between the two. The RDS operates from a World Wide Web address: *http://www.laneta.apc.org/rds*, and is being developed at present.

At this stage, the RDS Web site offers information on governmental organizations such as SEMARNAP, and specifically on two projects: (a) the Programme on Regional Sustainable Development (Programas de Desarrollo Regional Sustentable, or PRODERS), which is headed by SEMARNAP's Director General of Regional

Programmes, and (b) the National System of Information on Markets (Sistema Nacional de Información de Mercados, or SNIM), which is operated by the Ministry of Agriculture (SAGAR). The RDS also offers the possibility to connect to the Web home pages of four important international organizations that deal with environmental problems: the Food and Agriculture Organization of the United Nations, the United Nations Environment Programme (UNEP), UNDP, and the International Union for the Conservation of Nature. Of particular relevance to the RDS, UNEP's home page offers the possibility to connect to the Sustainable Development Networking Programme. This international programme links national efforts throughout the world to develop networks for sustainable development. Thus, through UNEP's Web node, the RDS can connect to other environmental networks in countries such as Brazil, Costa Rica, Bolivia, or India.

In addition to the connection to governmental, non-governmental, and international organizations, the RDS offers other services, inclùding: (a) electronic bulletins, (b) directories of environmental organizations, (c) discussion forums, (d) a listing of environmental regulations and standards, and (e) a listing of concrete proposals for sustainable development. The directories of environmental organizations consist of electronic versions of the "green" and the "blue" directories (SEDESOL 1994a, 1994b). The environmental forum is currently devoted to ongoing discussions on sensitive and controversial projects, such as the construction of a highway in the mountains that fringe Mexico City in the south-west of the basin. The listing of environmental regulations is basically an on-line electronic version of the published "Official Standards" (see SEDESOL 1994c).

Perhaps the most important feature of the RDS is its capacity to make information accessible to the public and to put different organizations in touch with each other. This network plays an important role in promoting discussions on environmental issues and bringing environmental groups together. Although the network is not so direct and open as a public hearing, it has brought an openness to the process of evaluating large-scale environmental projects that was previously unheard of in Mexico.

Appendix: List of acronyms and abbreviations

CECADESU: Centro de Estudios y Capacitación para el Desarrollo Sustentable
CECODES: Centro de Ecodesarrollo

CNA: Comisión Nacional del Agua
CNDH: Comisión Nacional de Derechos Humanos
CONABIO: Comisión Nacional para el Conocimiento y el Uso de la Biodiversidad
CONADE: Comisión Nacional de Ecología
CPCCA: Comisión para la Prevención y el Control de la Contaminación Ambiental en la Zona Metropolitana del Valle de México.
DDF: Departamento del Distrito Federal
IMTA: Instituto Mexicano de Ciencia y Tecnología del Agua
INE: Instituto Nacional de Ecología
INEGI: Instituto Nacional de Estadística, Geografía, e Informática
INIREB: Instituto de Investigaciones de los Recursos Bióticos
INP: Instituto Nacional de la Pesca
MAB: UNESCO's Man and the Biosphere Programme
MEM: Movimiento Ecologista Mexicano
NAFTA: North American Free Trade Agreement
NGO: non-governmental organization
PRODERS: Programa de Desarrollo Regional Sustentable
PROFEPA: Procuraduría Federal de Protección al Ambiente
RDS: Red de Desarrollo Sustentable
SAGAR: Secretaría de Agricultura, Ganadería y Desarrollo Rural
SDNP: UNEP's Sustainable Development Networking Programme
SEDESOL: Secretaría de Desarrollo Social
SEDUE: Secretaría de Desarrollo Urbano y Ecología
SEMARNAP: Secretaría de Medio Ambiente, Recursos Naturales y Pesca
SEP: Secretaría de Educación Pública
SMA: Subsecretaría de Mejoramiento del Ambiente
SNIM: Sistema Nacional de Información de Mercados
SSA: Secretaría de Salud
UNAM: Universidad Nacional Autónoma de México
UNCED: United Nations Conference on Environment and Development
UNDP: United Nations Development Programme
UNEP: United Nations Environment Programme
UNESCO: United Nations Educational, Scientific and Cultural Organization

8

Conclusions

Although environmental degradation in the Basin of Mexico has approached critical proportions in the late twentieth century, industrial development is not the only driving force. Urban and political centralism have been a tradition in Mexican society since Aztec times. The Basin of Mexico, for nearly two millennia one of the most densely populated areas of the world, has used its pre-eminent administrative and political position to obtain advantages over other areas of the nation. However, modern industrialization has exaggerated this trend to extraordinary dimensions, and is indeed responsible for the disproportionate urbanization and the biased distribution of population and wealth in the basin.

Since the Mexican Revolution, a brand of economic development, which Sandbrook (1986) has called "conservative modernization," developed in Mexico through the alliance of three dominant sectors: the paternalistic post-revolutionary government, local private enterprises, and foreign capital. The goal of this alliance has been massive industrial development, often at the expense of social equality. Public resources have been largely allocated to the industrial and financial sectors, and this, in turn, has accelerated urban growth. The Basin of Mexico concentrates government, public bureaucracy, a large middle class with high purchasing power, infrastructure such as electricity and roads, health services, and industries eager to profit from this growing market. These sectors have formed the "modern" part of the city, with skyscrapers, large shopping centres, highways, and residential suburbs. Most of the city, however, consists of poor districts inhabited by workers and underemployed people who only a generation ago were peasants in rural Mexico and who migrated into the basin looking for a share in some of the services and goods that industrialization seemed to promise.

Although population growth is decreasing, and many young middle-class professionals are now emigrating to medium-sized cities in search of a better quality of life (Izazola and Marquette 1995), the migration of peasants from impoverished rural regions into the megalopolis continues, and the city is still expanding over forests and fields. Furthermore, the consumption of fossil fuels, the number of cars, the replacement of forests by urban areas, and the pumping of ground water from a critically depleted aquifer are all still increasing at a rate that is often much higher than population growth.

Quite obviously, only a strong decentralization policy promoting migration to smaller cities, favouring life in rural areas, and heavily taxing residences in the Basin of Mexico can stop the process. But such a policy would cost hard currency in a country with a foreign debt of over US$100 billion, would go against the interests of both national and multinational industries, and might also go against the short-term interests of the workers of Mexico City. People must be made aware of the seriousness of the environmental problem before action on decentralization can proceed.

Resource exhaustion through inappropriate land use has produced extensive population decline in the past, demonstrating that there are limits to population growth in a closed basin with a given technological level. Air pollution, water shortages, the unbridled growth of the urban area, and the ever-rising economic and natural resources costs of maintaining the megalopolis suggest that a similar process of population curbing or even decline may occur in the future. The use of air, water, and soils as a commons is clearly unsustainable, and is already confronting the residents of Mexico City with a deterioration in their quality of life. Health problems that are typical of developed societies, such as heart diseases and malignant tumours, coexist in the basin with increasing problems related to air and water pollution, such as pneumonia and enteritis, at levels that are much higher than in the developed world.

In our opinion, it is inevitable that in the future subsidies will have to be eliminated, which will inevitably raise the cost of living and lead to a continuing deterioration in the quality of life for large sectors of the population. Governmental authorities have made several attempts in recent years to charge for water use at values nearer its real cost, but popular protests have aborted these initiatives. However, the capacity to subsidize water use is becoming more and more constrained and is likely to reach a limit soon.

Will awareness of the magnitude of the problem rise sufficiently to avert large-scale damage to the population? Or, contrariwise, will increasing frequencies of health problems and a generalized deterioration in the standard of living trigger greater awareness and potential solutions? This is hard to predict, but since late 1991 air pollution in winter has reached levels that under international standards are considered hazardous and unhealthy. In spite of emissions controls, with the car industry booming and the number of cars growing in the basin at an annual rate of more than 4 per cent, there is no reason to believe that in the near future the situation will improve substantially in any way. The rate of increase of consumption is simply higher than the improvements achieved by anti-pollution measures. Furthermore, the water shortage problem is likely to become more acute in the next few years, making the overall situation extremely critical.

At a juncture of rapid change in the international arena, the future of the Basin of Mexico seems to be inextricably linked with the economic future of Latin America and with the political and social model that the country adopts in the next decade. So far, the winds of economic liberalization have had little or no impact on the general environmental problem, as evidenced by the severe air pollution crises of most winters since 1991. This, of course, may change in the future, but a long-term government plan to deal with the problem is still lacking.

The story of the basin is one of growth, collapse, and cultural rebirth, of catastrophic disintegration and cultural reorganization (Whitmore et al. 1990). Centralism, resource dependence, and many other of the problems of the basin, although more acute than ever before, are not new. It is now in the hands of both government and society to find novel answers to the dramatic questions posed by the industrial development of the old Anahuac, the former capital of the Aztec empire.

Growing conflicts over water use, increasing air pollution, inadequate waste disposal, environmentally related health problems, and natural resource depletion are issues common to most of the third world megalopolises. The Basin of Mexico is a laboratory where many of the processes that drive changes in population, natural resources, and land use in the less developed nations are being tested. It provides both fascinating and terrible insights into what the future may hold for many of the megalopolises of Latin America and the third world.

Bibliography

AAMA. 1996. *World motor vehicle data*. American Automobile Manufacturers Association, Detroit, Michigan.

Aguilar, A. G. 1986. Contemporany urban planning in Mexico City. Its emergence, role, and significance. Unpublished Ph.D. thesis, University of London.

———— 1993. La Ciudad de México y las nuevas dimensiones de la reestructuración metropolitana. In: L. F. Cabrales (ed.), *Espacio urbano, cambio social y geografía aplicada*. Universidad de Guadalajara, Guadalajara, México, pp. 25–51.

———— 1997. Reestructuración económica y costo social en la Ciudad de México: Una metrópoli periférica en la escala global. In: A. Méndez (ed.), *Economía y urbanización: Problemas y retos del nuevo siglo*. Instituto de Investigaciones Económicas, UNAM, México, D.F.

Aguilar, A. G., and L. Godínez. 1989. Desigualdad del ingreso y expansión metropolitana en México. *Vivienda* (INFONAVIT, México, D.F.) 14(2): 138–157.

Aguilar, A. G., E. Ezcurra, T. García, M. Mazari-Hiriart, and I. Pisanty. 1995. The Basin of Mexico. In: J. X. Kasperson, R. E. Kasperson, and B. L. Turner II (eds.), *Regions at risk: Comparisons of threatened environments*. United Nations University Press, Tokyo, pp. 304–366.

Aguilar Sahagún, G. 1984. Reglamentación en problemas de desechos sólidos. In: *Memorias de la I Reunión Regional sobre Legislación Ambiental, Monterrey, Nuevo León*. Secretaría de Desarrollo Urbano y Ecología, México, D.F., pp. 35–45.

Alberro, J., and R. Hernández. 1990. Génesis de grietas de tensión en el Valle de México. In: *El subsuelo de la cuenca del Valle de México y su relación con la ingeniería de cimentaciones a cinco años del sismo*. Sociedad Mexicana de Mecánica de Suelos, A.C., 6–7 September, México, D.F., pp. 95–108.

Albert, L. A., and F. Badillo. 1991. Environmental lead in Mexico. *Reviews of Environmental Contamination, and Toxicology* 117: 1–49.

Álvarez del Villar, J. 1971. Panorama ecológico del Valle de México. In: IMERNAR, *Mesas redonadas sobre problemas de ecología humana en la cuenca del Valle de México*. Instituto Mexicano de Recursos Naturales Renovables, México, D.F., pp. 3–41.

Álvarez, J. R. (ed.). 1985. *Imagen de la Gran Capital*. Enciclopedia de México, Mexico, D.F.

AMCRESPAC (Asociación Mexicana para el Control de los Residuos Sólidos y Peligrosos). 1993. *Bosquejo histórico de los residuos sólidos en la Ciudad de México*. Edit. J. Sánchez-Gómez, México, D.F.

Anawalt, P. R. 1986. Los sacrificios humanos entre los Aztecas. *Mundo Científico (La Recherche)* 58: 564–573.

Anon. 1995a. Las 500 empresas más importantes de México. *Expansión* 27(672): 199–304.

——— 1995b. Las mayores empresas de América Latina. *Revista de Negocios de América Latina* 94–95: 2–176.

Armillas, P. 1971. Gardens on swamps. *Science* 174: 653–661.

Aznavourian, A. 1984. Normas de calidad del aire en México. In: *Memorias de la I Reunión Regional sobre Legislación Ambiental. Monterrey, México*. Secretaría de Desarrollo Urbano y Ecología, México, D.F., pp. 101–120.

Banco Nacional de México. 1996. *México social 1994–1995. Estadísticas Selecciona-das*. BANAMEX-ACCIVAL, División de Estudios Económicos y Sociales, México, D.F.

Barfoot, K. M., C. Vargas-Aburto, J. D. MacArthur, A. Jaidar, F. García-Santibáñez, and V. Fuentes-Gea. 1984. Multi-elemental measurements of air particulate pollution at a site in Mexico City. *Atmospheric Environment* 18: 451–467.

Barradas, V., and R. J-Seres. 1987. Los pulmones urbanos. *Ciencia y Desarrollo* 79: 61–72.

Barry, R. G., and R. J. Chorley. 1980. *Atmosphere, weather, and climate*. Omega, Barcelona.

Bataillon, C., and Rivière d'Arc, H. 1973. *La Ciudad de México*. Transl. by C. Montemayor and J. Anaya. Secretaría de Educación Pública, Colección SepSetentas, no. 99, México, D.F.

Bauer, L. I. 1981. *Efectos de los gases tóxicos en la vegetación*. Seminario sobre administración y tecnología del medio ambiente, Centro de Fitopatología, Colegio de Posgraduados, Chapingo, México.

Bauer, L. I., and S. V. Krupa. 1990. The Valley of Mexico: Summary of observational studies of air quality and effects on vegetation. *Environmental Pollution* 65: 109–118.

Bauer, L. I., T. Hernández Tejeda, and W. J. Manning. 1985. Ozone causes needle injury and tree decline in *Pinus hartwegii* at high altitudes in the mountains around Mexico City. *J. Air Pollut. Control Assoc.* 35(8): 838.

Bazdresch, C. 1986. Los subsidios y la concentración en la Ciudad de México. In: B. Torres (ed.), *Descentralización y democracia en México*. El Colegio de México, México, D.F., pp. 205–218.

Beaman, J. H. 1965. A preliminary study of the alpine flora of the Popocatépetl and Iztaccíhuatl. *Boletín de la Sociedad Botánica de México* 29: 67–75.

Birkle, P., V. Torres, and E. González. 1995. Evaluación preliminar del potencial de acuíferos profundos en la cuenca del valle de México. *Ingeniería Hidráulica en México* X(3): 47–53.

Blake, D. R., and F. S. Rowland. 1995. Urban leakage of liquefied petroleum gas and its impact on Mexico City air quality. *Science* 269(1995): 953–956.

Brambilia, C. 1987. Ciudad de México: La urbe más grande del mundo? In: G. Garza (ed.), *Atlas de la Ciudad de México*. Departamento del Distrito Federal and El Colegio de México, México, D.F., pp. 146–149.

Bravo, H. 1986. La atmósfera de la Zona Metropolitana de la Ciudad de México. Desarrollo y Medio Ambiente. *Fund. Mex. Rest. Ambiental* 2: 2–3.

———— 1987. *La contaminación del aire en México*. Fundación Universo Veintiuno, México, D.F.

Bravo, H., R. Sosa, and R. Torres. 1991. Ozono y lluvia ácida en la Ciudad de México. *Ciencias* 22: 33–40.

Bravo, H., G. Roy-Ocotla, P. Sánchez, and R. Torres. 1992. La contaminación atmosférica por ozono en la Zona Metropolitana de la Ciudad de México. In: I. Restrepo (ed.), *La contaminación del aire en México: Sus causas y efectos en la salud*. Comisión Nacional de Derechos Humanos, México, D.F., pp. 173–184.

Bribiesca, J. L. 1960. Hidrología histórica del Valle de México. *Ingeniería Hidráulica en México* 14(3): 43–62.

Bustamante C. 1993. Aspectos relevantes del sector informal. In: A. Bassols, G. González, and J. Delgadillo (eds.), *Zona Metropolitana de la Ciudad de México. Complejo geográfico, socioeconómico y político*. Departamento del Distrito Federal, Instituto de Investigaciones Económicas, UNAM, México D.F., Colección La estructura económica y social de México, pp. 246–275.

CAE (Consejo Asesor de Epidemiología). 1990. *Mexico: Información prioritaria en salud*. Secretaría de Salud, México, D.F.

Calderón, E., and B. Hernández. 1987. Crecimiento actual de la población de México. *Ciencia y Desarrollo* 76: 49–66.

Calderón-Garcidueñas, L., A. Osorno Velázquez, H. Bravo-Alvarez, R. Delgado-Chávez, and R. Barrios-Márquez. 1992a. Histopathologic changes of the nasal mucosa in southwest Metropolitan Mexico City inhabitants. *American Journal of Pathology* 140(1): 225–232.

Calderón-Garcidueñas, L., A. Hernández-Martínez, H. Bravo, and H. López. 1992b. Nasal cytology in southwest Metropolitan Mexico City inhabitants. *85th Annual Meeting & Exhibition of the Air & Waste Management Association*. Kansas City, Missouri, pp. 1–8.

Calneck, E. E. 1972. Settlement pattern and chinampa agriculture at Tenochtitlan. *American Antiquity* 36: 104–115.

Calvillo-Ortega, M. T. 1978. Areas verdes de la ciudad de México. *Anuario de Geografía* 16: 377–382.

Carrillo, C. 1995. *El Pedregal de San Ángel*. Coordinación de la Investigación Científica, Universidad Nacional Autónoma de México, Mexico, D.F.

Carrillo, N. 1969. Influencia de los pozos artesianos en el hundimiento de la Ciudad de México. In: *El hundimiento de la Ciudad de México. Proyecto Texcoco*. Secretaría de Hacienda y Crédito Público, México, pp. 7–14.

Carson, R. 1962. *Silent spring.* Houghton-Mifflin, Boston.

Castañeda, M. T. B., and M. L. Jiménez. 1986. Caracterización biológica de los residuos sólidos domésticos provenientes de la Delegación Azcapotzalco. Los límites del deterioro ambiental. *Memoria V Congreso Nacional de Ingeniería Sanitaria y Ambiental.* México, pp. 237–239.

Castillo, H. 1991. Para salvar la ciudad. *Proceso* 793: 32–36.

Castillo, H., B. Navarro, M. Perló, I. Plaza, D. Wilk, and A. Ziccardi. 1995. *Ciudad de México: Retos y propuestas para la coordinación metropolitana.* Universidad Autónoma Metropolitana and Universidad Nacional Autónoma de México, México, D.F.

CAVM (Comisión de Aguas del Valle de México). 1988. *Estudio para evitar la contaminación del acuífero del Valle de México,* ed. J. Durazo and R. N. Farvolden. Secretaría de Agricultura y Recursos Hidráulicos, México, D.F.

CEAS (Comisión Estatal de Agua y Saneamiento del Estado de México). 1993. Water supply. Unpublished report, México, D.F.

Ceballos, G., and C. Galindo. 1984. *Mamíferos silvestres de la Cuenca de México.* Publicación especial no. 12, Instituto de Ecología, A.C. MAB-UNESCO and Editorial LIMUSA, México, D.F.

CEC (North American Commission for Environmental Cooperation). In press. *State of the environment report for North America.* North American Commission for Environmental Cooperation, Montreal, Canada.

Cifuentes E., U. Blumenthal, G. Ruiz-Palacios, and S. Bennett. 1991. Health impact evaluation of wastewater use in Mexico. *Public Health Rev.* 19: 243–250.

CNA (Comisión Nacional del Agua). 1994. *Ley de aguas nacionales y su reglamento.* Comisión Nacional del Agua, Mexico, D.F.

CNI (Consejo Nacional de Investigación). 1995. *El agua y la Ciudad de México,* 2nd edition. Academia de la Investigación Científica A.C., Academia Nacional de Ingeniería, A.C., Academia Nacional de Medicina, A.C., and US National Research Council, Editorial Porrúa, México, D.F.

Coe, M. 1964. The chinampas of Mexico. *Scientific American* 211: 90–98.

CONADE (Comisión Nacional de Ecología). 1992. *Informe de la situación general en materia de equilibrio ecológico y protección ambiental 1989–1990.* Comisión Nacional de Ecología, México, D.F.

Constitución Política de los Estados Unidos Mexicanos. 1992. Editorial Porrúa, México, D.F.

Cook, M. 1947. The interrelation of population, food supply, and building in pre-Conquest Central Mexico. *American Antiquity* 8(1): 45–52.

Cornelius, W. A. 1975. *Politics and the migrant poor in Mexico City.* Stanford University Press, Stanford, Calif.

Corona, V. R. 1991. Confiabilidad de los resultados preliminares del XI Censo General de Población y Vivienda de 1990. *Estudios Demográficos y Urbanos* (El Colegio de México) 6(1): 33–68.

Coulomb, R. 1992. El acceso a la vivienda en la Ciudad de México. In: Consejo Nacional de Población, *La Zona Metropolitana de la Ciudad de México: Situación actual y perspectivas demográficas y urbanas.* Dirección General de Estudios de Población, México, D.F.

CPCCA (Comisión para la Prevención y el Control de la Contaminación Ambiental en la Zona Metropolitana del Valle de Mexico). 1992. *Estrategia para la pre-*

vención de desastres, minimización de riesgos y protección civil en la Zona Metropolitana de la Ciudad de Mexico. Comisión para la Prevención y el Control de la Contaminación Ambiental en la Zona Metropolitana del Valle de México, México, D.F.

Cruz, R. 1995. Sustentabilidad del desarrollo urbano: Medio ambiente, urbanización y servicios públicos, manejo de los residuos sólidos. In: A. G. Aguilar, L. J. Castro, and E. Juárez (eds.), *El desarrollo urbano de México a fines del siglo XX.* Sociedad Mexicana de Demografía, México. D.F., pp. 153–163.

DDF (Departamento del Distrito Federal). 1974. *Plantas de tratamiento de aguas negras en la Ciudad de México.* Departamento del Distrito Federal, Dirección General de Obras Hidráulicas, México, D.F.

———— 1975. *Memoria de las obras del sistema de drenaje profundo del Distrito Federal,* vols. I–IV. Talleres Gráficos de la Nación, México, D.F.

———— 1976. Estudio de economía urbana del plan director, vol. III. Unpublished.

———— 1977. *Volumen de agua potable para la Ciudad de México, datos estimativos 1976.* Departamento del Distrito Federal, Dirección General de Obras Hidráulicas, México, D.F.

———— 1979. *Monitoreo de la calidad del agua del sistema de drenaje de la Ciudad de México.* Departamento del Distrito Federal, Dirección General de Construcción y Operación Hidráulica, Technical Report, Mexico, D.F.

———— 1982. *Sistema de planificación urbana del Distrito Federal.* Departamento del Distrito Federal, México, D.F.

———— 1983. *La Ciudad de México antes y después de la Conquista* [a compilation of texts from early colonial times]. Colección Distrito Federal no. 2, México, D.F.

———— 1985. *Actividades geohidrológicas en el Valle de México.* Dirección General de Construcción y Operación Hidráulica, Contract no. 7-33-1-0403, México, D.F.

———— 1986. *Manual de planeación, diseño y manejo de las áreas verdes urbanas del Distrito Federal.* Departamento del Distrito Federal, México, D.F.

———— 1987a. Programas de desarrollo urbano del Distrito Federal, 1987–1988. Published in all Mexico City newspapers on 8 January 1987.

———— 1987b. *Geohidrología del Valle de México,* ed. J. M. Lesser, Contract no. 7-33-1-0211, México, D.F.

———— 1988a. *Manual de exploración geotécnica.* Secretaría General de Obras, México, D.F.

———— 1988b. *El sistema de drenaje profundo de la Ciudad de México.* Secretaría General de Obras, Dirección General de Construcción y Operación Hidráulica, México, D.F.

———— 1988c. *Manejo de los desechos sólidos: El caso del Distrito Federal.* Instituto Nacional de Administración Pública and Dirección General de Servicios Urbanos, México, D.F.

———— 1989. *Estrategia metropolitana para el sistema hidráulico del Valle de México.* Departamento del Distrito Federal y Gobierno del Estado de México, Mexico, D.F.

———— 1991. *Agua 2000. Estrategia para la Ciudad de México.* México, D.F.

———— 1992a. Inventario y políticas de gestión de desechos industriales en la ciudad de México. Unpublished report, México, D.F.

—— 1992b. *Compendio DGCOH 1992*. Dirección General de Construcción y Operación Hidráulica, México, D.F.

—— 1993. Fuentes de contaminación al agua subterránea y alternativas de saneamiento. Unpublished report, Contract no. 3-33-1-0172, Lesser et al., S.A de C.V., Mexico, D.F.

—— 1994. *Memoria de gestión del período diciembre de 1988 a agosto de 1994*. Dirección General de Servicios Urbanos, Mexico, D.F.

—— 1995. *Marco jurídico básico del Departamento del Distrito Federal*. Departamento del Distrito Federal, México, D.F.

—— 1997. *La Ciudad de México en cifras*. Departamento del Distrito Federal, México, D.F. (Internet homepage: http://www.regen.ddf.gob.mx/ag/index.html).

Deffis Caso, A. 1989. *La basura es la solución*. Editorial Concepto, México, D.F.

DGCOH (Dirección General de Construcción y Operación Hidraúlicas). 1989. *Plan maestro de agua potable*. Internal Report, Dirección General de Construcción y Operación Hidraúlicas, Departamento del Distrito Federal, México, D.F.

—— 1991. Distribución de pozos en la zona metropolitana de la Ciudad de México. Unpublished map. Dirección General de Construcción y Operación Hidraúlica, Departamento del Distrito Federal, México, D.F.

DGE (Dirección General de Epidemiología). 1989. *Registro nacional de cáncer. Resultados 1987, Ciudad de México*. Secretaría de Salud, Dirección General de Epidemiología, México, D.F.

DGE. (Dirección General de Estadística). 1990. *VI a XI Censo General de Población y Vivienda, Estados de Hidalgo, Mexico, Tlaxcala y el Distrito Federal, 1940–1990*. Secretaría de Industria y Comercio e Instituto Nacional de Estadística, Geografía e Informática (INEGI), México, D.F.

Diamond, J. M. 1984. Historic extinctions: A Rosetta stone for understanding prehistoric extinctions. In: P. S. Martin and R. G. Klein (eds.), *Quaternary extinctions: A prehistoric revolution*. University of Arizona Press, Tucson, Ariz., pp. 824–862.

Dickerson, R. R., S. Kondragunta, G. Stenchikov, K. L. Civerolo, B. G. Doddridge, and B. N. Holben. 1997. The impact of aerosols on solar ultraviolet radiation and photochemical smog. *Science* 278(5339): 827–830.

DOF (Diario Oficial de la Federación). 1971. Ley de Protección al Ambiente. *Diario Oficial de la Federación*, 23 March.

—— 1984. Ley Federal de Protección al Ambiente. *Diario Oficial de la Federación*, 27 January.

—— 1988. Ley General del Equilibrio Ecológico y la Protección al Ambiente. *Diario Oficial de la Federación*, 28 January.

—— 1992. Acuerdo por el que se crea la Comisión para la Prevención y el Control de la Contaminación Ambiental en la Zona Metropolitana del Valle de México. *Diario Oficial de la Federación*, 8 January.

—— 1993. Normas Oficiales Mexicanas que establecen los límites máximos permisibles de contaminantes en las descargas de diversas industrias. NOM-CCA-001 a 031. *Diario Oficial de la Federación*, 18 October: 2–119.

—— 1994a. Reglamento de la Ley de Aguas Nacionales. *Diario Oficial de la Federación*, 12 January.

—— 1994b. Decreto que reforma, adiciona y deroga diversas disposiciones de la Ley Orgánica de la Administración Pública Federal. *Diario Oficial de la Federación*, 28 December.

——— 1995. Normas Oficiales Mexicanas que establecen los límites máximos permisibles de contaminantes en las descargas de diversas industrias. NOM-063-ECOL-1994. *Diario Oficial de la Federación*, 5 January: 4–20, 6 January: 3–18, 9 January: 6–17, 11 January: 2–13.

——— 1996a. Norma Oficial Mexicana NOM-127-SSA1-1994, Salud ambiental, agua para uso y consumo humano. Límites permisibles de calidad y tratamientos a que debe someterse el agua para su potabilización. *Diario Oficial de la Federación*, 18 January: 41–46.

——— 1996b. Ley Ambiental del Distrito Federal. *Diario Oficial de la Federación*, 9 July.

——— 1996c. Reglamento Interno de la Secretaría de Medio Ambiente, Recursos Naturales y Pesca. *Diario Oficial de la Federación*, 8 July.

Domínguez, V. 1975. Estudio ecológico del volcán Popocatépetl, Estado de México. Unpublished thesis, Facultad de Ciencias, UNAM, México, D.F.

Durazo, J., and R. N. Farvolden. 1989. The groundwater regime of the Valley of Mexico from historic evidence and field observation. *J. Hydrology* 112: 171–190.

Duverger, C. 1983. *La flor letal. Economía del sacrificio azteca*. Fondo de Cultura Económica, México, D.F.

EPA (Environmental Protection Agency). 1994a. *Motor vehicles and the 1990 Clean Air Act*. Environmental Protection Agency, Doc. EPA 400-F-92-013, Fact Sheet OMS-11.

——— 1994b. National Emissions Standards for Hazardous Air Pollutants; Final Rule. Part III. 40 CFR Part 61/4. 402Z94001. *Federal Register* (15 July 1994) 59(135): 32280–36302.

Ezcurra, E. 1990a. *De las chinampas a la megalópolis: El medio ambiente en la Cuenca de México*. Fondo de Cultura Económica, Serie La Ciencia desde México, México, D.F.

——— 1990b. Basin of Mexico. In: B. L. Turner II, W. C. Clark, R. W. Kates, J. F. Richards, J. T. Mathews, and W. B. Meyer (eds.), *The Earth as transformed by human action. Global and regional changes in the biosphere over the past 300 years*. Cambridge University Press with Clark University, Mass., pp. 577–588.

——— 1991a. Las inversiones térmicas. *Ciencias* 22: 51–53.

——— 1991b. Qué mide el IMECA? *Ciencias* 22: 41–43.

——— 1992. Crecimiento y colapso en la Cuenca de México. *Ciencias* 25: 13–27.

——— 1995. Demographic and resource changes in the Basin of Mexico. In: B. L. Turner II, A. Gómez Sal, F. González Bernáldez, and F. di Castri (eds.), *Global land use change. A perspective from the Columbian encounter*. Consejo Superior de Investigaciones Científicas, Madrid, pp. 377–396.

Ezcurra, E., and M. Mazari-Hiriart. 1996. Are megacities viable? A cautionary tale from Mexico City. *Environment* 38(1): 6–15, 26–35.

Ezcurra, E., and J. Sarukhán. 1990. Costos ecológicos del crecimiento y del mantenimiento de la Ciudad de México. In: J. Kumate and M. Mazari (eds.), *Los problemas de la Cuenca de México*. El Colegio Nacional, México, D.F., pp. 215–246.

Fernández-Bremauntz, A. 1993. *Commuters' exposure to carbon monoxide in the Metropolitan Area of Mexico City*. Centre for Environmental Technology, Imperial College of Science, Technology, and Medicine, London.

Ferras, R. 1977. *Ciudad Nezahualcóyotl: Un barrio en vías de absorción por la Ciudad de México*. Centro de Estudios Sociológicos, El Colegio de México, México, D.F.

Flores, R. 1959. El crecimiento de la Ciudad de México: Causas y efectos económicos. *Investigación Económica* 19(74): 24–32.

Fuentes Gea, V., and A. A. C. Hernández. 1984. Evaluación preliminar de la contaminación del aire por partículas en el Area Metropolitana del Valle de México. *Memorias del IV Congreso Nacional de Ingeniería Sanitaria y Ambiental*. Sociedad Mexicana de Ingeniería Sanitaria y Ambiental, México, pp. 523–526.

Galindo, G., and J. Morales. 1987. El relieve y los asentamientos humanos en la Ciudad de México. *Ciencia y Desarrollo* 76: 67–80.

García-Mora, C. 1978. El medio y los barranqueños en San Miguel Atlautla. Informe. CISINAH, México.

——— 1979. Notas para la antropología ecológica de la subcuenca Chalca. *Biótica* 4(1): 13–22.

Garza, G. 1984. Concentración espacial de la industria en la Ciudad de México. *Revista de Ciencias Sociales y Humanidades* V(11). Universidad Autónoma Metropolitana-Azcapotzalco, México, D.F.

——— 1986. El desarrollo urbano de México: Realidades y conjeturas. In: B. Torres (ed.), *Descentralización y democracia en México*. El Colegio de México, México, pp. 237–280.

——— 1987a. Hacia la superconcentración industrial en la ciudad de México. In: G. Garza (ed.), *Atlas de la Ciudad de México*. Departamento del Distrito Federal and El Colegio de México, México, D.F., pp. 100–102.

——— 1987b. Introducción. In: G. Garza (ed.), *Atlas de la Ciudad de México*. Departamento del Distrito Federal and El Colegio de México, México, D.F.

——— 1990. Metropolización en México. *Ciudades* 6. Red Nacional de Investigación Urbana, México, D.F.

Garza, G., and A. Damián. 1991. Ciudad de México. Etapas de crecimiento, infraestructura y equipamiento. In: M. Schteingart (ed.), *Espacio y vivienda en la Ciudad de México*. El Colegio de México and Asamblea de Representantes del Distrito Federal, pp. 21–49.

Garza, G., and S. Rivera. 1994. *Dinámica macroeconómica de las ciudades en México*. INEGI, Colegio de México, and Instituto de Investigaciones Sociales, UNAM, México, D.F.

Garza, G., and M. Schteingart. 1978. Mexico City: The emerging megalopolis. In: W. A. Cornelius and R. Kemper (eds.), *Metropolitan Latin America: The challenge, and the response*. Latin America Urban Research 6, Sage Publications, Calif.

——— 1984. Ciudad de México: Dinámica industrial y estructuración del espacio en una metrópoli semiperiférica. *Demografía y Economía* XVIII, 4(60): 581–604.

GAVM (Gerencia de Aguas del Valle de México). 1995. Informe interno. Uso del Agua. Comisión Nacional del Agua, unpublished.

Goldani, A. M. 1976. Impacto de la inmigración sobre la población del Area Metropolitana de la Ciudad de México. Unpublished Master's thesis, El Colegio de México, México, D.F.

——— 1977. Impacto de los inmigrantes sobre la estructura y el crecimiento del área metropolitana. In: H. Muñoz, O. de Oliveira, and C. Stern (eds.), *Migración y desigualdad social en la ciudad de México.* Instituto de Investigaciones Sociales, Univ. Nac. Aut. de México and El Colegio de México, México, D.F., pp. 129–137.

González Angulo, J., and Y. Terán Trillo. 1976. *Planos de la Ciudad de México 1785, 1853 y 1896.* Instituto Nacional de Antropología e Historia, Colección Científica 50, México, D.F.

González Salazar, G. 1993. Acerca de la calidad de vida. In: A. Bassols Batalla and G. González Salazar (eds.), *Zona Metropolitana de la Ciudad de México. Complejo geográfico, socioeconómico y político.* Instituto de Investigaciones Económicas, UNAM, and Departamento del Distrito Federal, México, D.F.

Graizbord, B., and H. Salazar. 1987. Expansion física de la Ciudad de Mexico. In: G. Garza (ed.), *Atlas de la Ciudad de México.* Departamento del Distrito Federal and El Colegio de México, México, D.F., pp. 120–125.

Guerrero, G., A. Moreno, and H. Garduño. 1982. *El sistema hidráulico del Distrito Federal.* Departamento del Distrito Federal, DGCOH, México, D.F.

Guevara, S., and P. Moreno. 1987. Areas verdes en la zona metropolitana de la ciudad de México. In: G. Garza (ed.), *Atlas de la Ciudad de México.* Departamento del Distrito Federal and El Colegio de México, México, D.F., pp. 231–236.

Halffter, G., and E. Ezcurra. 1983. Diseño de una política ecológica para el valle de México. *Ciencia y Desarrollo* 53: 89–96.

Halffter, G., and P. Reyes-Castillo. 1975. Fauna de la cuenca del Valle de México. In: *Memoria de las Obras del Sistema del Drenaje Profundo del Distrito Federal,* vol. I, Talleres Gráficos de la Nación, México, D.F., pp. 135–180.

Harner, M. 1977. The ecological basis for Aztec sacrifice. *American Ethnologist* 4: 117–135.

Hernández Tejeda, T., and L. I. de Bauer. 1986. Photochemical oxidant damage on *Pinus hartwegii* at the "Desierto de los Leones," Mexico, D.F. *Phytopathology* 76(3): 377–383.

Hernández Tejeda, T., L. I. de Bauer, and S. V. Krupa. 1985. Daños por gases oxidantes en pinos del Ajusco. *Memoria de los Simposia Nacionales de Parasitología Forestal II y III.* Secretaría de Agricultura y Recursos Hidraúlicos, Publicación Especial no. 46, México, D.F., pp. 26–36.

Hernández Tejeda, T., L. I. de Bauer, and M. L. Ortega Delgado. 1985. Determinación de la clorofila total de hojas de *Pinus hartwegii* afectadas por gases oxidantes. *Memoria de los Simposia Nacionales de Parasitología Forestal II y III.* Secretaría de Agricultura y Recursos Hidraúlicos, Publicación Especial no. 46, México, D.F., pp. 334–341.

Herrera, I., and A. Cortés. 1989. El sistema acuífero de la cuenca de México. *Ingeniería Hidráulica en México* IV(2): 60–66.

Hiriart, F., and R. J. Marsal. 1969. El hundimiento de la Ciudad de México. In: *El hundimiento de la Ciudad de México.* Proyecto Texcoco, Secretaría de Hacienda y Crédito Público, México, D.F., pp. 109–147.

Huerta García, R. 1993. Aspectos monográficos de la industria manufacturera. In: A. Bassols Batalla and G. González Salazar (eds.), *Zona Metropolitana de la Ciudad de México. Complejo geográfico, socioeconómico y político.* Instituto de Investigaciones Económicas, UNAM, and Departamento del Distrito Federal, México, D.F.

Humboldt, A. von 1811. *Ensayo político sobre el reino de la Nueva España.* Editorial Porrúa, Mexico, D.F., 1984 (first edition in French, 1811).

Ibarra, V., F. Saavedra, S. Puente, and M. Schteingart, 1986. La ciudad y el medio ambiente: El caso de la zona metropolitana de la ciudad de México. In: V. Ibarra, S. Puente, and F. Saavedra (eds.), *La ciudad y el medio ambiente en América Latina: Seis estudios de caso.* El Colegio de México, México, D.F., pp. 97–150.

Icazuriaga, C. 1992. *La metropolización de la Ciudad de México a través de la instalación industrial.* CIESAS, Ediciones de la Casa Chata, México, D.F.

IGUNAM (Instituto de Geografía, Universidad Nacional Autónoma de México). 1989. Sistema urbano. Crecimiento espacial de las principales ciudades. In: *Atlas Nacional de México.* Instituto de Geografía, UNAM, México, D.F.

IIUNAM (Instituto de Ingeniería, Universidad Nacional Autónoma de México). 1993. *Plantas de tratamiento de aguas residuales.* Instituto de Ingeniería, UNAM, Mexico, D.F.

INAP (Instituto Nacional de Administración Pública). 1991. El municipio y la ecología. *Gaceta Mexicana de Administración Pública Estatal y Municipal,* nos. 39, 40, 41: 1–87.

INEGI (Instituto Nacional de Estadística, Geografía e Informática). 1990. *El área metropolitana de la Ciudad de México.* Instituto Nacional de Estadística, Geografía e Informática, México, D.F.

—— 1991. *XI Censo general de población y vivienda.* Instituto Nacional de Estadística, Geografía e Informática, Mexico, D.F.

—— 1994a. *Cuentas nacionales de México* (text and CD-ROM). Instituto Nacional de Geografía e Informática, Aguascalientes, Mexico.

—— 1994b. *Censo económico: Industria, comercio y servicios.* Instituto Nacional de Estadística, Geografía e Informática, Aguascalientes, Mexico.

—— 1995. *Inventario nacional de empleo urbano, segundo cuatrimestre, abril–junio 1995.* Instituto Nacional de Estadística, Geografía e Informática, Aguascalientes, Mexico.

—— 1997. *Banco de información económica INEGI.* Instituto Nacional de Estadística, Geografía e Informática, Aguascalientes, Mexico (Internet homepage: http://www.inegi.gob.mx/).

Instituto de Geografía. 1990. Sistema urbano, crecimiento espacial de las principales ciudades. In: *Atlas Nacional de México.* Universidad Nacional Autónoma de México, México, D.F.

Izazola, H., and C. M. Marquette. 1995. Migration in response to the urban environment: Out-migration by middle-class women and their families from Mexico City after 1985. *Geographia Polonica* 64: 225–256.

Jáuregui, E. 1971. La erosión eólica en los suelos vecinos al Lago de Texcoco. *Rev. de Ingeniería Hidráulica* 25(2): 103–118.

—— 1983. Variaciones de largo periodo de la visibilidad en la Ciudad de México. *Geofísica Internacional* 22–23: 251–275.

—— 1987. Climas. In: G. Garza (ed.), *Atlas de la Ciudad de México.* Departamento del Distrito Federal and El Colegio de México, México, D.F., pp. 37–40.

—— 1990. *Algunos efectos antropogénicos sobre el clima de las grandes ciudades.* Atlas de México, Instituto de Geografía, UNAM, map no. V.2.5.

Krupa, S., and L. I. de Bauer. 1976. La ciudad daña los pinos del Ajusco. PAN-AGFA 4(31): 5–7.

Lara, O. 1988. El agua en la Ciudad de México. *Gaceta UNAM* 45(15): 20–22.

Lavín, M. 1983. Cambios en las áreas verdes de la zona metroplitana de la Ciudad de México de 1940 a 1980. Unpublished internal report, Instituto de Ecología, México, D.F.

Legorreta, J. 1988. El transporte público automotor en la Ciudad de México y sus efectos en la contaminación atmosférica. In: S. Puente and J. Legorreta (eds.), *Medio ambiente y calidad de vida. Proceedings of the Seminar "La Dinámica de la Ciudad de México en la perspectiva de la investigación actual,"* vol. 3. Departamento del Distrito Federal, Colección Desarrollo Urbano, México, D.F., pp. 263–300.

———— 1995. *Transporte y contaminación en la Ciudad de México*, 2nd edition. Centro de Ecología y Desarrollo, México, D.F.

León Portilla, M., A. M. Garibay, and A. Beltrán. 1972. *Visión de los vencidos: Relaciones indígenas de la conquista.* UNAM, México, D.F.

Lerner, D. N. 1986. Leaking pipes recharge ground water. *Ground Water* 24(5): 654–662.

Lesser, J. M., F. Sánchez, and D. González. 1986. Hidrogeoquímica del acuífero de la ciudad de México. *Ingeniería Hidráulica México* September–December: 64–77.

Logan, M. H., and T. W. Sanders. 1976. The model. In: E. R. Wolf (ed.), *The Valley of Mexico: Studies in prehispanic ecology and society.* University of New Mexico Press, Albuquerque, pp. 31–58.

López Rosado, D. 1988. *El abasto de productos alimenticios en la ciudad de México.* Fondo de Cultura Económica, México, D.F.

Lorenzo, J. L. 1981. Los orígenes mexicanos. In: D. Cosío Villegas (coord.), *Historia general de México*, 3rd edition. El Colegio de México, México, D.F., vol. 1, pp. 83–123.

MacGregor, M. T. G., J. González-Sánchez, and E. Cervantes. 1989. *Crecimiento espacial de las principales ciudades: Ciudad de México.* Atlas de México, Instituto de Geografía, UNAM, map no. III.3.5.

MacNeish, R. S. 1976. Early man in the New World. *American Scientist* 64: 316–327.

Marcus, L. F. and R. Berger. 1984. The significance of radiocarbon dates for Rancho La Brea. In: P. S. Martin and R. G. Klein (eds.), *Quaternary extinctions: A prehistoric revolution.* University of Arizona Press, Tucson, Ariz., pp. 159–183.

Margulis, S. 1992. *Back-of-the-envelope estimates of environmental damage costs in Mexico.* Policy Research Working Papers, World Bank.

Marsal, R. J., and M. Mazari. 1969. *El subsuelo de la Ciudad de México*, vol. I. Congreso Panamericano de Mecánica de Suelos y Cimentaciones, Facultad de Ingeniería, UNAM, México, D.F.

———— 1987. *El subsuelo de la Ciudad de México. Variación de propiedades mecánicas con la profundidad.* Series Instituto de Ingeniería no. 505, UNAM, México, D.F.

———— 1990. Desarrollo de la mecánica de suelos en la Ciudad de México. In: *El subsuelo de la cuenca del Valle de México y su relación con la ingeniería de cimentaciones a cinco años del sismo.* Sociedad Mexicana de Mecánica de Suelos, A.C., México, D.F., pp. 3–25.

Martin, P. S. 1984. Prehistoric overkill: The global model. In: P. S. Martin and R. G. Klein (eds.), *Quaternary extinctions. A prehistoric revolution*. University of Arizona Press, Tucson, Ariz., pp. 354–403.

Martínez de Muñoz, D., O. Chávez, and M. A. Maza. 1992. Incendio en la empresa Agricultura Nacional de Veracruz (ANAVERSA). Efectos bioquímicos de una muestra representativa de la población de Córdoba, Veracruz, relacionados con la toxicidad de los pesticidas organofosforados. In: *Memorias de la Reunión anual del Programa Universitario de Medio Ambiente*. Programa Universitario del Medio Ambiente, UNAM, vol. II, pp. 1–4.

Martínez González, L., and A. Chacalo Hilu. 1994. *Los árboles de la Ciudad de México*. Universidad Autónoma Metropolitana, Unidad Azcapotzalco, Mexico, D.F.

Martínez-Palomo, A., and J. Sepúlveda. 1990. La investigacion biomedica basica en America Latina. *Ciencia* (número especial): 7–13.

Matos Moctezuma, E. 1987. The Templo Mayor of Tenochtitlan: History and interpretation. In: J. Broda, D. Carrasco, and E. Matos Moctezuma (eds.), *The Great Temple of Tenochtitlan. Center and periphery in the Aztec world*. University of California Press, Berkeley, pp. 15–60.

Mazari, M., and J. Alberro. 1990. Hundimiento de la Ciudad de México. In: J. Kumate and M. Mazari (eds.), *Los problemas de la Cuenca de México*. El Colegio Nacional, México, D.F., pp. 83–114.

Mazari, M., R. J. Marsal, and J. Alberro. 1984. *Los asentamientos del Templo Mayor analizados por la Mecánica de Suelos*. Instituto de Ingeniería, UNAM, México, D.F.

Mazari, M., M. Mazari-Hiriart, C. Ramírez, and J. Alberro. 1992. Efectos de la extracción de agua en la zona lacustre de la Cuenca de México. In: R. J. Marsal (ed.), *Volumen especial*. Sociedad Mexicana de Mecánica de Suelos, A.C., México, D.F., pp. 37–48.

Mazari-Hiriart, M. 1992. Potential groundwater contamination by organic compounds in the Mexico City Metropolitan Area. Unpublished D. Env. dissertation, University of California, Los Angeles, Calif.

Mazari-Hiriart, M., and M. Bellón. 1993. Sustentabilidad del desarrollo urbano: Agua. In: *Memorias Seminario Nacional sobre Movilidad Territorial, Distribución Espacial de la Población y Proceso de Urbanización*. Sociedad Mexicana de Demografía and El Colegio de México, 10 and 11 November.

Mazari-Hiriart, M., and D. M. Mackay. 1993. Potential for groundwater contamination in Mexico City. *Environmental Science & Technology* 27(5): 794–801.

Mazari-Hiriart, M., S. Saval, R. Iturbe, and A. Noyola. 1996. *Caracterización de sitios de canal en la zona industrial de la subcuenca de Chalco*. X Congreso Nacional de Ingeniería Sanitaria y Ambiental.

Mejía Maravilla, S. 1987. Sistema hidráulico del Distrito Federal. In: G. Garza (ed.), *Atlas de la Ciudad de México*. Departamento del Distrito Federal and El Colegio de México, México, D.F., pp. 183–186.

Menéndez Garza, F. 1993. *Mexico City information*. Mexico City Metropolitan Commission for the Prevention and Control of Environmental Pollution, Mexico, D.F.

Miller, A. A. 1975. *Climatology*. Omega, Barcelona.

Millon, R. 1970. Teotihuacan: Completion of a map of the giant ancient city in the valley of Mexico. *Science* 170: 1077–1082.

Monroy Hermosillo, O. 1987. Manejo y disposición de residuos sólidos. *Desarrollo y Medio Ambiente* 2: 2–7.

Mosser, F. 1987. Geología. In: G. Garza (ed.), *Atlas de la Ciudad de México.* Departamento del Distrito Federal and El Colegio de México, México, D.F., pp. 23–29.

Mulás, P. 1995. Energía y desarrollo sostenible: El caso de México. In: L. García-Colín and M. Bauer (eds.), *Energía, ambiente y desarrollo sustentable. El caso de México.* El Colegio Nacional and Universidad Nacional Autónoma de México, México, D.F., pp. 121–135.

Murillo, R. 1990. Sobre explotación del acuífero de la cuenca del valle de México: Efectos y alternativas. In: *El subsuelo de la cuenca del Valle de México y su relación con la ingeniería de cimentaciones a cinco años del sismo.* Sociedad Mexicana de Mecánica de Suelos, México, D.F., pp. 109–118.

Negrete, M. E., and H. Salazar. 1986. Zonas Metropolitanas en México. 1980. *Estudios Demográficos y Urbanos* 1(1), El Colegio de México, México, D.F.

———— 1987. Dinámica de crecimiento de la población de la ciudad de México (1900–1980). In: G. Garza (ed.), *Atlas de la Ciudad de México.* Departamento del Distrito Federal and El Colegio de México, México, D.F., pp. 125–128.

Niederberger, C. 1979. Early sedentary economy in the Basin of Mexico. *Science* 203: 131–142.

———— 1987a. De la prehistoria a los primeros asentamientos humanos en la Cuenca de México. In: G. Garza (ed.), *Atlas de la Ciudad de México.* Departamento del Distrito Federal and El Colegio de México, México, D.F., pp. 40–43.

———— 1987b. *Paléopaysages et archéologie pré-urbaine du bassin de Mexico (Mexique),* 2 vols. Centre d'études mexicaines et centraméricaines, Etudes mésoaméricaines, Mexico, D.F.

NRC (National Research Council). 1995. *Mexico City's water supply. Improving the outlook for sustainability.* National Research Council, Academia de la Investigación Científica, A.C., and Academia Nacional de Ingeniería, A.C., National Academy Press, Washington, D.C.

Ortega, A., and R. N. Farvolden. 1989. Computer analysis of regional groundwater flow and boundary conditions in the Basin of Mexico. *Journal of Hydrology* 110: 271–294.

Ortega-Guerrero, A., J. A. Cherry, and D. L. Rudolph. 1993. Large-scale aquitard consolidation near Mexico City. *Ground Water* 31(5): 708–718.

Ortiz de Montellano, B. 1975. Empirical Aztec medicine. *Science* 188: 215–220.

Palacio, A., A. Rodríguez, M. Mazari-Hiriart, P. Magaña, I. Navarro, J. Padilla, V. Olvera, F. Pérez, M. Sotelo, P. González. 1994. *Evolución de la calidad del agua del embalse del Proyecto Hidroeléctrico Zimapán, Hidalgo,* 2 vols. Instituto de Ingeniería, UNAM, and Comisión Federal de Electricidad, México, D.F.

Palerm, A. 1973. *Obras hidráulicas prehispánicas en el sistema lacustre del valle de México.* Instituto Nacional de Antropología e Historia, Cordoba, Mexico.

Páramo, V. H., M. A. Guerrero, M. A. Morales, R. E. Morales, and D. Baz Contreras. 1987. Acidez de las precipitaciones en el Distrito Federal. *Ciencia y Desarrollo* 72: 59–66.

Parsons, J. R. 1976. Settlement and population history of the Basin of Mexico. In: E. R. Wolf (ed.), *The Valley of Mexico: Studies in prehispanic ecology and society.* University of New Mexico Press, Albuquerque, pp. 69–100.

Partida, V. 1987. El proceso de migración a la ciudad de México. In: G. Garza (ed.), *Atlas de la Ciudad de México.* Departamento del Distrito Federal and El Colegio de México, México, D.F., pp. 134–139.

Pisanty, I. 1979. Introducción al estudio de los ecosistemas transformados en el área Chalco-Amecameca: El Maíz. Unpublished thesis, Facultad de Ciencias, UNAM.

Pitre, C. V. 1994. Analysis of induced recharge from a waste water canal through fractured clays in Mexico City. Unpublished M.Sc. thesis in Earth Sciences, University of Waterloo, Ontario, Canada.

Pitre, C. V., and D. L. Rudolph. 1991. Evolution of waste water infiltrating through natural clay sediments beneath a sewage canal in Mexico City. *AGU 1991 Fall Meeting.* Program and Abstracts, 9–13 December: 166.

Ponciano, G., R. Moreno, R. M. Espinosa, A. Báez, E. Díaz, G. Arriaga, A. Guzmán. 1996. Situación actual de México. In: O. Rivero Serrano, G. Ponciano Rodríguez, and S. González Martínez (eds.), *Los residuos peligrosos en México.* Programa Universitario de Medio Ambiente, UNAM, México, D.F., pp. 11–42.

Pradilla Cobos, E. 1993. Reconstrucción del centro histórico de la Ciudad de México. *Ciudades* (Red Nacional de Investigación Urbana) 17: 14–21.

Quadri, G. 1990. Una breve historia del ecologismo en México. *Ciencias* No. especial 4: 56–64.

RAMA (Red Automática de Monitoreo Atmosférico). 1996a. *Informe anual de la calidad del aire en la Ciudad de México 1995.* Departamento del Distrito Federal, Dir. Gral. de Prevención y Control de la Contaminación, México, D.F.

——— 1996b. *Programa precipitaciones acidas en la Zona Metropolitana de la Ciudad de México. Informe Anual 1994.* Departamento del Distrito Federal, Dir. Gral. de Prevención y Control de la Contaminación, México, D.F.

Ramírez, C. 1990a. El agua en la Cuenca de México. In: J. Kumate and M. Mazari (eds.), *Los problemas de la Cuenca de México.* El Colegio Nacional, México, D.F., pp. 61–82.

——— 1990b. Planeación de corredores urbano-industriales. In: J. Kumate and M. Mazari (eds.), *Los problemas de la Cuenca de México.* El Colegio Nacional, México, D.F., pp. 287–300.

Reséndiz, D., and J. Zonana. 1969. La estabilidad a corto plazo de excavaciones a cielo abierto en la arcilla de la Ciudad de México. In: *El hundimiento de la Ciudad de México.* Proyecto Texcoco, Secretaría de Hacienda y Crédito Público, México, D.F., pp. 203–227.

Reséndiz Meza, J. 1989. En ruinas, la planta para procesar basura en Aragón. *Ovaciones*, 8 March: 1–2 B.

Restrepo, I. (ed.). 1992. *La contaminación del aire en México: Sus causas y efectos en la salud.* Comisión Nacional de Derechos Humanos, México, D.F.

——— 1995. Variables, los niveles de plomo en las gasolinas. *La Jornada Ecológica* 3(34): 4–5.

Restrepo, I., and D. Phillips. 1985. *La basura: Consumo y desperdicio en el Distrito Federal.* Centro de Ecodesarrollo, México, D.F.

Restrepo, I., G. Bernache, and W. Rathje. 1991. *Los demonios del consumo. Basura y contaminación*. Centro de Ecodesarrollo, México, D.F.

Reyes, J. E. 1984. Instalará el DDF incineradores de basura: No hay lugar para tiraderos. *Uno más uno*, 31 May: 23.

Riva Palacio, E. 1986. Contaminación del ecosistema de la ciudad de México. In: *Atlas de la Ciudad de México*. Departamento del Distrito Federal and El Colegio de México, México, D.F., pp. 229–230.

Rivera, L., J. C. Sugasty, F. Viniegra, A. Castorena, and R. Benítez. 1980. *Efectos sobre la salud pública del reuso de aguas residuales en el Distrito de Riego 03, zona poniente de Tula, Hidalgo*. Internal Report, Escuela de Salud Pública, México, D.F.

Riveros, H. G. 1995. Hidrocarburos en la atmósfera de la Ciudad de México: Quién los emite? *Ciencia y Desarrollo* 125: 13–15.

Riveros, H. G., J. Tejeda, L. Ortiz, A. Julián-Sánchez, and H. Riveros-Rosas. 1995. Hydrocarbons and carbon monoxide in the atmosphere of Mexico City. *Journal of the Air & Waste Management Association* 45: 973–980.

Rojas Rabiela, T. 1985. La cosecha del agua. Pesca, caza de aves y recolección de otros productos biológicos acuáticos de la cuenca de México. *Cuadernos de la Casa Chata* (CIESAS-SEP, Museo Nacional de Culturas Populares) 116: 1–112.

Rojo, A. (ed.). 1994. *Reserva Ecológica "El Pedregal" de San Ángel: Ecología, historia natural y manejo*. Universidad Nacional Autónoma de México, México, D.F.

Rudolph, D. L., J. A. Cherry, and R. N. Farvolden. 1991. Groundwater flow and solute transport in fractured lacustrine clay near Mexico City. *Water Resources Research* 27(9): 2187–2201.

Ruiz Chiapetto, C. 1986. Ciudad de México: Dinámica industrial y perspectivas de descentralización después del terremoto. In: B. Torres (ed.), *Descentralización y democracia en México*. El Colegio de México, México, D.F., pp. 219–236.

Ryan, C. M. 1989. An investigation of inorganic nitrogen compounds in the groundwater in the Valley of Mexico. *Geofísica Internacional* 28(2): 417–433.

Rzedowski, J. 1954. Vegetación del Pedregal de San Ángel. *Anales de la Escuela Nacional de Ciencias Biológicas* 8(1–2): 59–129.

——— 1969. Notas sobre el bosque mesófilo de montaña en el Valle de México. *Anales de la Escuela Nacional de Ciencias Biológicas* 18: 91–106.

——— 1975. Flora y vegetación en la cuenca del Valle de México. In: *Memoria de las Obras del Sistema del Drenaje Profundo del Distrito Federal*, vol. I. Talleres Gráficos de la Nación, México, D.F., pp. 79–134.

——— 1979. *Vegetación de México*. Ed. Limusa-Wiley, México, D.F.

SAHOP (Secretaría de Asentamientos Humanos y Obras Públicas). 1977. *Memoria descriptiva del flujo de agua, energéticos y alimentos en el área metropolitana de la ciudad de México*. Secretaría de Asentamientos Humanos y Obras Públicas, Subsecretaría de Asentamientos Humanos, Dirección General de Ecología Urbana, México, D.F.

——— 1978. *Diagnóstico de la calidad atmosférica del Valle de México*. Secretaría de Asentamientos Humanos y Obras Públicas, Subsecretaría de Asentamientos Humanos, Dirección General de Ecología Urbana, México, D.F.

Sala Catalá, J. 1986. La localización de la capital de Nueva España, como problema científico y tecnológico. *Quipu* 3: 279–298.

Salazar, S., J. L. Bravo, and Y. Falcón. 1981. Sobre la presencia de algunos metales pesados en la atmósfera de la Ciudad de México. *Geofísica Internacional* 20: 41–54.

Sandbrook, R. 1986. Crisis urbana en el Tercer Mundo. In: V. Ibarra, S. Puente, and F. Saavedra (eds.), *La ciudad y el medio ambiente en América Latina: Seis estudios de caso.* El Colegio de México, México, D.F., pp. 19–27.

Sanders, W. T., 1976a. The agricultural history of the Basin of Mexico. In: E. R. Wolf (ed.), *The Valley of Mexico: Studies in prehispanic ecology and society.* University of New Mexico Press, Albuquerque, pp. 101–159.

——— 1976b. The natural environment of the Basin of Mexico. In: E. R. Wolf (ed.), *The Valley of Mexico: Studies in prehispanic ecology and society.* University of New Mexico Press, Albuquerque, pp. 59–67.

Sanders, W. T., J. R. Parsons, and R. S. Santley. 1979. *The Basin of Mexico: Ecological processes in the evolution of a civilization.* Academic Press, New York.

Sandoval, J. M., and I. Semo. 1985. Los movimientos sociales del ecologismo en México. In: E. Leff (ed.), *México: Biosociología.* Programa Universitario Justo Sierra, UNAM, México, D.F.

Santos-Burgoa, C., and L. Rojas-Bracho. 1992. Los efectos de la contaminación atmosférica. In I. Restrepo (ed.), *La contaminación del aire en México: Sus causas y efectos en la salud.* Comisión Nacional de Derechos Humanos, Mexico, D.F., pp. 205–250.

SARH (Secretaría de Agricultura y Recursos Hidráulicos). 1985a. Dirección General de Distritos Generales de Riego, Oficina de Riego y Drenaje, unpublished data.

——— 1985b. *Sistema Cutzamala, segunda etapa: Captación Valle de Bravo.* Secretaría de Agricultura y Recursos Hidráulicos, México, D.F.

Schteingart, M. 1989. *Los productores del espacio habitable. Estado, empresa y sociedad en la Ciudad de México.* El Colegio de México, Centro de Estudios Demográficos y de Desarrollo Urbano, México, D.F.

SEDESOL (Secretaría de Desarrollo Social). 1993. *Informe de la situación general en materia de equilibrio ecológico y protección al ambiente.* Instituto Nacional de Ecología, México, D.F., pp. 181–206.

——— 1994a. *Directorio de programas académicos sobre áreas ambientales en instituciones nacionales de educación superior.* Instituto Nacional de Ecología, Secretaría de Desarrollo Social, México, D.F.

——— 1994b. *Directorio verde de organismos no gubernamentales*, 2nd edition. Instituto Nacional de Ecología, Secretaría de Desarrollo Social, México, D.F.

——— 1994c. *Normas Oficiales Mexicanas en materia de protección ambiental.* Instituto Nacional de Ecología, Secretaría de Desarrollo Social, México, D.F.

——— 1994d. *Informe de la situación general en materia de equilibrio ecológico y protección al ambiente 1993–94.* Instituto Nacional de Ecología, Secretaría de Desarrollo Social, México, D.F.

SEDUE (Secretaría de Desarrollo Urbano y Ecología). 1985. *Indice metropolitano de calidad del aire.* Secretaría de Desarrollo Urbano y Ecología and Corporación Internacional TECNOCONSULT, México, D.F.

——— 1986. *Informe sobre estado del medio ambiente en México.* Secretaría de Desarrollo Urbano y Ecología, México, D.F.

——— 1987. *Legislación Básica.* Secretaría de Desarrollo Urbano y Ecología, Dirección General de Asuntos Jurídicos, México, D.F.

Segura Burciaga, S. G., and M. Martínez Ramos. 1994. La introducción de especies acomunidades naturales: El caso de Eucaliptus resinifera Smith (Myrtaceae) en la reserva "El Pedregal" de San Ángel. In: A. Rojo (ed.), *Reserva Ecológica "El Pedregal" de San Ángel: Ecología, historia natural y manejo.* Universidad Nacional Autónoma de México, México, D.F., pp. 177–186.

SEMARNAP (Secretaría de Medio Ambiente, Recursos Naturales y Pesca). 1996a. Estrategia del Proyecto de Descentralización de la SEMARNAP: Primera versión para discusión. Internal unpublished document, Secretaría de Medio Ambiente, Recursos Naturales y Pesca.

——— 1996b. *Programa de Áreas Naturales Protegidas de México 1995–2000.* Instituto Nacional de Ecología, Secretaría de Medio Ambiente, Recursos Naturales y Pesca, Poder Ejecutivo Federal, México, D.F.

——— 1996c. *Programa de Medio Ambiente 1995–2000.* Instituto Nacional de Ecología, Secretaría de Medio Ambiente, Recursos Naturales y Pesca, México, D.F.

——— 1996d. *Programa para mejorar la calidad del aire en el Valle de México 1995–2000.* Instituto Nacional de Ecología, Secretaría de Medio Ambiente, Recursos Naturales y Pesca, Departamento del Distrito Federal, Gobierno del Estado de México, Secretaría de Salud, México, D.F.

——— 1996e. *México: La transición hacia el desarrollo sustentable.* Secretaría de Medio Ambiente, Recursos Naturales y Pesca, México, D.F.

——— 1996f. *México: Hacia el desarrollo sustentable. Bases para la transición.* Secretaría de Medio Ambiente, Recursos Naturales y Pesca, México, D.F.

Serra Puche, M. C. 1988. *Los recursos lacustres en la cuenca de México durante el Formativo.* Universidad Nacional Autónoma de México, Colección Posgrado, México, D.F.

——— 1990. El Pasado. Una forma de acercarnos al futuro? In: J. Kumate and M. Mazari (eds.), *Los problemas de la cuenca de México.* El Colegio Nacional, México, D.F., pp. 3–29.

Serra Puche, M. C., and R. Valadez Azúa. 1989. Importancia de los venados en Terremote-Tlaltenco. *Ciencia y Desarrollo* 15(85): 63–72.

Siebe, C., and W. R. Fischer. 1991. Schwermetallbelastung von Boden durch landwirtschaftliche Nutzung städtischer Abwässer in Zentral-Mexico. *Mitteilungen Dt. Bodenkundl. Gesellschaft* 66(II): 1189–1192.

Sierra, C. J. 1984. *Historia de la navegación en la Ciudad de México.* Departamento del Distrito Federal, Colección Distrito Federal no. 7, México, D.F.

Sigler Andrade, E., V. Fuentes Gea, and C. Vargas Aburto. 1982. Análisis de la contaminación del aire por partículas en Ciudad Universitaria. *Memorias del III Congreso Nacional de Ingeniería Sanitaria y Ambiental,* vol. II. Sociedad Mexicana de Ingeniería Sanitaria y Ambiental, México, D.F., pp. 1–13.

Simonian, L. 1995. *Defending the land of the jaguar. A history of conservation in Mexico.* University of Texas Press, Austin.

Skärby, L., and G. Sellden. 1984. The effects of ozone on crops and forests. *Ambio* 13: 68–72.

SMA (Subsecretaría de Mejoramiento del Ambiente). 1978a. *Fuentes emisoras en México. Industrias altamente contaminantes.* Secretaría de Salubridad y Asistencia, Subsecretaría de Mejoramiento del Ambiente, México, D.F.

——— 1978b. *Situación actual de la contaminación atmosférica en el área metropolitana de la Ciudad de México.* Secretaría de Salubridad y Asistencia, Subsecretaría de Mejoramiento del Ambiente, México, D.F.

——— 1978c. *Desechos sólidos*. Secretaría de Salubridad y Asistencia, Subsecretaría de Mejoramiento del Ambiente, México, D.F.

Soms García, E. 1986a. *La hiperurbanización en el Valle de México*, vol. I. Universidad Autónoma Metropolitana, México, D.F.

——— 1986b. *La hiperurbanización en el Valle de México*, vol. II. Universidad Autónoma Metropolitana, México, D.F.

Sorchini, H. A., and S. Contreras. 1982. *Planta de tratamiento Cerro de la Estrella*. DGCOH, Departamento del Distrito Federal, México, D.F.

Stern, C. 1977a. The growth of Mexico City: Varying sources of its migrant inflow, 1900–1970. Unpublished Ph.D. dissertation, Washington University, USA.

——— 1977b. Cambios en los volúmenes de migrantes provenientes de distintas zonas geoeconómicas. In: H. Muñoz, O. de Oliveira, and C. Stern (eds.), *Migración y desigualdad social en la ciudad de México*. Universidad Nacional Autónoma de México and El Colegio de México, México, D.F., pp. 115–128.

Strauss, M. 1986. About wastewater reuse in Mexico. In: U. Blumenthal (ed.), *Epidemiological aspects of use of wastewater in agriculture in Mexico*. Technical Report, London School of Hygiene and Tropical Medicine, London.

——— 1988. Examples of wastewater and excreta use practices in agriculture and aquaculture. In: Human wastes: Health aspects of their use in agriculture, and aquaculture. *IRCWD News* 24–25: 1–3. International Reference Centre for Waste Disposal, Switzerland.

Suárez, L. 1974. *De Tenochtitlan a México*. Fondo de Cultura Económica, Series Archivo del Fondo no. 16, México, D.F.

Tamayo, L. M., C. Valverde, and A. G. Aguilar. 1990. Desigualdad social en las tres principales áreas metropolitanas, 1980, Escala 1: 700 000. In: *Atlas Nacional de México*. Instituto de Geografía, UNAM, México, D.F.

Thom, G. C., and W. R. Ott. 1975. *Air pollution indices. A compendium and assessment of indices used in the United States and Canada*. Council on Environmental Quality and the Environmental Protection Agency, Washington, D.C., US Government Printing Office.

Trabulse, E. 1983. *Cartografía mexicana: Tesoros de la nación, siglos XVI a XIX*. Archivo General de la Nación, México, D.F.

Trejo Vázquez, R. 1987. La disposición de desechos sólidos urbanos. *Ciencia y Desarrollo* 74: 79–90.

Turner II, B. L., and K. W. Butzer. 1992. The Columbian encounter and land-use change. *Environment* 43(8): 16–20, 37–44.

Unikel, L. 1974. *La dinámica del crecimiento de la Ciudad de México*. Secretaría de Educación Pública, colección SEP-Setentas, México, D.F.

Unikel, L., C. Ruiz Chiapetto, and G. Garza. 1976. *El desarrollo urbano de México. Diagnóstico e implicaciones futuras*. El Colegio de México, México, D.F.

Valverde C., and Aguilar A. G. 1987. Localización geográfica de la Ciudad de México. In: G. Garza (ed.), *Atlas de la Ciudad de México*. Departamento del Distrito Federal and El Colegio de México, México, D.F.

Velasco Levy, A. 1983. La contaminación atmosférica en la ciudad de México. *Ciencia y Desarrollo* 52: 59–68.

Villegas, M. 1976. *Malezas de la Cuenca de México*. Publicación Especial No. 1, Instituto de Ecología, A.C., México, D.F.

Villegas Tovar, J. 1988. Zona Metropolitana de la Ciudad de México: Localización y estructura de la actividad industrial 1975–1985. In: O. Terrazas and E. Preciat (eds.), *Estructura territorial de la Ciudad de México*. Plaza y Valdez Editores, Departamento del Distrito Federal, México, D.F.

Ward, P. 1981. Mexico City. In: M. Pacione (ed.), *Problems and planning in third world cities*. Croom Helm, London.

———— 1991. *México: Una megaciudad. Producción y reproducción de un medio ambiente urbano*. Ed. Alianza, México, D.F.

Whitmore, T. M., and B. L. Turner II. 1986. *Population reconstruction of the Basin of Mexico: 1150 B.C. to present*. Technical Paper no. 1, Millennial Longwaves of Human Occupance Project, Clark University, Worcester, Mass.

———— 1992. Landscapes of cultivation in Meso-America. In: K. W. Butzer (ed.), *The Americas before and after 1492: Current geographical research*. Special edition, *Annals of the Association of American Geographers* 82(3): 401–425.

Whitmore, T. M., B. L. Turner II, D. L. Johnson, R. W. Kates, and T. R. Gottschang. 1990. Long-term population change. In: B. L. Turner II, W. C. Clark, R. W. Kates, J. F. Richards, J. T. Mathews, and W. B. Meyer (eds.), *The Earth as transformed by human action. Global and regional changes in the biosphere over the past 300 years*. Cambridge University Press with Clark University, Mass., pp. 25–39.

WHO and UNEP (World Health Organization and United Nations Environment Programme). 1992. *Urban air pollution in megacities of the world*. Blackwell Scientific Publications, Oxford.

WRI (World Resources Institute). 1994. *World Resources 1994–95*. Oxford University Press, New York and Oxford.

Index

Commission for Mexican Tropical Forests 180
Commission for the Regularization of Land Tenure (CORETT) 121
communal land ownership 120, 160
Constitution, modification of 160
Consultative Council on Sustainable Development 180
Coyoacán (Mexico City area) 38, *52*, 63, 64
Ecological Association 176, 180
population growth *52*, 63
subsidence *87*
Cuautitlán–Izcalli *52*, 122
Cuautla-Yautepec 71
Cuernavaca-Temixco-Jiutepec 71, 136
Cuicuilco (Mexico) 32
Cumbres del Ajusco national park 37, 138
currency devaluation crisis 180
Cutzamala Basin, water imported from 79, *81*, *82*, 83, 122, *144*, 145, *149*

Dacca (Bangladesh)
GNP per capita *2*
population data *2*
decentralization policies 122, 185
deforestation
causes 8, 33, 37, 169
effects 35, 37, 143, 156, 169, 170
demographic changes 29–38
dependence on neighbouring ecosystems 8–9, 29
desertification 33
Desierto de los Leones national park 37, 81, 138
Díaz, Porfirio (President) 36, 171
see also Porfirian dictatorship
drainage of basin 8, 35–36, 67, 68
effects 70, 84–86
drainage system 89–91
deep drainage system 90, *146*
energy costs *147*
effects of subsidence 145, *146*
leakage 90, 148
drinking-water provision 119, 129
drinking-water regulations 88
dust storms 75

earthquake 38
air pollution after 177
re-location of populations after 121
Ecatepec 47, 48, *52*, 120
Echeverría, Luis (President) 156, 157
ecological activism 173–174, 175–177
ecological crisis, factors causing 5
ecological productivity 28–29
ecological reserves 158
ecological subsidies 8, 113, 122
Ecologist Green Party 162
economic crisis, environmental action affected by 157
economic policy, change to neo-liberal approach 49–50
economic pre-eminence (of Mexico City and Basin of Mexico) xiv, 59–60, 119, 122, 184
economic subsidies 7, 113, 123–129, 184, 186
economy 55–59
educational institutions 59
ejido land-tenure system 120, 160
El Pedregal de San Angel *14*, 18, 20–21, 64–65, 137, 138
lead levels in air *103*
see also pedregal
energy consumption *113*
by water supply/drainage system 145, 147
England, lead content of gasoline *153*
enterprises in Mexico *131*
number in Mexico City 130
environmental conscience 155–156
environmental history 7–38
environmental networks 181–182
environmental policies
current government policies 163–169
evolution 156–159
new economic and political approaches 160–162
paradigm shift 159–160
Environmental Protection Attorney General (PROFEPA) 160, 163
environmental sustainability
as major concern 162–163
Mexico City as laboratory 4, 187
Escandón *hacienda* 65

209

213

215